The Poetry
of Ezra Pound

The Poetry
of Ezra Pound

HUGH KENNER

NEW DIRECTIONS
Norfolk, Connecticut
U.S.A.

KRAUS REPRINT CO.

Millwood, N.Y.

1974

KRAUS REPRINT CO.

A U.S. Division of Kraus-Thomson Organization Limited

ISBN 0-527-48500-4   LC 51-12356

Printed in U.S.A.

To

MARSHALL McLUHAN

'*A catalogue, his jewels of conversation*'

'It doesn't, in our contemporary
world, so much matter where you begin
the examination of a subject, so long as
you keep on till you get round again to
your starting point. As it were, you
start on a sphere, or a cube: you must
keep on till you have seen it from all
sides.'
                    —*ABC of Reading.*

When the mind swings by a grass-blade
    an ant's forefoot shall save you
the clover leaf smells and tastes as its
    flower
                    —Canto LXXXIII.

The 'Rays' ideogram from the Fenollosa collection (front cover) is glossed by Pound as (left half) 'bright'—fire above a walking man, abbreviated to the light and the moving legs; 'I should say it might have started as the sun god moving below the horizon.' (Right half) 'flying'— moving wings above short-tailed bird. Bright + Flying = Rays.

With its sun-god component and its emphasis on winged and propagated light (= intelligence), the ideogram, which Pound has several times employed as a motto, engages profoundly with his conception of poetic efficacy.

CONTENTS

11

CONTENTS

PART THREE: THE CANTOS

APPENDICES

ACKNOWLEDGMENT

The author gratefully acknowledges the permission to reproduce quotations from the works of Mr. T. S. Eliot given by Messrs Harcourt, Brace and Co.

INTRODUCTION

This book is intended for the reader who does not need to be persuaded about contemporary writing in general—who knows, for instance, his Eliot and his Joyce—but whom thickets of misunderstanding have hitherto kept at a distance from the poetry of Ezra Pound. Since my object is simply to help as many people as possible to read Pound for themselves, I have attempted a consecutive attack on the more obvious misunderstandings, limiting myself to those specifically related to the reading of a specific body of poetry. Because it is about Pound's poetry, this book eschews both his personality and the externals of his biography, which largely depend on his personality. This should not be taken to imply a schism in the subject, but a necessary limitation in the treatment. I have had to choose, and I have chosen rather to reveal the work than to present the man.

The peripheral booby-traps evaded, there remains the irreducible difficulty of the work itself. It is difficult as all poetry is difficult, but the hard shell of difficulty is in most places very thin. No poet is less mysterious once we have entered his world, or more inexhaustibly enjoyable.

It is important to bear in mind that the poet does not state a doctrine or embroider an assemblage of sentiments. He projects an intelligible world. The difficulties of Pound's world are those of any intelligible order: the eye sees without effort, the mind only with tension. They are not specifically difficulties of erudition: I haven't found it necessary to burden the reader with many even of the sources and allusions that I happen to know. What the reader of the *Cantos* should try to grasp is not where the components came from but how they go together. The components of Pound's poetic world— Homer, Cavalcanti, Dante; Confucius; Jefferson and the Adamses; distributive economics and the corporate states of the thirties; Flaubert and Chinese linguistics—appear, it is true, in mere listening, haphazard and heterogenous to an unsupportable degree. The same, for that matter, could be said of the shoal, the poisoned chalice, the trumpet-tongued angels, and the naked babe of one of Macbeth's speeches; and nothing would more discourage a new reader than a list of the more important kinds of learning built into Dante's *Commedia*. But no one thinks it necessary to postpone Dante until he has worked through Averroes and solved in the abstract the problem how Odysseus imprisoned in a horned flame can be brought into stereoscopic focus with a succession of commentaries on the Sentences of Peter Lombard. It is enough to be satisfied that there is a nodal point at which the diversely collected rays meet and are brought under simultaneous control.

Every great writer operates from some such node. It is the point—to change the metaphor—at which the local operation of words in lines and passages becomes continuous with the operation of passages in the main design, and of whole works in the poise and thrust of a lifetime's output. To see, for instance, a hierarchy of parodies in the sentence as in the situation, in the situation as in the book, in the book as in the cycle, is to occupy the point of leverage in the world of James Joyce. Pound has made it especially easy to locate this point in his own work, by telling us repeatedly what and where it is. No poet has given his readers more help. Hence I have been able to write the first section of this book by compiling, with some abridgment and paraphrase, a little anthology of Pound's luminous and coherent prose.

Certain enigmatic juxtapositions in the book are intentional; the patient reader will find that many matters, especially in the first part, are dropped for resumption in a more opportune context. The reader should keep the volumes of early poems and the Cantos (both in print) at hand, and take every hint to refer to them. If he declines this trouble his bargaining position *vis-à-vis* the commentator is weak.

The problem of bringing Pound's procedures to focus is that of seeing a large number of factors distinctly and at the same time. 'I shall go on', says Pound somewhere, 'patiently trying to explain a complex of phenomena, without pretending that its twenty-seven elements can with profit to the reader be considered as five.' Nor is it only commentators who lump and entangle. With the best will in the world, the reader striving to connect Confucius, Dante, Fenollosa, and Flaubert with what he knows already is apt to dissipate his energy on non-existent short-cuts. I have tried to mark out a safe route, but no book is foolproof; and it is not in any case this book but the *Cantos* that I ask the reader to try to understand.

It may be worth while to set down my awareness that what I have undertaken is exposition, not 'criticism'. The time-lag in apprehension of even the decade of Pound's most spectacular activity is now almost forty years. It seems fair to say that most even of those who have looked at his pages have not *read* them. One cannot 'place' a poet by one's maturest standards (not merely literary standards) until one has first surrendered oneself to his world, and scrupulous critical rigour is frequently no more than a mask of the self-possession that will not make that surrender. The only criticism of the *Cantos* worth reading is Mr. Eliot's *Coriolan* sequence, a profound and witty utilization of their techniques to effect a displacement of the Poundian centre.

My thanks are due to Messrs. John Reid, H. M. McLuhan, Cleanth Brooks, F. B. Rainsberry, and Ambrose Gordon Jr. for reading the manuscript and making helpful suggestions; to the editors of *The Hudson Review* for permission to reprint portions that first appeared in their pages; and to the John Addison Porter prize committee of Yale University for increasing my confidence in the efficacy of the book by naming it for their 1950 award.

HUGH KENNER.

Santa Barbara College,
University of California.

Chapter 1

A PREFATORY DISTINCTION

Something for the modern stage;
Not, at any rate, an Attic grace.

There is no great contemporary writer who is less read than Ezra Pound; yet there is none who can over and over again appeal more surely, through 'sheer beauty of language', to the man who generally would rather talk about poets than read them. The *Pisan Cantos*, for instance, were during a few months of 1949 more 'in the news' (for irrelevant reasons) than perhaps any volume of poetry in modern times. They were widely written off as a dead loss, and all sorts of alarming implications were read into their author's receipt of the Bollingen Prize for Poetry at the hands of a committee of fellow-poets. And yet a reader who opened the book would have found on the first page:

yet say this to the Possum: a bang, not a whimper,
    with a bang not with a whimper,
To build the city of Dioce whose terraces are the colour of stars.
The suave eyes, quiet, not scornful,
                    rain also is of the process.
What you depart from is not the way
and olive tree blown white in the wind
washed in the Kiang and Han
what whiteness will you add to this whiteness,
                                what candour?

Such verse moves with incomparable assurance. Its ellipses, which may trouble the understanding of one who knows not

'Possum' or 'the process', offer no impediment to his ear. We have not to deal with a tense fellow talking in epigrams. The reader is not subjected to that brow-knotting strain, invariably betraying itself in incompetent rhythms, which in lesser work admonishes him to keep screwed to the sticking-place his awareness of assisting at a hushed rite among the eggshell teacups of poesy.

There is still no one, Mr. Eliot has said of these latest *Cantos*, who can write like that. Were it not that relations between poet and audience have deteriorated steadily since at least the eighteenth century,[1] it would be merely presumptuous to say more. What kind of importance the *Cantos* have, or are going to have, is not for an immediate contemporary to decide; and of the language one can remark only, within its own standards, the perfection. Things being as they are, though, to offer the reader some insight into his own presumptive neglect of one of the few comprehensive masters of technique in the history of English verse may be a legitimate function for the commentator.

It is not that there is, for the purpose at least of bringing the reader into initial contact with *Personae* and the *Cantos*, anything new to explain. Pound has spent nearly forty years explaining himself incomparably. Unfortunately, little of the *forma mentis* he and the other trail-blazers of this century desiderate has taken widespread hold, even among those who conscientiously and concurrently tried to 'keep up'. A phrase like 'ideogrammic method' has become, like 'objective correlative', at the hands of exhorters and detractors alike both a blur and a bore. So it is worth while making another try. Again, the greater number of the books to which the honest student of today should turn for light—*Instigations; Gaudier-Brzeska; Culture; ABC of Reading*—are out of print[2] and hard to come by in libraries. A little anthologizing may show him why they are worth the effort of procurement, and what kind

---

[1] It is supposed, that by the act of writing in verse an Author makes a formal engagement that he will gratify certain known habits of association; that he not only thus apprises the reader that certain classes of ideas and expressions will be found in his book, but that others will be carefully excluded.—Wordsworth, *Preface* of 1800.

[2] *ABC of Reading* reissued by Faber and Faber, and New Directions 1951.

of attention, transcending the exigencies of bygone pamphlet-
eering, they deserve.

The curiosity of the reader here borne in mind—one who,
decently motivated, is fairly familiar with the work of the
more accepted contemporary reputations, and probably
thinks of Pound, with some piety, as a mysteriously-function-
ing but potent 'influence'—his curiosity may perhaps be
jogged in this way: how is it, now that Joyce, Eliot, and Yeats
are getting assimilated—not, certainly, on their own terms,
but to some extent assimilated—how is it that Pound's
reputation alone remains so much a matter of inert convention? Why is the master whose crucial support Mr. Eliot
has always acknowledged, to whom he dedicated *The Waste
Land* as *il miglior fabbro,* and to whom he has devoted at least
four long essays; who was probably the efficient cause in the
abolition of Yeats' early 'poetical' manner; of whom Joyce
said 'We all owe him a great deal, and I most of all surely';
why is his poetry so little discussed and, one suspects, less
read?

The same question might be asked of Ben Jonson, Landor,
and Browning, who languish today in the shade of, respectively,
Shakespeare, Shelley, and Tennyson, as Pound in the shade of
Eliot. Pound, with his multi-lingual erudition, his orientation
toward politics rather than psychology, his exact critical sense
issuing in precise, unequivocal, but apparently random
judgments, his abrupt handling of fools, and his 'poetry of the
surface', which as Eliot said of Jonson's 'cannot be understood
without study, for to deal with the surface of life, as Jonson
dealt with it, is to deal so deliberately that we too must be
deliberate, in order to understand'; Pound on all these counts
has many claims to be considered the contemporary Ben
Jonson. If that be so, the popularity of Eliot rather than
Pound is analogous to the popularity, in our time, of Donne
rather than Jonson. And explaining this popularity Eliot has
said of a group of poets antithetic to Jonson, including
Shakespeare, Donne, Marlowe, and Webster, that while in the
end more difficult, 'they offer something at the start to encourage the student or to satisfy those who want nothing

more; they are suggestive, evocative, a phrase, a voice. . . . But the polished veneer of Jonson reflects only the lazy reader's fatuity; unconscious does not respond to unconscious; no swarms of inarticulate feelings are aroused.' His words, like Pound's, have not that 'network of tentacular roots reaching down to the deepest terrors and desires'. That is why so many readers feel that Pound has 'nothing to say' to the modern mind; no relevance to the problems of contemporary living.

It is on this latter kind of relevance, manifested by the rousing of 'swarms of inarticulate feelings', that the placing of poets during their lifetime is based. No one now reads Tennyson's longer works very avidly, and no more sermons are likely to take heart from *In Memoriam*; but for the nineteenth century relevance to contemporary emotional problems was decidedly what Tennyson had and Browning had not. This is not to imply that Browning suffers today a wholly undeserved neglect, though it was not a response to his real strength that made him the congenial lay preacher of Presbyterians, and in their concession to popular romantic psychology his best-known poems are probably his worst: Pound is right in singling out for praise the 'unreadable' *Sordello*. But the contrast is instructive. Browning in the passage from *Sordello* that Pound exhibits in the *ABC of Reading* is an incomparably better writer of English—is more aware of the resources of his medium and less hamstrung by his conceptions of technique—than Tennyson ever was. Yet no man could have been more unfortunate in his adherents (hence his present semi-jocular status) and they adhered to him for irrelevant reasons (as have most of Pound's). The reading public put its money on Tennyson, unconscious responding to unconscious, swarms of inarticulate feelings being aroused.

Pound is a far more important figure than Browning or Landor, Eliot than Tennyson or Shelley. One must return to the contrast between Jonson and his darkly articulate contemporaries for an analogy similar in magnitude as well as in principle. But the principle, that on which literary reputations are formed, has been valid since the overt collapse, contemporary with Shakespeare, of the moral and political structure

19

of western Europe. Ever since then the artist has been looked to for psychological ordering, for a cathartic action in which the moral fears and confusions of the audience could be implicated and purged. (The development of the headline and the thriller as purgatives of more obvious efficiency is not unrelated to an eighty years' decline in the size of the audience for poetry.) That is why Aristotle's metaphor of catharsis has been so violently disputed: in the Greek drama of which he wrote the cathartic function, united with a body of political and religious conventions, took place less in the recesses of the psyche than at a level of ritual, of habituated intelligibility, which corresponds to the philosopher's detached, almost offhand tone. It is also why the recent vogue of Dante, the exponent of a corresponding Christian order, is even in Eliot a bit wistful; and why Chaucer, who is strongly in the Ben Jonson–Pound tradition, is not read as literature but as philology.

Many of Mr. Eliot's phalanx of readers undoubtedly draw this sort of psychic comfort from his pages. It is the main thing poetry is now thought to be for; and it is so far antipathetic to Pound's desiderated 'nutrition of impulse' that he may almost be said, as a poet, to have conscientiously precluded its possibility. Our deliberateness must match his, but he has not been deliberate because he had made poetry the art of a consummate mechanic, or because he was 'uninspired'. He asks complex acts of discernment, not immolation.

We were speaking, however, of some of Mr. Eliot's readers. 'It's so beautifully *morbid*,' said a debutante to the present writer, of *The Hollow Men*; and Anne Morrow Lindberg has taken to quoting his later poetry in *The Readers' Digest*. The author of a recent volume of commentary has taken heart from the resemblance of Eliot's dramatic situations to the stages of the process of psychic individuation as expounded by Jung; that this sort of interest proliferates is not, of course, a judgment on Mr. Eliot, since the same has come to be true of Donne and Shakespeare. It goes far, however, to explain the fluctuations of his reputation as his foci of interest have shifted and one body of admirers, with a feeling of being

cruelly cheated, has been replaced by another: involvement
to that degree in a poet's rhythms and personae has little to
do with a daylit rational delight in his proceedures. It also
explains why Pound, who is not susceptible of this kind of
misreading, has had, in an age that does not really care for
poetry except as therapeutic, except among certain other
writers next to no reputation at all. In Canto LXXX Pound
adverts to this state of affairs in his own way:

> Curious, is it not, that Mr. Eliot
> has not given more time to Mr. Beddoes
>   (T. L.) prince of morticians
>   where none can speak his language
> centuries hoarded
> to pull up a mass of algae
>   (and pearls)
> or the odour of eucalyptus or sea wrack.

and in further allusion to the connoisseur of Practical Cats:

> Prowling night-puss leave my hard squares alone
>   they are in no case cat food . . .
> You can neither eat manuscript nor Confucius
>   nor even the Hebrew scriptures . . .
> the cat-faced eucalyptus nib
>   is where you cannot get at it
>   Tune: kitten on the keys
>   radio steam Calliope
> following the Battle Hymn of the Republic
>   where the honey-wagon cease from stinking
>   and the nose be at peace
> 'mi-hine eyes hev'
>   well yes they *have*
> seen a good deal of it
>   there is a good deal to be seen
> fairly tough and unblastable
>   and the hymn . . .
> well in contrast to the *god*-damned crooning
>   put me down for the temporis acti

21

When Pound thus sets The Battle Hymn of the Republic against the 'crooning', his alignment with Browning, and Eliot's in some respects with Tennyson, is plain. The crooner in Tennyson, the voice that in the HMV recordings declaims the more unctuous periods of *Little Gidding*, have a temporary appeal to temporary psychic dislocations. This is not, once more, to devalue Eliot's position as one of the greatest poets in the language, past or present. It is merely to indicate that he is not much enjoyed at his own level: that much of his appeal is a therapeutic, cathartic appeal. Tennyson's reputation was *merely* so based, or more nearly. But beneath the cathartic crooner so indulged in by so many, there lies the great Eliot whom nobody reads. Just as there is a Pound whom, more literally, nobody reads, because he does not even afford the illusion of crooning.

Part One

'Ching Ming'

━━◁◁◁◁◁◁◁◁◁◁◁◁▷◁▷◁▷▷▷▷▷▷▷▷▷━━

At its start the book speaks of the one principle, it then spreads into a discussion of things in general, and concludes by uniting all this in the one principle. Spread it out and its arrows reach to the six ends of the universe, zenith and nadir; fold it again and it withdraws to serve you in secret as faithful minister. Its savour is inexhaustible. It is, all of it, solid wisdom. The fortunate and attentive reader directing his mind to the solid, delighting in it as in a gem always carried, penetrating into its mysterious purity, when he has come to meridian, to the precise understanding, can use it to the end of his life, never exhausting it, never able to wear it out.

—THE UNWOBBLING PIVOT
(Ciu Hsi's Preface)

Chapter 2

SOME MEANINGS OF
'INFLUENCE'

'But for Kuan Chung', sd/Confucius
'we shd/still be buttoning our coats tother way on.'

There is no ready-typed role in which the essentially
melodramatic imagination of the literary historian
can cast Ezra Pound, except perhaps the role of bar-
barian; hence he has little chance of starring in the academic
extravaganzas of the 1960's and '70's. Like Jonson or even
Landor, he seems destined to cliché status as a name on a
reading-list with perhaps a few malaprop tags: 'imagism' and
'ideogram', like 'humours' or 'lapidary verse'. Meanwhile the
shade of Eliot will be permitted to extend over his quarter-
century much of the uninspected supremacy which that of
Shakespeare exerts over a correspondingly turbulent age.
Not that the mills of literary journalism are being slow to
grind down Eliot also to cliché size: waste-land followed by
anxious faith, with footnotes on Laforgue and Saint John of
the Cross.

Those whose interest in academic sociology is clinical rather
than participant may observe this set of deformations already
in progress in numerous survey volumes which, whatever their
orientation, are alike in not having the slightest idea what to
do about Pound. One carries away, on the whole, an impression
of Pound as one who spat on the floor of the Palladian temple
and had somehow at the same time something to do with Mr.
Eliot's present eminence as high priest.

It gets more and more obvious that only Eliot's frequent tributes to the mentor and *miglior fabbro* have kept Pound's stock on the exchange at all (the left-wing *avant garde* in 1949 persistently implied that the Nobel prizewinner had rigged the Bollingen Committee). Shakespeare on the other hand never claimed to have been influenced by Ben Jonson, so Jonson has been jettisoned from literary small talk without embarrassment. The problem, then, for the academic historian, is to describe this Poundian 'influence', and to describe it in terms of the mechanical-Darwinian metaphor of 'influence' which he inherited from his nineteenth-century masters who founded the higher study of literature. He finds it, to his exasperation, a devil of a job.

This sort of metaphor can remain roughly plausible so long as its data are in the past. Keats, Milton, Wordsworth, Virgil, can exist in the mind of the historian as little foci of intricate vibration; the appropriate 'period' as a tank of vehicular fluid or a section of ether. The exact equation of the waves emanating from the bullfrog Virgil by the time, interacting with other sets of vibrations, they joggled the cork Tennyson, is a legitimate object of critical calculus. Nobody with a career to advance is going to object to the *poems* of Virgil and Tennyson being regarded simply as documents in the case. Pound and Eliot, on the contrary, are, and for some decades will within living memory have been, very much alive, with all the complexity that living in a specific overpopulated milieu entails. Until many data have perished, the kind of initial simplification entailed by these little problems in wave-mechanics cannot be convincingly performed. Hence the embarrassment of the historian of contemporary letters.

From one fact alone he draws approximate salvation. The intellectual physiognomy of Ezra Pound seems intrinsically, opaque (it would not be polite to the historian to say 'baffling'). Not a mind but a muscle; a Bohemian; a mid-Westerner; a frenzy behind a beard. Accordingly, he can be treated as a thick-skulled bull in a china-shop, or as a golf-ball bouncing around a room full of mouse-traps, depending upon one's opinion of the results. Eliot is then the new proprietor unhappily disposing of his fragmented stock, or else the biggest mousetrap, which was struck the directest hit and went off with the loudest snap: a snap that deafened everybody for twenty years. Of course the analyst need spend no pains on the golf-ball: that random missile from the Idaho wilderness.

It will be noted that in seeking to describe the notion of 'influence' employed by literary historians one is invariably driven for analogy towards mindless objects. Poets, by such an accounting, cease to be more or less learned and more or less rational human beings doing jobs of perception and vitalization: categories reserved in contemporary journalism for tycoons and diplomats. Poets exist to keep professors and editors in jobs, and perhaps to give purchasers of books a few pleasant afternoons in a hammock. Hence 'the tradition of art', etc., belongs to everybody except the poet, who qualifies as hired help; and every genuine innovation of expression (as distinguished from the pseudo-innovations of a Sitwell or a Dali, which are accepted as titillating) becomes an affront to decorum, i.e. to long-hoarded lecture-notes, to the investment contained in tons of stereotype metal, to the stability of arrangements of mental furniture, or the non-obsolescence of mechanisms of sensibility that came off the assembly-lines of a previous epoch.

Here, however is Pound on the same subject:

'It appears to me quite tenable that the function of litera-ture as a generated prize-worthy force is precisely that it does incite humanity to continue living; that it eases the mind of strain, and feeds it, I mean definitely as *nutrition of impulse*.

'This idea may worry lovers of order. Just as good literature does often worry them. They regard it as dangerous, chaotic, subversive. They try every idiotic and degrading wheeze to tame it down. They try to make a bog, a marasmus, a great putridity in place of a sane and active ebullience. And they do this from sheer simian and pig-like stupidity, and from their failure to understand the function of letters.'

Polite Essays, p. 163.

The reader will be ready to suppose from this that Pound, the 'influencer' *par excellence*, envisions the relations existing among artists rather differently. The listing of the kinds and degrees of writers in 'How to Read', *Polite Essays*, p. 167, runs (condensed) as follows:

'(*a*) *The inventors*, discoverers of a particular process or of more than one mode and process. Sometimes these people are known or discoverable; for example, we know that Arnaut Daniel introduced certain methods of rhyming, and we know that certain finenesses of perception appeared first in such a troubadour or in G. Cavalcanti....

'(*b*) *The masters*. This is a very small class, and there are very few real ones. The term is properly applied to inventors who apart from their own inventions, are able to assimilate and co-ordinate a large number of preceding inventions....

'(*c*) *The diluters*, those who follow either the inventors or the "great writers", and who produce something of lower intensity. . . .

'(*d*) The men who do more or less good work in the more or less good style of a period. . . . At their faintest "*Ils n'existent pas, leur ambiance leur confert une existence.*" . . .

'(*e*) *Belles Lettres* . . . who can hardly be said to have originated a form, but who have nevertheless brought some mode to a very high development.

'(*f*) . . . the starters of crazes, the Ossianic McPhersons . . . whose wave of fashion flows over writing for a few centuries or a few decades, and then subsides, leaving things as they were.'

It would clarify immensely the bulk of literary discussion to keep such classifications as these in view; one might even venture, as an illustration of principle, to suggest contemporary candidates:

(*a*) *The inventors*. In our time, pre-eminently Pound.
(*b*) *The masters*. Eliot, Joyce.
(*c*) *The diluters*. Auden, Spender, the Sitwells, 'the thirties'.
(*d*) *Workers in 'the style of the period'*. To be filled in *ad lib.* W. C. Williams? Hemingway?

(*e*) *Belles Lettres*. Ford Madox Ford, perhaps.

(*f*) *Starters of crazes*. Gertrude Stein.

Pound, needless to say, is not responsible for the above nominations, from some of which he might be expected to register emphatic dissent. They may serve however to emphasize one or two points.

FIRST, critical categories are meaningless except in particular terms. The reader should pay line-by-line attention to the entire 'How to Read' essay and to Pound's contention that a knowledge of the books and poems where formulable technical innovations, incorporation into literature of new provinces of thought and feeling, take place, is essential to informed critical judgment. Technical innovation is not necessarily to be confused with orthographic or syntactic high-jinks; innovation can always be counterfeited, and this need not invalidate gilt-edged issue. A major poem, any major poem, IS such an innovation. The innovator handles language in novel ways because his expression is too deeply engaged with his sensibility, his sincerity is too urgent, for received moulds to suffice. The *juvenilia* of every major poet consist of a series of attempts to learn the lessons of his predecessors while purging his sensibility of their mannerisms. His period of fecundity starts when he has invented a language of his own.

SECOND, Pound as literary historian, especially in 'How to Read', *ABC of Reading*, and *Make it New*, keeps our interest focused with scientific precision on discoveries: the masterworks are those in which discoveries are embodied. He has frequently adduced a scientific parallel which is of more than strategic significance:

'People regard literature as something vastly more flabby and floating and complicated and indefinite than, let us say, mathematics. Its subject-matter, the human consciousness, is more complicated than are number and space. It is not, however, more complicated than biology, and no one ever supposed that it was. . . .

'And we could, presumably, apply to the study of literature a little of the common sense that we currently apply to physics or to biology. In poetry there are simple procedures, and there are known discoveries, clearly marked. . . . In each age one or two men of genius find something, and express it. It may be only in a line or in two lines, or in some quality of a cadence; and thereafter two dozen, or two hundred, or two or more thousand followers repeat and dilute and modify.

If the instructor would select his specimens solely from works that contain these discoveries and solely on the basis of discovery. . . .'

Polite Essays, pp. 160–1.

(Such a 'discovery' is not of course to be thought of as a recipe for poetasters. We shall consider later the frequent complaints that Pound in the *Cantos* 'can only translate', 'i, nothing but a technician,' etc., charges which presuppose the *mode* of valid creation to be parthenogenesis, and which imply as he nowhere implies, a separation between technique and perception, or between the eye and sight.)

THIRD, available literary histories are not being impotently spat at, it is their basis that is challenged. The historian of *reputations* would shuffle the names in the example above quite differently. He might put Miss Sitwell in class (*f*) or Auden *et al.* in classes (*b*) or (*d*). Pound is concerned, however, with the progress of an art whose subject-matter and equipment are alike to be sought in the human consciousness; an art, moreover, international and interlingual in a way that our present hypertrophied neuro-muscular sensitivity to the morphologies of racial sensibility scarcely permits us to suspect. (See, for example, his notes on the metamorphosis of Tuscan song in Renaissance England: *Make It New*, pp. 396–407). He ranks Donne as he does, and not among the 'masters', with an eye on Cavalcanti. He places Virgil and Petrarch as 'dubious cases' with an eye on Homer and the troubadours. The enormous historical importance of Virgil and Petrarch to the European historian, and later of Donne to the English, does not bear a direct relation to their specific gravity. Which is not to say that they are negligible poets, ungifted men, foolish men, or a waste of even the busy reader's time.

It should also be noted that sherry-party ammunition has not been provided here in the form of a neat declension of ranks. Ford Madox Ford brought the impressionist novel to a very high development, notably in his memoirs. He has no English rival. He knew more, did more, and means more than, say, Mr. Auden. To stick him among the belle-lettrists would not imply otherwise.

What has often seemed the impiety or obtuseness of Mr. Pound's judgments on dead writers is generally explained by his sharp focus not on Johnsonian personality nor on historical accident of the kind that has placed Milton where he is, but on actual written achievement, on the doing of what had not hitherto been done, on new consolidations of values. The reading of Elizabethan translators, for instance, persuaded him that the credit due Milton for developing the resonance of the English blank verse paragraph was 'probably much less than other people have until now supposed' ('Now'=1916. The results of this piece of research have not yet, over thirty years later, been absorbed into the literary histories. Whether such time-lags are tolerated in other sciences it is vain to inquire.)

Chapter 3

RESEARCH

'Thass a funny lookin' buk' said the Baronet . . .
'Wu . . . Wu . . . wot you goin' eh to do with ah . . .
. . . ah read-it?'

The preceding discussion should suggest that Pound's 'influence' on the foremost writers of his time has not been confined merely to the energy with which he procured them a hearing; though it was in fact he who picked nearly every winner in his generation, a credential sufficiently rare among critics. His importance lies much more in his technical discoveries, in the amelioration he has afforded to the art he practised. It is inseparable, in other words, from major achievement. So it makes no sense to pay Pound lip-service on this score, and yet continue writing off the *Cantos*.

Again, there has been some point in isolating to some degree the spirit in which he has gone to the literature of the past. 'I began an examination of comparative European literature in or about 1901; with the definite intention of finding out what had been written, and how. The motives I presumed to differ with the individual writers.' On the other hand, 'English and American criticism of the generation preceding mine . . . has been occupied chiefly with the inane assertion of the non-existence of the giraffe, and not of the giraffe alone, but of whole tribes of animals, the puma, the panther, the well-known Indian buffalo.'

He set out, that is, to acquire professorial expertise in Comparative Letters (in particular, Romance literature) by the detailed examination of actual specimens.

Such knowledge is usually acquired from handbooks, lecture-courses, etc., to be used as 'background' for a lifetime of specialization on a figure or a period. Rings of interest radiate outward from a single point of impact to lose themselves in inanition. The possessor of the knowledge is seldom razor-certain of what he does or doesn't know.

'The difference between what is known and what is merely faked or surmised has at all times seemed to me worth discovering. Obviously the more limited the field the more detailed can the demarcation become.'

As an example of such delimitation he cites his edition of Guido Cavalcanti, with MS. facsimiles and necessary apparatus. The attention there focused on one author does not differ in principle from that focused elsewhere in Pound's prose on much larger bodies of literature. That Joyce in *Ulysses* brought to consummation what Flaubert undertook in *Bouvard et Pécuchet* is knowledge of this kind. That 'Catullus, Ovid, Propertius, all give us something we cannot find now in Greek authors' is knowledge of this kind. A remark about Shelley's 'lyrical soul' probably isn't.

In this connection *The Spirit of Romance* (1910) is worth reading both as a mine of information and as evidence of the spirit in which Pound from the very beginning undertook his critical labours. The paragraphs in that book are mostly very short. Each one adds a brick. The bricks are not gathered to be heaved at anyone, but to be cemented into an edifice of the known and examined. The quality of perception consolidated in a certain poem is as much a datum as is the date of its composition. A certain poet's ability to maintain an unbroken melodic line, the skill of another at compelling intricate rhymes to *function*, rather than ornament his song, are not swamped in handbook generalizations about the 'troubadours'. The labelling of guesswork as such, the dissociation of lumps into elements, the discarding of unearned reputations, the definition of what was actually achieved by whom, are the marks of a considerable labour of purification.

There are two forms of the impulse to generalize. The

commoner substitutes a statement for a set of facts in order
to disembarrass the mind of further consideration of those
facts: dealing with a recalcitrant watch by melting it down.
The contrary generalizing power that is not a form of sloth is
akin to poetic creation, building out of data an intelligible
form in as it were an act of homage to the nourishing virtue
of the particular perceptions. The first kind of mind takes its
revenge in proscribing or deriding the analogies, epigrams, and
parabolic locutions in which the second is fertile. Pound's
comparison of Dante and Villon issues in remarks like these:

'Where Dante has boldness of imagination, Villon has the
stubborn persistency of one whose gaze cannot be deflected
from the actual fact before him; what he sees, he writes.
Dante is in some ways the most personal of poets; he holds the
image up to nature, but he is himself that mirror. . . .

'Dante is many men, and suffers as many. Villon cries out
as one. He is a lurid canto of the "Inferno", written too late
to be included in the original text.'

Spirit of Romance, pp. 178, 189.

These are not blocks of picturesque phraseology. They are
vigorously worded not because their author has a 'gift for
epigram' but because he possesses and is possessed by a detailed familiarity with two large bodies of writing. For some
reason the alertness of Pound's prose suggests to many
readers that he has barely glanced at his text as a stimulus to
saying something clever. Hence it is of paramount importance
to realize the amount of close reading that went into this early
book. It is fatal to suppose that we are dealing with a sparking-
mechanism that explodes on contact.

Curiously, this critic who is accused of slapdash formulation
inhabits the same body with the poet who is accused of being
unable to get beyond his documents. To the stereoscopic gaze
of plenary critical judgment Pound the critic and Pound the
poet are the same organism. The cross-eyed supposition that
we are in the presence of two unblended functions breeds
nothing but confusion. *The Spirit of Romance* abounds both
in aphorisms of the kind cited above, and in extensive bodies

of quotation. The entire interest of the author is engaged in both kinds of presentation. Similarly the *Cantos* abound both in brilliantly realized fusions of multiform experience (e.g. XXXIX) AND in bundles of unvarnished transcriptions out of prose sources (e.g. XXXIII). The alert quest of defined and realized experience that fused certain overtones of a whole book of the *Odyssey* into:

> Eurilochus, Macer, better there with good acorns
> Than with a crab for an eye, and 30 fathom of fishes
> Green swish in the socket,

was the same that prized and conserved this unaltered morsel of Jeffersonian incision:

'removal wd. be necessary to more able commissaries rather than to a more plentiful country. (T. J. on provisions.)'

And the 'esemplastic power' that built a memorable canto out of visions of the first kind was functioning equally, selecting, weighing, relating, juxtaposing, in the building of another canto out of quotations of the second kind.

Pound's critical writings ('critical' need not be restricted to literary materials) are reports on investigations into bodies of writing. His poetry constitutes a series of reports on investigations into wider ranges of experience. The critic set out to dissipate guesswork, to dissociate facts, to uncover procedures, to define reputations in terms of achievement. The poet set out to embody emotions actually undergone, to discriminate modes of moral and passionate being, to afford volitional nutriment, to define phases of civilization in terms of human realization.

Shortly before the commencement of the *Cantos*, Pound undertook two long surveys of Elizabethan translators and translators of Greek (both in *Make It New*). In these essays he was concerned to assess the adequacy with which successive workers had realized in the linguistic materials available to them certain transcendent bodies of poetic perception. In the *Cantos*, especially the opening thirty, he assesses the embodiment in divers men and civilizations of moral potentials as real

35

to his mind as the text of Homer. The Homeric wisdom, for example, manifests itself in the life of Greece and Venice as the Homeric poem in the pages of Pope and Chapman.

The relationship between these critical and poetic undertakings should not be overlooked.

Chapter 4

CHING MING

et qu'on n'employât que des termes propres
(namely CH'ing ming)

The whole key to Pound, the basis of his *Cantos*, his music, his economics, and everything else, is this concern for exact definition. The worried reader may rest assured that we shall proceed to illustrate and justify this statement. A conspectus of what lies before us may be secured by transcribing the fourth paragraph of Pound's final version of the Confucian *Ta Hio*, a work which he has repeatedly cited as 'what I believe'.

'4. The men of old wanting to clarify and diffuse throughout the empire that light which comes from looking straight into the heart and then acting, first set up good government in their own states; wanting good government in their own states, they first established order in their own families; wanting order in the home, they first disciplined themselves; desiring self-discipline, they rectified their own hearts; and wanting to rectify their hearts, they sought precise verbal definitions of their inarticulate thoughts (the tones given off by the heart); wishing to attain precise verbal definitions, they set to extend their knowledge to the utmost. The completion of knowledge is rooted in sorting things into organic categories.'

(A more obviously literary analogue may be secured by substituting 'their own arts' for 'their own families'.)

Starting at the bottom of the scale, we have indicated the beginnings of Pound's endeavour to 'extend his knowledge to the utmost' in the interest of 'precise verbal definitions'. The 'Ching Ming' ideograph of this latter principle makes its first appearance in the *Cantos* at the end of Canto LI and recurs throughout the following nineteen cantos, whose orientation is explicitly political (e.g. *Cantos LII to LXXI*, pp. 79, 98, 128, 133, 146). This scale extending from philology to government and ultimately to that extension of enlightenment (not necessarily coterminous with Great Books Course enterprises) which may be taken as convertible with 'civilization' ('the men of old wanting to clarify and diffuse throughout the empire that light which comes from looking straight into the heart and then acting') is both the major principle of unity in the *Cantos* and in Pound's career of usefulness to letters. To say that the unity of the *Cantos* is Pound is not as limiting a judgment as might at first appear.

正名

The Ching Ming[1] ideograph has levels of signification beginning with orthography and ending with the most intimate moral discriminations. 'Call things by their right names.' Don't, for example, call a man Comptroller of the Currency unless he really controls it. Less literally, finding 'the precise words for the inarticulate heart's tones' relates conduct scrupulously to motives, motives to perceptions, formulations to observations, theory to practice, poetry to things seen and sensations undergone. 'Orthography is a discipline of morale and of morals.'

[1] More properly chêng[4] ming[2], according to one dictionary, but there is no uniformity in these matters. The left-hand component, according to Pound, means 'Governor' (hitching-post or king-pin uniting various levels of being, ground and sky, perhaps); the right-hand component is the sign of the waning moon over the mouth: terminology drifting through successive phases and requiring to be re-aligned with fact.

Chapter 5

CHISEL VS. DAISY-CHAIN

**The fourth; the dimension of stillness.
And the power over wild beasts.**

A further couple of chapters had better be inserted at this point simply for the sake of emphasis. Here, if anywhere, it is relevant to heap up instances. We are saying nothing that isn't in *Polite Essays* (notably 'How to Read') or in the 'Date Line' preface to *Make It New*. Both these volumes are, at the time of writing, more or less readily obtainable. But what may be described as the relation of politics to letters is one of Pound's two key insights, failure to grasp which has perhaps more than anything else debarred perfectly willing readers from access to the *Cantos*. (The other key insight, to which we shall shortly come, is the fact that juxtaposed objects render one another intelligible without conceptual interposition.)

In Canto LXXIV the following exchange occurs:

> the useful operations of commerce
> stone after stone of beauty cast down
> and authenticities disputed by parasites
> (made in Ragusa) and: what art do you handle?
> 'The best' And the moderns? 'Oh, nothing modern
> we couldn't sell anything modern.'

In *Polite Essays* (p. 53) the same conversation (with a New York art dealer loose on a quai in Venice) is related as evidence of the meaning of a word like 'the best' when 'rotted by commerce'.

'The word, rotted by commerce, affects us all where we live. It has built up a set of counterfeit "idealists" who jeopard every man's life, mind, and food.'

The reader will have no difficulty confirming this statement in respect of such words as 'bread' (see Seigfried Giedion's *Mechanization Takes Command*), 'education' (as lately as 1890 an 'educated' man could read *The Odyssey*), 'literature' (now applied to snake-oil pamphlets: 'Send the coupon for FREE literature'), 'democracy,' 'artist' (=pansy or doodler), 'poem,' 'justice,' 'accuracy' (connotes measurement only), 'politics,' 'beautiful.'

It should be noted that the violence of an art-dealer to a word is equated in Canto LXXIV with the violence of commercial demolition or bombardment: 'stone after stone of beauty cast down.'

Consideration of these facts may engender some *a priori* suspicion that the man who devotes a lifetime to the amelioration of poetry does not necessarily incur the limiting connotations of 'aestheticism'. Purer-hearted Lotus-eaters than those of Bloomsbury are as a matter of fact consigned to the cadres of parasitism in a memorable passage in the *Cantos*:

Floating. Below, sea churning shingle.
Floating, each on invisible raft
On the high current, invisible fluid,
Borne over the plain, recumbent,
The right arm cast back,
    the right wrist for a pillow. . . .

              Reclining,
With the silver spilla,
The ball as of melted amber, coiled, caught up, and turned.
Lotophagoi of the suave nails, quiet, scornful,
Voce profondo:
      'Feared neither death nor pain for this beauty;
If harm, harm to ourselves.'

                      (Canto XX).

Some work, some float. The counterweight is given previously in the preternatural alertness of Cantos VIII–XI, and subsequently in the chorus of the 'clear bones' of the drowned mariners.[1]

The drama of *Mauberley*, the climactic poem of Pound's second period, commands similar tensions:

> For three years, diabolus in the scale,
> He drank ambrosia . . .
>
> .   .   .   .
>
> To be certain . . . certain . . .
> (Amid aerial flowers) . . . time for arrangements—
> Drifted on
> To the final estrangement;
> Unable in the supervening blankness
> To sift TO AGATHON from the chaff
> Until he found his sieve . . .
> Ultimately, his seismograph . . .

'Le parfum des violettes un tonnerre.' This metamorphosis of down-drifting lotus-petals into seismic tremors demanding a radical alteration in the daisy-gatherer's analytic equipment both parodies the onset of clumsy post-war conceptions of the poet's 'social responsibility' (Auden and Isherwood) and parallels the overhaul our conceptions of the artist's usefulness must undergo before we are equipped to understand the passion of Pound's and Flaubert's concern for *le mot juste*.

' "Artists are the antennae of the race." They are the registering instruments, and if they falsify their reports there is no measure to the harm that they do. If you saw a man selling

---

[1] If we can rid our minds of the expectation of sulphur and brimstone, we can see, by juxtaposing this passage and a comment of Charles Williams on Dante, the sense in which the first thirty Cantos correspond to an Inferno. Apropos of Dante's sentence, 'The proper function is not in existence for the sake of the being, but the being for the sake of the function' (*De Monarchia*, I, iii), Williams writes, 'This is the primal law for all the images, of whatever kind; they were created for their working, and in order to work. Hell is the cessation of work and the leaving of the images to be, without any function, merely themselves.' (*The Figure of Beatrice*, p. 40). The 'if harm, harm to ourselves' of the Lotophagoi is in this sense only a more stoical mask of Francesca's 'Love led us to one death' (*Inferno* V, 106).

defective thermometers to a hospital, you would consider him
a particularly vile kind of cheat.'

Polite Essays, p. 116.

John Adams observes in Canto LXII:

Magazines, daily pamphlets in hands of men of no character
in fact one bookseller said to me: can get 'em at a guinea a day
to write pro or con anything. Hired!

In an important formulation of *circa* 1928 Pound thus describes
the function of literature in the State:

'It has to do with the clarity of 'any and every' thought
and opinion. It has to do with maintaining the very cleanliness
of the tools, the health of the very matter of thought itself.
Save the rare and very limited instances of the plastic arts, or
in mathematics, the individual cannot think or communicate
his thought, the governor and legislator cannot act effectively
or frame his laws, without words, and the solidarity of these
words is in the care of the damned and despised *literati*. When
their work goes rotten—by that I do not mean when they express indecorous thoughts—but when their very medium, the
very essence of their work, the application of word to thing
goes rotten, i.e. becomes slushy and inexact, or excessive or
bloated, the whole machinery of social and individual thought
and order goes to pot.'

Polite Essays, p. 164.

Such a pronouncement would not have been understood either
by the English writers from whose hands Pound received
the tradition of the language at the turn of the century, or by
the Edwardian and Georgian journalist-poets from whom he
has always, with understandable exasperation, tried to defend
it:

'I doubt if any of us in 1911 clearly articulated the proposition: there ought to be an active literature for if its literature
be not active a nation will die at the top. When literature is
not active; when the word is not constantly striving towards
precision, the nation decays in its head. There may be to-day

42

some conception of the nation as a whole, but the sense of the nation as a total intellectual organism is, to put it mildly, deficient. . . .'

Polite Essays, p.5.

Yeats' emblematic tower—

> Is every modern nation like the tower,
> Half dead at the top?

—receives sardonic emendation in *The Pisan Cantos*:

My dear William B. Y. your $\frac{1}{2}$ was too moderate.

In the *Cantos* as elsewhere Pound has indicated that the contention against bloat and rot is permanent, rising occasionally to a pitched battle. Mr. Eliot's intuition of continual new beginnings against

> the general mess of imprecision of feeling,
> Undisciplined squads of emotion

has made this motif fairly familiar in the past ten years. But the *Quartets* are subtler than their commentators, and the studied nervelessness of their rhythms has led many to suppose that all that is in question is a harassed and fastidious sense of being overwhelmed peculiar to Mr. Eliot. It is, on the contrary, as clear to him as to Pound that the poet in revising a line, the scholar reclaiming from half-opinion a text or a tradition, are repeating the stand of a Hercules against Hydra-headed irruption and aerating the very blood of civilization.[1] Here, for example, is a Poundian account of the Renaissance:

'And in the midst of these awakenings Italy went to rot, destroyed by rhetoric, destroyed by the periodic sentence and by the flowing paragraph, as the Roman Empire had been destroyed before her. For when words cease to cling close to things, kingdoms fall, empires wane and diminish. Rome went because it was no longer the fashion to hit the nail on the head. They desired orators. . . .

'Quintillian "did for" the direct sentence. And the Greek

[1] 'Flaubert said of the War of 1870: "If they had read my *Education Sentimentale*, this sort of thing wouldn't have happened".'—*Make It New*, p. 254.

43

language was made an excuse for more adjectives. . . . The attempt to reproduce Greek by Latin produced a new dialect that was never spoken and had never before been read. The rhetoric got into painting. The habit of having no definite convictions save that it was glorious to reflect life in a given determined costume or decoration "did for" the painters. . . .

'The Renaissance sought a realism and attained it. It rose in a search for precision and declined through rhetoric and rhetorical thinking, through a habit of defining things always "in terms of something else".'

Gaudier-Brzeska, pp. 136–41.

Opposition to 'rhetoric' is a far from simple position; it should not be supposed that anything so naïve as simple impatience with a multiplicity of words is involved in the above diagnosis. Nor are Pound's strictures on rhetoric to be confused with the romantic-Ockhamist opinion of Croce (the most familiar modern anti-rhetorician) that once the aesthetic intuition is formulated no expanding, re-shaping, or re-handling is valid. It would be puzzling if Pound, the technician *par excellence*, could be identified with an opposition to rhetorical artifice that was really a disguise for the romantic opposition to the artist's employment of conscious procedures.

In decrying the classical and renaissance cult of verbosity Pound's alignment is with the line of tirelessly moral aphoristic wisdom running from Seneca through Montaigne into the French Enlightenment. It was this tradition, as Gilson's *Héloise et Abelard* makes clear, that was congenial to the Christian distrust of magnificence. During the Renaissance itself Senecan and Ciceronian party-lines were drawn in such a way as to engage the widest moral and theological issues. The Senecan utilized rather the aphorism than the periodic sentence, and so exalted the sage rather than the orator, private virtue leavening the *res publica* rather than the flamboyant man of affairs. It is this tradition that opposes the Jonsonian spareness, his witty flexibility of tone rather than trope, to the lavish magniloquence of Marlowe. It is in this tradition that Bacon eschews the appearance of system in the delivery of knowledge, since aphorisms encourage men to enquire further.[1] It is to this tradition, with its almost Confucian progression between empirical enquiry, linguistic sincerity, private worth, and public benefit, that Pound may be said to belong.

It may be gathered from this account that Pound's apparent dissipation of energy is a post-Victorian illusion. His centre of operations is a tradition that last came to focus in Europe early in the eighteenth century. In England Dryden's and Milton's 'magniloquence' distended it, and the Latinate diction of Pound's *Lustra* period marks an attempt to create, with French help, an English 'eighteenth century' sensibility without Milton, to serve as a new starting point: a way of getting English poetry back on the road at the point of derailment. His earlier Romance studies correspond to the enthusiasms that fed the precedent Renaissance. His aphoristic prose should be compared, as to form, with the *Pensées* and with Jonson's *Timber*. The French Enlightenment, if its weakness was Cartesian, drew its strength from the Senecan (we have adduced Montaigne). And it was the Enlightenment that discovered Confucius for Europe. The elegant ironic Latinisms of Pound's society verse,

> His brother has taken to gypsies,
> But the son-in-law of Mr. H. Styrax
> Objects to perfumed cigarettes.

[1] Bacon's words are sufficiently relevant to the rationale of such a volume as *Culture* to be worth quoting at length:

'. . . the writing in aphorisms hath many excellent virtues, whereto the writing in method doth not approach.

'For first it trieth a writer whether he be superficial or solid: for aphorisms, except they should be ridiculous, cannot be made but of the pith and heart of sciences: for discourse of illustration is cut off; recitals of examples are cut off; discourse of connexion and order is cut off; descriptions of practice are cut off; so there remaineth nothing to fill the aphorisms but some good quantity of observation. . . . Secondly, methods are more fit to win consent or belief, but less fit to point to action; for they carry a kind of demonstration in orb or circle, one part illuminating another, and therefore satisfy. But particulars being dispersed, do best agree with dispersed directions. And lastly, aphorisms, representing a knowledge broken, do invite men to inquire further; whereas methods carrying the show of a total, do secure men as if they were at farthest.'
Advancement of Learning, Bk. II.

In the parlance of Niccolo Machiavelli:
'Thus things proceed in their circle';
And thus the empire is maintained.

correspond to a tone, mightily present in Laforgue, that has not lost its power to tincture English speech whenever, as with Pope and Rochester, the latter has come into contact with post-seventeenth century French. (Voltaire and the *Dunciad* have a component in common. Pope, like his friend Swift, was thoroughly Senecan both in his concern for keeping the channels of language uncluttered and in his tireless insistence on private morals as the leaven of public. It was these ingredients of the Augustan poise that made possible its intercourse with contemporary French thought.) The milieu of Jefferson and Adams was, again, the eighteenth-century French vanguard; so there is nothing fortuitous about Pound's juxtaposition of China and young America in Cantos LII to LXXI. And there is, finally, enough of the tradition of Christian Senecanism (not to be confused with the Elizabethan re-emphasis, chronicled by Mr. Eliot, on the Senecan dramatic experiments) in the bloodstream of Europe to render Mr. Pound's attempted infusion of Confucius not impossibly exotic. Which is not to say that his operations have been either old hat or unnecessary.

Concern for the health of language and thought should not be thought to have been a virtue exclusive to Senecans: witness Joyce's demonstration, in the wake of Saint Augustine, of the possibilities of tension and sincerity within an elaborate style, and his concurrent satirization of irresponsible ornament and made-to-order cliché. But with the Senecans as with Pound these concerns received an unwavering centrality of emphasis.

'The serious artist', therefore, whom Pound in an early essay describes, in the terms outlined above, as the maintainer of the mental health of the state, has concerns identical with those of the serious philosopher, the serious ruler, the serious editor or publisher, the serious teacher. He keeps up values. As long ago as 1910, long before doctrinaire emphasis could be suspected of warping his eye for fact, Pound had noted, as a perfectly natural phenomenon, Dante's grouping of the usurers and the violent against art in the same quarter of Hell. The widely-anthologized Canto XLV adduces multiple analogies for the same perception:

> with usura
> seeth no man Gonzago his heirs and his concubines
> no picture is made to endure nor to live with
> but is made to sell and sell quickly
> with usura, sin against nature,
> is thy bread ever more of stale rags
> is thy bread dry as paper,
> with no mountain wheat, no strong flour
> with usura the line grows thick
> with usura is no clear demarcation. . . .

These are not merely arguable economic statements. They furnish, in their collectivity, an ideogram of a state of mind and its contrary. Unless the distinction between 'clear demarcation' and its opposite can become vivid to the reader, and unless he can overcome the notion that the former is the property of the mathematical sciences, whereas poetry is a matter of imprecisions and shifting roseate veils, there is no hope of his penetrating the *Cantos* or even of reading Shakespeare. It was a poet who remarked of metaphysics,

'Unless a term is left meaning one particular thing, and unless all attempt to unify different things, however small the difference, is clearly abandoned, all metaphysical thought degenerates into a soup. A soft terminology is merely an endless series of indefinite middles.'

Make It New, p. 389.

It was a poet who attributed the decline of the Renaissance to the growing habit of talking about things 'in terms of something else', and in the same volume quoted Barzun's invective against 'poésie farcie de "comme" '.

Pound sees the racial or national consciousness, from its poetry down to its pig-selling, as a continuum. The distinction of the poet is simply that he deals in ideas that are more, not less, definite than those of the grocer. 'Not the idea but the degree of its definition determines its aptitude for reaching to music.' Music: not necessarily a lilt or unbroken vowels, but 'music of ideas', a phrase frequently tossed into a gap in the speaker's knowledge during discussions of Eliot, but actually susceptible of definite exemplification—the tension, interplay, and mutual modification among juxtaposed units each of which is the verbal embodiment of a sharply defined perception.[1] Such verbal exactitudes, taken from the correspondence of John Adams, are set in motion in the un-canorous Cantos LXII–LXXI. It is the essence of Pound's praise of Adams, and intimately related to Adams' political efficiency, that his casual phrases are so closely derived from his sense of fact as to permit of this use. The early Chinese editors anthologized Confucian dicta in the same way. These Cantos are the Analects of Adams, as comparable technical devices in Pound's new translation of the Confucian Analects make plain. The poetic rationale of the *Pisan Cantos*, with the 'items' largely phrased or re-phrased by Pound and drawn from a very wide variety of sources, is identical in principle. No-one will deny the unforgettable lucidity of any fragment of that sequence. The difficulty, with which we shall eventually be dealing, is only to see how they belong side by side.

[1] 'Dante lives in his mind; to him two blending thoughts give a music perceptible as two blending notes of a lute. He is in the real sense an idealist. He sings of true pleasures; he sings as exactly as Villon; they are admirably in agreement: Dante to the effect that there are supernormal pleasures, enjoyable by man through the mind; Villon to the effect that the lower pleasures lead to no satisfaction.'

Spirit of Romance, p. 188.

Chapter 6

HARMONY

... and with one day's reading a man may have the key in his hands ...

There should by now be no difficulty in seeing how Pound, who introduced the author of *Little Gidding* to the permanent significance of Dante, cannot be neglected as an implicit component in the 'familiar compound ghost' who among the ruins of a burning world confronts the fire-watching Eliot in incarnate magistracy: Tradition confronting the Individual Talent.

> Since our concern was speech, and speech impelled us
> 　　To purify the dialect of the tribe
> 　　And urge the mind to aftersight and foresight. ...

It is true, and a commentator's commonplace, that Mallarmé, with his 'Donner un sens plus pur aux mots de la tribu', is prominently represented in that second line; but the voice, no matter whose the phrase, is the voice of Pound. A final sheaf of instances:

'The WORD built out of perception of COMPONENT parts of its meaning reaches down and through and out into all ethics and politics. Clean the word, clearly define its borders, and health pervades the whole human congeries, *in una parte più e meno altrove.*'

Polite Essays, p. 52.

'An artist's technique is a test of his personal validity. Honesty of the word is the writer's first aim, for without it he can communicate nothing efficiently. . . . Orthology is a discipline both of *morale* and of morals.'

Polite Essays, p. 193.

'. . . As language becomes the most powerful instrument of perfidy, so language alone can riddle and cut through the meshes. Used to conceal meaning, used to blur meaning, used to produce the complete and utter inferno of the past century . . . against which, SOLELY a care for language, for accurate registration by language avails.'

Make It New, p. 7.

'The history of literary criticism is the history of a vain struggle to find a terminology which will define something.'

The Spirit of Romance, p. 3.

In the 'Don'ts for Imagists' of 1913:

'Use no superfluous word, no adjective, which does not reveal something.

'Don't use such an expression as 'dim lands *of peace*'. It dulls the image. It mixes an abstraction with a concrete. . . .

'Go in fear of abstractions. Do not re-tell in mediocre verse what has already been done in good prose. . . .'

Reprinted in *Make It New*, p. 337.

In the 'Digest of the Analects' which opens *Culture*, where the political bearings of exact terminology are explicated:

'Tseu-Lou asked: If the Prince of Mei appointed you head of the government, to what wd. you first set your mind?

'KUNG[1]: To call people and things by their names, by the correct denominations, to see that the terminology was exact. . . .

' "You mean that is the first?" said Tseu-Lou. "Aren't you dodging the question? What's the use of that?"

'KUNG: You are a blank. An intelligent man hesitates to talk of what he don't understand, he feels embarrassment.

'If the terminology be not exact, if it fit not the thing, the governmental instructions will not be explicit, if the instruc-

[1] Kung-fu-tse: Confucius.

50

tions aren't clear and the names don't fit, you can not conduct business properly.

'If business is not properly run the rites and music will not be honoured, if the rites and music be not honoured, penalties and punishments will not achieve their intended effects, if penalties and punishments do not produce equity and justice, the people won't know where to put their feet or what to lay hold of or to whom they shd. stretch out their hands.'

Culture, pp. 16–17.

A small paradigm of the organization of the *Cantos*, or rather one dimension of that organization, may be had by setting beside this the third section of *The Unwobbling Pivot*. The above conversation reaches from the Ching Ming ideogram towards the Jefferson-Adams-Chinese 'political' Cantos. The following citation expands the Ching Ming ideogram, or the Imagist Manifesto, in the opposite direction, into ethics and metaphysics, that is, into the 'lyric' Cantos, with their imagery of rain, light, and sculpturesque demarcation:

'. . . He who defines his words with precision will perfect himself and the process of this perfecting is in the process [that is, in the process *par excellence* defined in the first chapter, the total process of nature.]

'Sincerity is the goal of things and their origin, without this sincerity nothing is.

'On this meridian the man of breed respects, desires sincerity, holds it in honour and defines his terminology.

'. . . The inborn nature begets this activity naturally, this looking straight into oneself and thence acting. These two activities constitute the process which unites outer and inner, object and subject, and thence constitutes a harmony with the seasons of earth and heaven.

'Hence the highest grade of this clarifying activity has no limit, it neither stops nor stays.

'. . . With this penetration of the solid it has effects upon things, with this shining from on high, that is with its clarity of comprehension, now here, now yonder, it stands in the emptiness above with the sun, seeing and judging, interminable in space and in time, searching, enduring, and therewith it perfects even external things. . . .

'The celestial and earthly process pervades and is substantial; it is on high and gives light, it comprehends the light and is lucent, it extends without bound, and endures.'

The Unwobbling Pivot, III, xxv–xxvi.

'Harmony with the seasons of earth and heaven': compare—

> Know then:
> Toward summer when the sun is in Hyades
> Sovran is Lord of the Fire
> to this month are birds.
> with bitter smell and with the odour of burning
> To the hearth god, lungs of the victim
> The green frog lifts up his voice
> and the white latex is in flower. . . .

and the rest of the Canto (LII). In the next Canto this sense of ordered process gathered up in ritual is affiliated with art as the embodiment of a cognized overall harmony:

> Chun to the spirit Chang Ti, of heaven,
> moving the sun and stars
> que vos vers expriment vos intentions,
> et que la musique conforme

(French has been since the eighteenth century the modern European language of comparable precision. The polyglot features of the *Cantos* are far from fortuitous.)

'. . . It is on high and gives light, it comprehends the light and is lucent . . .' Compare, from Canto LXXIV,

> Light tensile immaculata
> the sun's cord unspotted
> 'sunt lumina' said the Oirishman to King Carolus,
> 'OMNIA,
> all things that are are lights'

'The Oirishman' is Scotus Erigena, the Catholic context of whose philosophy is fused with the Chinese sages elsewhere in the same Canto:

and this day the air was made open
for Kuanon of all delights,
Linus, Cletus, Clement
whose prayers,
the great scarab is bowed at the altar
the green light gleams in his shell
plowed in the sacred field and unwound the silk worms early
in tensile
in the light of light is the *virtù*
'sunt lumina' said Erigena Scotus
as of Shun on Mt Taishan
and in the hall of the forebears
as from the beginning of wonders
the paraclete that was present in Yao, the precision
in Shun the compassionate
in Yu the guider of waters

(For Yao, Shun, and Yu see the opening of Canto LIII. Linus, Cletus, and Clement are corresponding saints of the very early church who turn up in the prayers at the Mass. The scarab-shell is the priest's chasuble.)

Ching Ming—the purification of the Word—leads us in this way into a zone of perception, reaching naturally to poetry, common to all high civilizations. In how wide a field Pound's interests constitute a total unity of discriminate perception may be indicated by adducing a portion of his translation of the Cavalcanti *Donna Mi Prega*: it is of *Amor*, but the imagery is that of Confucius on The Process:

...yet is found the most
Where folk of worth be host.
And his strange property sets sighs to move
And wills man look into unformed space
Rousing there thirst
that breaketh into flame.
None can imagine love
that knows not love;
Love doth not move, but draweth all to him;

Nor does he turn
>> for a whim
>>>> to find delight
Nor to seek out, surely,
>>>> great knowledge or slight. . . .
There, beyond colour, essence set apart,
In midst of darkness light light giveth forth
Beyond all falsity, worthy of faith, alone
That in him solely is compassion born.

Make It New, pp. 354–5.

Another version of this canzone, registering as it does a summit in the definition and demarcation, through music, of certain crystalline perceptions, follows, in Canto XXXVI, the moral chaos of Mitteleuropa. It functions within the Cantos, that is, as a poetic image, naturally associating with other poetic images as we have seen it associating with Confucian terminology. Every poet's stock of imagery—Eliot's hyacinths, dove's wing, wheel, and 'eyes I dare not meet in dreams'; Donne's bones, devotions, and astrological lore; Baudelaire's 'prostitutes, mulattoes, Jewesses, serpents, cats, corpses,'—is capable of what at least seem, after he has made the connections, to be intrinsic associations, and serves to delimit point by point a particular world of perceptions. All that makes Pound's imagery seem unwieldy or pedantic is its independent status on the pages of anthologies, memoirs, and text-books. The juxtaposition of Cantos XXXV and XXXVI, or of the elements (Neo-Platonists, Curie, Stesichoros, De Maensac, Anchises) within Canto XXIII, obey precisely the same poetic principle as Donne's celebrated juxtaposition of two words in 'A bracelet of bright hair about the bone'. An articulated ultimate like the *Donna Mi Pregha* goes into a cultural plenum as a crucial word or image goes into a poem. Pound's learning is less haphazard than it has been fashionable to suppose, as we shall see in examining the uses to which it is put in the *Cantos*. That use is a poet's use: it is care for the word—the Ching Ming ideograph—that reaches towards political efficiency on the one hand and lyric intensity on the

54

other. We have seen this in Confucian texts, and we shall see it again in the *Cantos*.

Mr. Eliot has worked the same mine: his 'word' assailed by the shrieking voices of quotidian chatter becomes 'The Word in the desert' attacked by voices of temptation, and his intuition of order in *Little Gidding* is strikingly like that of Pound:

> And every phrase
> And sentence that is right (where every word is at home,
> Taking its place to support the others,
> The word neither diffident nor ostentatious,
> An easy commerce of the old and the new,
> The common word exact without vulgarity,
> The formal word precise but not pedantic,
> The complete consort dancing together)
> Every phrase and every sentence is an end and a beginning,
> Every poem an epitaph. . . .

It is ultimately in the spirit behind these lines that the heritage of Imagism, that much-epitaphed movement, is to be found.

Chapter 7

WHY IMAGISM?

so that you cd/ crack a flea on eider wan
ov her breasts
sd/ the old Dublin pilot
             or the precise definition

It is usual to outline Imagist internal politics with a smile and to judge the 'movement' by what happened to it at the hands of Amy Lowell ('Amygism'). It is also customary to say that H. D.'s poems are 'slight', or that the whole affair is reducible to the easily-learned trick of saying 'Butcher elbowed Baker in Threadneedle Street' instead of 'The street was full of people'. These are futile lines of approach. What Imagism in fact meant is perhaps easier to see if one starts at the beginning.

'In the spring or early summer of 1912, "H. D.", Richard Aldington and myself decided that we were agreed upon the three principles following:

'1. Direct treatment of the "thing" whether subjective or objective.

'2. To use absolutely no word that does not contribute to the presentation.

'3. As regarding rhythm: to compose in the sequence of the musical phrase, not in the sequence of a metronome. . . .

'The school was later "joined" or "followed" by numerous people who, whatever their merits, do not show any signs of agreeing with the second specification. *Vers Libre* has become as prolix and verbose as any of the flaccid varieties of prose that preceded it. It has brought in faults of its own. The actual language and phrasing of it is often as bad as that of our elders, without having even the excuse that the words are shovelled in to fill a metric pattern or to complete the noise of a rhyme-sound....'

Make It New, pp. 335–6.

An important corollary appears in the *ABC of Reading* (1934):

'The defect of earlier Imagist propaganda was not in misstatement but in incomplete statement. The diluters took the handiest and easiest meaning, and thought only of the STATIONARY image. If you can't think of imagism or phanopoeia as including the moving image, you will have to make a really needless division of fixed image and praxis or action.

'I have taken to using the term phanopoeia to get away from irrelevant particular connotations tangled with a particular group of young people who were writing in 1912.'

ABC of Reading, p. 36.

It should be noted that 'praxis' is Aristotle's term for the 'actions' by the imitation of which ('plot'), he says, the poet is known. His remarks on plot, which should be looked up, are entirely relevant to the present discussion.[1]

What exactly happened to the pioneer imagists need not concern us. The essentially feminine and 'poetical' sensibility of H. D. and Aldington, which joined itself only in a frigid and precious way with the new marmoreality *aere perennius*, and the incursion of Amy Lowell (whose work appeared in the first anthology because the group needed money, and whose talents, Pound said at the time in a letter to Margaret Anderson, 'will always be political rather than literary or artistic)

[1] e.g. *Poetics* VI, 2. 'All human happiness or misery takes the form of action; the end for which we live is a certain kind of activity, not a quality. Character gives us qualities but it is in our actions—what we do— that we are happy or the reverse. In a play accordingly they do not act in order to portray the characters; they include the characters for the sake of the action.'

When it is recalled that action (praxis) includes deeds, fortunes, and mental and emotional happenings, 'plot' will be seen to be applicable to a lyric as well as a tragedy. A sonnet, a *hokku*, depend on 'peripeteia' and 'discovery' as much as the *Œdipus*. The consequences of Fenollosa's perception that even the simplest sentence has a plot and imitates an action will be examined later.

eventually drove Pound away and into collaboration with Wyndham Lewis and 'Vorticism'. The Vortex, besides its emphasis, as above, on the *moving* (dynamic; dramatic) image, lent itself at Pound's hands to the ethical and metaphysical implications which were only consolidated with his Chinese studies at a later period. By 1916, with the republication of the long exposition of Vorticist aesthetics in *Gaudier-Brzeska: a Memoir*, the whole of Pound is present in embryo. It is thus important to keep one's eyes on Pound's texts, and avoid generalities about Imagism. The history of the Imagist Movement is a red herring.

The primary datum about the world into which Pound launched these corrective movements is given by his retrospective remark in the Harold Monro obituary:

'One of the densest, almost ubiquitous, English stupidities of that time was the disbelief that poetry was an art. Dozens of blockheads expected the crystal Helicon to gush from their addled occiputs "scientiae immunes . . . anseres naturali." ' (*De Volg. Eloq.*)

Polite Essays, p. 7.

Of the attempts to set things right, he adds in the same essay:

'. . . You have a period of muddle, a few of the brightest lads have a vague idea that something is a bit wrong, and nobody quite knows the answer. As a matter of fact, Madox Ford knew the answer but no one believed him. . . . Mr. Hulme is on the way to mythological glory; but the Hulme notes, printed after his death, had little or nothing to do with what went on in 1910, 1911, or 1912.[1] Mr. Yeats had set an example (specifically as to the inner form of the lyric or short poem containing an image), this example is obscured for posterity and for the present "young"—meaning Mr. Eliot and his juniors—by Mr. (early) Yeats's so very poetic language.'

The principle of the enduring reform did not spring fullgrown from Pound's or anyone else's brain. How far Ford and Yeats got is noted above, and we shall be paying Ford further

[1] See Appendix I.

attention. Pound's own insight appears to have arisen from his study of Dante. As a young man he had written,

'The true poet is most easily distinguished from the false, when he trusts himself to the simplest expression, and when he writes without adjectives.'

The Spirit of Romance, p. 219.

and again,

'. . . to speak of the "Vita Nuova" as "embroidered with conceits" is arrant nonsense. The "Vita Nuova" is strangely unadorned; more especially is this evident if it be compared with work of its own date. It is without strange, strained similes.

'Anyone who has in any degree the faculty of vision will know that the so-called personifications are real and not artificial. Dante's precision in both the "Vita Nuova" and in the "Commedia" comes from the attempt to reproduce exactly the thing which has been clearly seen. The "Lord of terrible aspect" is no abstraction, no figure of speech. There are some who can not or will not understand these things.'

The Spirit of Romance, p. 114.

The parallel with Mr. Eliot's celebrated remarks, in his essay on Dante, on the 'high dream' and the allegorical habit (*Selected Essays*, p. 204) will escape no-one; it has not escaped at least one professor. More important than finding Eliotic parallels is an understanding of what the words mean. Elsewhere in *The Spirit of Romance*, Pound says of a certain sonnet,

'Here the preciseness of the description denotes, I think, a clarity of imaginative vision. In more sophisticated poetry an epithet would suffice, the picture would be suggested. The dawn would be "rosy-fingered" or "in russet mantle clad".'
. . . The use of epithet is an advance on this method only when it suggests a vision not less clear, and its danger is obvious. In Milton or Swinburne, for example, it is too often

merely a high-sounding word, and not a swift symbol of vanished beauty.'

p. 92.

So far, so good. The image is to be presented to the mind's eye without superfluous words, and without the opposite danger of presenting merely a pretty noise. And it is by understanding only so far that the usual critiques of imagism have gone astray. Pound is *not* thinking of poetry as a kind of painting. What he is thinking of may be stated, short-circuiting much more quotation from *The Spirit of Romance*, by skipping to the 'Don'ts for Imagists':

'Don't use such an expression as "dim lands *of peace*". It dulls the image. It mixes an abstraction with the concrete. It comes from the writers' not realizing that the natural object is *always* the adequate symbol.'

Make It New, p. 337.

And again, in the Monro essay,

'. . . a presented image . . . the perfectly adequate expression or exposition of *any* urge, whatsoever its nature.'

Polite Essays, p. 13.

It is the superlative and not the principle that is unfamiliar in this last statement. The three or four urges in which the commercial cinema deals have always been presented in terms of images; the fog shot to 'key' a thriller, waving grass and blossoms for the healthy animality of red-blooded young America, the shiny convertible for opulent nonchalance. Anyone who has seen the famous Russian silent films will remember the careening baby-carriage that epiphanizes the massacre in *Potemkin*. There need not be thought to be anything intrinsically clumsy in this method of presentation as opposed to the intricacies of the periodic sentence. It was lack of things to say, not of expressive resources, that made the Soviet films so bull-headed. The principles were sound. Eisenstein's theoretical writing, notably in the posthumous collection, *Film Form*, is closely apropos, particularly his account (pp. 103–5) of the resources on which he proposed to draw to present a murderer's 'interior monologue' in *An American Tragedy*.

The example of cinema makes it easy to see how a concatenation of images adds up to Aristotle's *praxis*. It should also remind us of Pound's caution against supposing that by 'image' here is meant something stationary, snapshotted, only. To the statement that the presented image is the perfectly adequate expression or exposition of *any* urge, one has only to add the *moving* image, and one has:

'The only way of expressing emotion in the form of art is by finding an "objective correlative"; in other words, a set of objects, a situation, a chain of events which shall be the formula of that *particular* emotion; such that when the external facts, which must terminate in sensory experience, are given, the emotion is immediately evoked.'

Eliot, Selected Essays.

These famous words were written in 1917. The Poundian equivalent, seven years earlier, is this:

'Poetry is a sort of inspired mathematics, which gives us equations, not for abstract figures, triangles, spheres, and the like, but equations for the human emotions. If one have a mind which inclines to magic rather than science, one will prefer to speak of these equations as spells or incantations; it sounds more arcane, mysterious, recondite.'

Spirit of Romance, p. 5.

Chapter 8

THE MOVING IMAGE

For the nobleness of the populace brooks nothing below its own altitude.
One must have resonance, resonance and sonority . . . like a goose.

The 'motion' of the moving image is contained, ultimately, in the word-to-word jostle of language itself. The simplest sentence 'moves'. A charge of some kind is transferred from subject to predicate: Man s—e—e—s—> Horse. In inflected languages the predicate is actually spelled in an altered way to indicate the damage it sustains or the addition it incurs. This key insight of Fenollosa's is one of the neglected points of contact between his essay on the Chinese written character and general poetics. In the same way, every lyric poem has a plot. The action of the simplest category of lyric, the two-line Japanese *hokku* with which Pound experimented extensively, depends on Aristotle's central plot-device, *peripeteia*, or 'reversal of the situation':

> Fu I loved the high cloud and the hill,
> Alas, he died of alcohol.
>
> *Personae.*

Hokku deals in '*perspective* by incongruity', not in the merely visceral incongruity characterized by Pound as 'any decayed cabbage cast upon any pale satin sofa'. It is not enough simply to produce contrasts:

'I am not saying that Baudelaire is nothing but cabbages cast upon satin sofas, but merely that in many poems one "unpleasant" element is no more inevitable than another . . .'

Imaginary Letters, p. 49.

In judging epigrammatic verse the reader must distinguish between the rhetorical gesture that chucks in one component to negate another, and the *peripeteia* that juxtaposes two worlds of perception to strike light from their interaction. The rotten cabbage strikes the satin sofa with a gesture of contempt. Fu I's sozzled exit doesn't debunk his love of the high cloud and the hill, but inflects it with a wry pathos of inadequacy.

The *Pisan Cantos* are full of *hokku*:

And Margherita's voice was clear as the notes of a clavichord
tending her rabbit hutch . . .

O moon my pin-up,
                    chronometer . . .

Arachne, che mi porta fortuna, go spin on that tent rope . . .

In longer passages the principle of action is identical:

Came Eurus as comforter
And at sunset la pastorella dei suini
    driving the pigs home, benecomata dea
        under the two-winged cloud
        as of less and more than a day

                                    Canto LXXVI.

The point to be noted here is that the next word or phrase is always *unexpected*. With the addition of each new component the trajectory changes direction:[1]

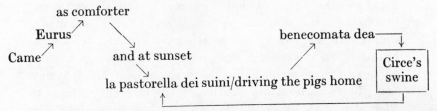

[1] In *The Spirit of Romance*, p. 166, Pound speaks of 'compressed or elliptical expression of metaphorical perception, such as antitheses suggested or implied in verbs or adjectives'. The example we are considering should be related to the discussion of ideogram as metaphor (chapters 10–11, below).

It will be seen, for what help the parallel may prove to be, how this corresponds to cinematic montage, the succession of timed, computed, and carefully composed shots. The Shakespearean running metaphor is like a double-exposure, again in the literal sense a case of the moving image:

> Witness this army of such mass and charge,
> Led by a delicate and tender prince,
> Whose spirit, with divine ambition puffed,
> Makes mouths at the invisible event,
> Exposing what is mortal and unsure
> To all that fortune, death, and danger dare,
> Even for an eggshell.

On top of the successive unexpectedness of the words is imposed a ghostly sequence of firing cannon: 'mass and charge'; 'puffed'; 'mouths at the invisible event' (cannon elevated to a target beyond the horizon; the shouting face of the officer; a nose thumbed at destiny; these in triple-exposure). The coming to rest of the whole upon 'eggshell' is pure Imagism.

The reason why these principles are so little understood, and why the 'objective correlative' has been the target of so much irrelevant disputation, is that it is in precisely this dimension that poetry is most resistant to exegesis. The criticism stemming from Empsonian dissection of symbol-clusters has made everyone familiar with intellectual complexity, at the level of workmanship at which the images are fitted together. It is obvious how much more the critic can find to say about the example from *Hamlet* above than about, say, Canto IV, where he is generally reduced to source-hunting. But this order of complexity, which may or may not be purely mechanical as in the decadence of Metaphysical 'wit', bears no *necessary* relation to the inherent voltage, to the value of the work in question as a human product. The assumption that what can be taken apart equals what has been put together has accustomed the analyst and his victim the reader to a brilliant but drastically limited range of emotional complexes: abrupt, wry, witty, and so on. Assuming that the successful parts of the new—or old—poetry are coterminous with the apparatus of the new criticism, commentators have tended to suppose that whatever Pound thought he was driving at isn't there at all. Indeed, except in *Propertius* and *Mauberley*, Empsonian methods find no handles by which to take hold of Pound's verse. Hence by such criteria, Pound's poetry, before *Propertius* and after *Mauberley*, simply isn't there. Analysis can't reveal the presence of an emotion; the analyst's fingers detect, as it were, palette-knife techniques, disturbances of the surface, that may or may not be engendering valuable emotion. Ivory medallions or varnished brush-work present a finish of which fingers so trained yield negative or misleading reports. Why paintings should be judged with closed eyes is not obvious.

This is not to be ungrateful to Empson, who has forged analytic tools of the utmost value for rehabilitating a body of poetry and of poetic techniques that the nineteenth century had thrown into desuetude. But one cannot be grateful to the obfuscators who have confused the dialectical-rhetorical analytics of Messrs. Empson and Richards with the 'new criticism' instigated by Mr. Eliot, who even in the justly celebrated Philip Massinger essay is careful not to becloud his perceptions with the brilliance of his dissections.

Pound has remarked that the leopards and juniper-trees of *Ash-Wednesday* are just as inexplicable (not incomprehensible) as anything in the *Cantos*. And *Ash-Wednesday*, despite its just reputation, is not a poem of which contemporary criticism has been able to find much to say.

The first requisite for judging any poetry is not analytic skill but a trained sensibility. Dr. Leavis, despite his stern disapproval of most of Pound's work, is nowhere more surprisingly Poundian than in his realization of this, though the training he desiderates smacks rather strenuously of moral rearmament. The prestige of rationalized rhetorical analysis à la Empson and Richards has cloaked such anomalies as the affection of the literal-minded counter proposition that a poem is a *statement*, and a statement 'about' an experience, and that experience one which the poet has had. It is easy to see why the objective correlative, the image as sensory equivalent of an emotion, the Aristotelian equation of a poem with an action, and Eliot's claim that emotions the poet has never experienced will serve his turn as well as familiar ones, should seem in such eyes impossibly muddle-headed and esoteric.

The same obfuscations have also contributed to the fictions (*a*) that such a poem as *Ash-Wednesday* is pretty but impenetrable; (*b*) that the excision of certain glamorous adjectives from poetry was the sole result of the Imagist movement; (*c*) that Ezra Pound is a blockheaded publicist of sporadic skill, or, as one critic neatly puts it, 'a sensibility without a mind.'

Pound has defined the phrase, 'break with tradition' as 'desert the more obvious imbecilities of one's immediate elders'. This is not necessarily a wholesale ritual slaughter of poetic fathers: 'Dryden and the precursors of Dryden did not react against *Hamlet*' but against adjacent 'katachrestical vigours'. The imagist 'revolution' was against, for example, the suet in the *Idylls*, not against *The Eagle* or *Cold in the Earth*.

These things being so, the embodiment of emotions in images, *aliter* the objective correlative, may be examined in a few instances selected for maximum contrast.

(1)   The clouds have gathered and gathered,
       and the rain falls and falls,
The eight ply of the heavens
       are all folded into one darkness,
And the wide, flat road stretches out.
I stop in my room toward the East, quiet, quiet,
I pat my new cask of wine.
My friends are estranged, or far distant.
I bow my head and stand still. . . .
            To-Em-Mei's 'The Unmoving Cloud'.

(2)   The chestnut casts his flambeaux, and the flowers
Stream from the hawthorn on the wind away,
The doors clap to, the pane is blind with showers.
Pass me the can, lad; there's an end of May.

There's one spoilt spring to scant our mortal lot,
One season ruined of our little store.
May will be fine next year as like as not:
Oh, aye, but then we shall be twenty-four. . . .

                                        A. E. Housman.

A rough similarity in the intended emotions is obvious. And it
is likely that purely rhetorical analysis—analysis dwelling on
the way the emotion is worked up—could by concentration
on such details as 'away' in the second line and 'blind' in the
third, and on the interaction of scene and dialogue, make the
second seem much the more impressive, and even, by concentration on the particularized 'hawthorn' and the banging
door, make it seem the more 'Imagistic'. But to substantiate
one's judgment of facility and tawdriness in the Housman
stanzas, one would isolate, in addition to the threadbare
rhythm (note the meaningless jerk after 'flambeaux'), the
element of continual melodramatic *comment*. This is not only
to say that the second stanza explains unnecessarily what the
feelings are, or that the feelings are melodramatic in a purely
adolescent way ('Oh, aye, but then we shall be twenty-four').
More important, the appeal is not to an inherent decorum
between the emotions and the objects, but rather to the
suitable reader's memory of boyhood disgust with rainy
days. The barest shorthand ('The doors clap to, the pane is
blind with showers') imports the reader *into* the situation,
and he can then be trusted to know what feelings are expected
of him: feelings that in any case he is already itching to
release.

It will not be easy to convince a reader who cannot see it
for himself that the Pound stanza works in a totally different
way. The objects, the images, clouds, rain, darkness, the wide
flat road, exist not as stage-dressing, as atmospheric props for
a display of the writer's chagrin, but as a constellation intrinsically and inevitably related to the inherent mood. (This
is a manner of speaking; whether these relationships 'existed'
before the poet made his stanza is irrelevant to our technical
inquiry). They are allotropic components into which the
mood, the initial poetic 'idea', has been fragmented. Nor is the

mood threadbare and familiar, existing for the reader as an evoked memory. It is particular and new. Its delicacy matches the delicacy of presentation: a delicacy inherent in the quiet opening tone. The reader is not being exhorted: 'Pass me the can, lad; there's an end of May' functions as exhortation. The function of 'I pat my new cask of wine', in *complicating* rather than underlining the emotion, is totally different. And this emotion, calm, complexly regretful, civilized, is made available for steady contemplation, still there whenever we return. No more than the Great Pyramid is it altered by imperfect apprehension. It depends on no personal vagary of the reader, nor is it wrenched from him by a series of neural assaults. It is there on the page—there among the images.

A better understanding of principles of this kind would relax many anxious readers. There would be less disputation about such a line as (in *The Waste Land*)

Et O, ces voix d'enfants, chantant dans la coupole,

if the prevalent critical tradition could relax from its digging among sources and accept as functional the inherent emotional weight of a given image or passage. Of course, since emotional weight cannot be rationalized except in such bad examples as Housman here provides, the kind of commentator who fattens by providing the totally unskilled reader with an illusion of understanding what he has never contemplated would be left jobless. Pound's impatience with critics has very largely such a basis.

Another pair of examples, which point up rather a difference in method (vividly present vs. elegiac-ruminative) than a simple contrast between a sound method and a vicious one is to be had by juxtaposing Pound's Lotus-eaters with Tennyson's.

And from floating bodies, the incense
    blue-pale, purple above them.
Shelf of the lotophagoi,
Aerial, cut in the aether.
                Reclining,
With the silver spilla,
The ball as of melted amber, coiled, caught up, and turned.

Lotophagoi of the suave nails, quiet, scornful,
Voce-profondo:

> 'Feared neither death nor pain for this beauty;
If harm, harm to ourselves.'

(Canto XX.)

Tennyson:

But, propt on beds of amaranth and moly,
How sweet (while warm airs lull us, blowing lowly)
With half-dropt eyelids still,
Beneath a heaven dark and holy,
To watch the long bright river drawing slowly
His waters from the purple hill—
To hear the dewy echoes calling
From cave to cave thro' the thick-tented vine—
To watch the emerald-coloured water falling
Thro' many a wov'n acanthus-wreath divine!
Only to hear and see the far-off sparkling brine,
Only to hear were sweet, stretch'd out beneath the pine.

Actually, the Tennyson, though not in its way, for at least the first five lines, inconsiderable *melopoeia*, bears much the same relation to the corresponding Pound as did the Housman example previously cited. Its mode of working is kinetic; that is to say, since somnolence is the theme, soporific. The reader is being invited once more to get inside the situation and feel like a Lotus-eater. The vowel-music, the rhymes re-echoed, lingering and lingering, the uncoiling rhythms, are modes of imitation only superficially. Their avowed function, from the opening 'How sweet it were . . .', is to offer emotions for participation, not contemplation. The excitement with which the Pound passage infects us is on the contrary that of inspecting, as it were from behind glass, a new and exotic mode of being. The presentation is not 'cold', the Lotus-eater feelings are 'there'. but the passion is attached to cognition, not submersion. It is hunger for the latter, an extension of the endemic Romantic wish for a vicarious day-dream, that makes many readers dismiss Pound's verse as cold and uninteresting.

A trip to his zoo or his treasure-house doesn't send 'em. They yearn for the belly-punch.

Such verse simply does not invite the immolation of the intellect or the critical conscience. Unless a writer's output be restricted to metaphysics or bills of lading, that is perhaps as far from 'a sensibility without a mind' as it is possible for him to get.

Chapter 9

VORTEX

'as the sculptor sees the form in the air
before he sets hand to mallet,
and as he sees the in, and the through,
the four sides
'not the one face to the painter . . .'

The next chapter will bring us into the province of ideogram; some consolidation of the precedent matter may first be useful. The relation between the Confucian calling of things by their right names (Ching Ming) and the Imagist programme of (1) presentation, not yatter 'about'; (2) no unnecessary word; (3) intrinsic, rather than superimposed, musical schemes, will be obvious. The essential seriousness of the Imagist procedures as a means of restoring language to health is brought out by considering, in this new context, yet another of Pound's 'Ching Ming' formulations:

'It does not matter whether the author desire the good of the race or acts merely from personal vanity. The thing is mechanical in action. In proportion as his work is exact, i.e. true to human consciousness and to the nature of man, as it is exact in formulation of desire, so is it durable and so is it "useful"; I mean it maintains the precision and clarity of thought, not merely for the benefit of a few dilettantes and "lovers of literature", but maintains the health of thought outside literary circles and in non-literary existence, in general individual and communal life.

'Or "*dans ce genre on n'émeut que par la clarté* ". One "moves" the reader only by clarity. In depicting the motions of the

71

"human heart" the durability of the writing depends on the exactitude. It is the thing that is true and stays true that keeps fresh for the new reader.'

Polite Essays, p. 165.

It is perhaps not easy to realize how totally these poetic devices are rooted in the traditions of pre-Cartesian Europe. Descartes' distrust of language as an autonomous matrix, his dialectician's confidence that language provides at best a desperate, deceptive, and (from the enlightened thinker's point of view) ignoble shorthand has introduced into the channels of communication a vehement determination to effect between poet and audience a transfusion of personality rather than of perception. Like foreigners stumbling imperfectly with pidgin, writer and reader strive more or less desperately to get inside one another. Market research and autographing teas take the place of a sane milieu. This is an evident feature of the post-Cartesian Romantic Movement; by the time of Tennyson it has become a *procédé* to be manipulated fairly calmly. But in Tennyson as much as in Housman[1] (a much more naïve and anxious person) or Shelley (a self-consciously primitive, vehement person) there is visible an identical distrust of the possibility of any communication, especially of emotional states, without constant comment, constant overt appeal to the reader's experience, habits, and day-dreams. Poetic, that is, has given way to rhetoric. The poet in a dialectical milieu is conscious of an audience to be influenced rather than of a poem to be made. And the quality of what is communicated suffers in consequence, so that technical judgments are inseparable from moral.

Pound, Eliot, Joyce, and Yeats mark by contrast a return to the Aristotelian benison. (Pound has several times cited approvingly Aristotle's assertion that the genius of a poet is manifested in his forging of metaphors). A poem is an *imitation* in the sense that it offers an image, an action, a chain of events such as, on contemplation, may yield the intelligible species

---

[1] It is Housman, rather than Pound, whom most people think of as *the* 'classical' technician.

proper to the initial experience. This may have little to do with the action or chain of events that initiated the emotional experience originally. (Conrad's preface to *The Secret Agent* offers valuable illustration of such a statement.) Pound, again, in *Gaudier-Brzeska: a Memoir*, describes his lengthy search for the verbal equivalent of the feelings with which an emergence into the crowd in a Paris underground inspired him. After several decreasingly wordy attempts, over a period of months, he succeeded in boiling away the contingent distractions of the original experience;

> The apparition of these faces in the crowd:
> Petals on a wet, black bough.[1]

Concerning this example he makes an important dissociation:

' "The one-image poem" is a form of super-position, that is to say, it is one idea set on top of another. . . . In a poem of this sort one is trying to record the precise instant when a thing outward and objective transforms itself, or darts into a thing inward and subjective.

'This particular form of consciousness has not been identified with impressionist art. I think it is worthy of attention.'

Gaudier, p. 103.

The imagist, in other words is not concerned with getting down the general look of the thing. Nor does he praise or blame; nor does he tell the reader *what* to feel. (It is the reader panting for his emotional marching-orders who dismisses such juxtapositions, whether in two lines or as the structural unit of twenty, as 'trivial' or 'personal' or 'obscure'.) The imagist's fulcrum—a point to which we shall recur—is the process of cognition itself. How this is related with the Aristotelian mimesis comes out in the following example:

'The pine-tree in mist upon the far hill looks like a fragment of Japanese armour.

---

[1] This is as good a place as any to refer to 'Dichten = Condensare': Pound's statement (see *ABC of Reading*, p. 20) that verse differs from prose only by superior concentration. Its rhythmic and melodic accessories afford extra emotional weight without extra words. To put it another way, 400 pages of prose may 'by sheer architectonics' achieve the weight of 40 lines of verse.

'The beauty of the pine-tree in the mist is not caused by its resemblance to the plates of the armour.

'The armour, if it be beautiful at all, is not beautiful *because* of its resemblance to the pine in the mist.

'In either case, the beauty, in so far as it is beauty of form, is the result of "planes in relation".

'The tree and the armour are beautiful because their diverse planes overlie in a certain manner.

'. . . And the poet? "Pourquoi doubler l'image?" asks Barzun, in declaiming against this "poésie farcie de 'comme'"· The poet, whatever his "figure of speech", will not arrive by doubling or confusing an image.

'Still the artist, working in words only, may cast on the reader's mind a more vivid image of either the armour or the pine by mentioning them close together or by using some device of simile or metaphor, that is a legitimate procedure of his art, for he works not with planes or with colours but with the names of objects and of properties. It is his business so to use, so to arrange, these names as to cast a more definite image than the layman can cast.'

Gaudier, pp. 146–7.

'Planes in relation' reminds us that these words are roughly contemporary with analytic cubism, with Gaudier's sculpture, and with the first impact of Wyndham Lewis: a period of visual discovery which succeeding painters and sculptors have largely failed to consolidate, but which remains closely related to Pound's procedures with language, precisely because its practice was to seek ways of penetrating the particularity of the object under scrutiny, rather than divagating into that object's likeness to some other. Under the burning-glass of Vorticist scrutiny pine-trees and suits of armour yielded up their formal secrets in muscular arrangements of pigment into flying wedges. To 'generalize' the suit of armour—to paint it as a massive 'type'—or else to focus on the merely haphazard 'individuality' of its contingent dents and rust-spots, would be equally far from the Vorticist idea of realizing in arrangements of colour the peculiar energy of its special *mode* of being.

In the same way, 'poésie farcie de "comme",' a streaming reduplication of images to caress the reader's nerves or to be elucidated by reference to his own memories or feelings of suits of armour, is to be distinguished from the Poundian pursuit of epigrammatic quiddities. The energy required to maintain these perceptions in focus amid the down-drifting circumambience of the decade 1910–20 accounts for the precipitate of unassimilated violence in the Vorticist sensibility. It was natural that the *Blast* coterie should have had the reputation of wild men; it was perhaps unnecessary that they should have played the role with such gusto.

A fuller account of the bearings of Vorticism on verbal manifestation would utilize Lewis' 'pictorial' writing in *The Enemy of the Stars* and its technical affiliations with the 'Circe' episode in *Ulysses*: that Cyclopean drama of whirling images.

Chapter 10

IDEOGRAM: SEEING

Deo similis quodam modo
hic intellectus adeptus.

Ideogram, at least as a poetic principle, is not a Sinophile fad. It inheres in Aristotle on metaphor. Nothing could more conclusively document the capture of Aristotle by the thirteenth-, seventeenth-, and twentieth-century dialecticians than the fact that it took Ernest Fenollosa's essay on 'The Chinese Written Character as a Medium for Poetry' to bring a useful theoretical basis of poetics squarely once more before the attention of the West. We shall sketch in a later chapter historical alignments that the student may find useful; it is first of all the *nature* of the 'Ideogrammic method' that concerns us.

(1) The mind lays hold only on particular things. It can NOT know an abstraction it has not itself made. Hence the fundamental scholastic principle, 'Nothing is in the intellect that is not first in the senses.'

(2) You can NOT pour 'clear and distinct ideas' into another man's head. You can try, but the result will surprise you. One of three things will happen. He will ask for examples. Or he will consult his own storehouse of examples, taking your statement as a directing-rod for his own perceptions. Or he will make an assenting noise and forever after parrot your formulation, thinking he knows 'all about horses' from hearing a definition. Every teacher knows these things. The reader should look at the second chapter of Dickens' *Hard Times* before going further.

Our first axiom concerns epistemology. Our second concerns communication. They follow from one another. They delimit the same facts. Any theory of poetics, any theory of language, is, implies, follows from, a theory of knowledge. The old grammarians applied identical exegetical techniques to the book of Nature and a book of words. They saw that the same process of apprehension goes on in reading words as in reading things. Hence the grip of the doctrine of the Logos on the western mind for fifteen hundred years: the creative Word, the focus of all intelligibility, was made flesh in one sense at the Creation of *things*, in another with the Incarnation, in another with the writing of the sacred books. Pope's

> Unerring NATURE, still divinely bright,
> One clear, unchanged, and universal light,
> Life, force, and beauty doth to all impart,
> At once the source, and end, and test, of Art.

—this is still the Logos, A.D. 1711.

Looking about the world, we know *things*. On a page of poetry there are set in motion the intelligible species of *things*. Words are solid, they are not ghosts or pointers. The poet connects, arranges, defines, *things*: pearls and eyes; garlic, sapphires, and mud.

Since Descartes *the* epistemological proposition has been that what we know is *ideas*. Locke imported this notion to England, and English poetry started to flounder. Throughout the nineteenth century artists in England either trifled apologetically with dream-worlds that 'didn't matter', or were driven into endless self-protective theorizing. Blake, Wordsworth, Coleridge, Shelley all sought to draw about their poetic practices a ring of fire which the juggernaut of mechanically linked ideas couldn't cross. They had neither the fulcrum nor the theoretical equipment to smash its totality. It had too firm a hold on the 'practical' worlds of commerce, philosophy, politics, for amateur extirpation. But they tried at least to keep its hands off poetry. Hence the separation between literature and life. A poem like Tennyson's *Palace of Art* is a representative document of this struggle. We shall fill out this account in chapter 12; this much summary is given here so that the reader can see where he is being led.

The mind knows things; as Aristotle knew; though Aristotle's reputation as the father of syllogism and logic-chopping makes it almost impossible to invoke him, at present, in such a connection. Aristotle, Pound tells us, 'doesn't get as far as Kung' (i.e. in ethics and politics) 'but he at least knew how generals are known from particulars'. 'From' particulars: *through* particulars, *in* particulars.[1] The mind lays hold of nothing else.

> ... as says Aristotle
> philosophy is not for young men
> their *Katholou* can not be sufficiently derived from
> their *hekasta*
> their generalities cannot be born from a sufficient phalanx
> of particulars
> lord of his work and master of utterance
> who turneth his word in its season and shapes it
> (Canto LXXIV).

'A sufficient phalanx of particulars'. The mind can't know *one* thing by itself. You have to look at a lot of dogs to extract the idea of 'dog' with any validity. If you saw but one dog in your life your mind could do nothing with it. You would cherish only the memory of a queer sensation. It would be like encountering, just once, the Dong with the Luminous Nose.

But a congeries of related sensory experiences fertilizes the mind; sets it in motion; stores it with forms. When you see twenty different dogs lined up in a row you can form some solid idea of dogdom. The same applies if you see them one after another; they are lined up in a row to be dealt with in the memory. (The epistemology of Cavalcanti's *Canzone d'Amore* —'In quella parte dove sta memoria'—starts from this point.) In the same way, the experiences of a lifetime clarify one another, illuminate one another. And as one both relates and distinguishes one's experiences with dogs, so the more points

---

[1] 'Ante rem, in re, post rem'—St. Thomas Aquinas, *In Sent.*, II, *dist.*, III, *qu.* 3.

at which one succeeds in connecting one's memories and experiences, the more the individuality of any one of them is penetrable. (This interpenetration of experiences is wisdom; going into action, it is ethics. The Confucian *Ta Hio* starts from this point: 'Wanting to rectify their hearts, they sought precise verbal definitions of their inarticulate thoughts [the tones given off by the heart]; wishing to attain precise verbal definitions, they set to extend their knowledge to the utmost. This completion of knowledge is rooted in sorting things into organic categories.' There is nothing here that would have puzzled the encyclopaedic Augustine). That is why the *Cantos*, which seek to establish 'a hierarchy of values', must handle an incredible variety of materials.

Knowledge—the digestion of particulars—may for some purposes be formulated: 'Cats have tails;' 'All men are mortal.' It need not be formulated. In any case the formulation has communicative value only as a director of the audience's perceptions; as an electromagnet which may pull their perceptions into the same pattern as the speaker's. Without the audience's perceptions to work with, the formulation is void.[1] You can't talk readily about elephants to a man who has never seen one, or a picture of one. He will do his best with the storehouse of forms he possesses; in his mind he will hang a stocking-shaped object, endowed with the strength and flexibility of a bull-snake, from the muzzle of a grey-hided horse. He won't really see an elephant, however clear and distinct the idea possessed by the communicator.

If the matter were important enough, you might try to help your interlocutor out of his bewilderment by supplying analogies with what he does know and has handled: stockings, snakes, horses. If you did this with sufficient efficiency, his mind might lay hold of a fairly sound simulacrum. You would

[1] Compare Francis Bacon (*Advancement of Learning*, Bk. II):
'. . . a man may revisit and descend unto the foundations of knowledge and consent; and so transplant it into another, as it grew in his own mind. For it is in knowledges, as it is in plants, if you mean to use the plant, it is no matter for the roots; but if you mean to remove it to grow, then it is more assured to rest upon roots than slips: so the delivery of knowledges, as it is now used, is as of fair bodies of trees without the roots; good for the carpenter, but not for the planter.'

have achieved your little triumph of communication by use of sensory particulars. The poet, with intangibles to communicate, works in this way. Seeking to register the quality of Platonic intuition, he doesn't supply definitions and propositions. He talks of

'. . . the reality of the *nous*, of mind, apart from any man's individual mind, of the sea crystalline and enduring, of the bright as it were molten glass that envelops us, full of light.

Culture, p. 44.

Strengthening the contours of this by drawing upon the further definition available through rhythmic means, we have:

> Cythera potens, κύθηρα δεινά
> no cloud, but the crystal body
> the tangent formed in the hand's cup
> as live wind in the beech grove
> as strong air amid cypress
> (Canto LXXVI).

In the same way, an impression of Henry James:

'The massive head, the slow uplift of the hand, *gli occhi onesti e tardi*, the long sentences piling themselves up in elaborate phrase after phrase, the lightning incision, the pauses, the slightly shaking admonitory gesture with its "wu-a-wait a little, wait a little, something will come"; blague and benignity and the weight of so many years' careful, incessant labour of minute observation always there to enrich the talk,

Make It New, pp. 251–2.

takes on in Canto VII the contours of a Dantean vision:

> And the great domed head, *con gli occhi onesti e tardi*
> Moves before me, phantom with weighted motion,
> *Grave incessu*, drinking the tone of things,
> And the old voice lifts itself
> weaving an endless sentence.

To take a simpler case. Pound, following Fenollosa, tells us in the *ABC of Reading*,

80

'In Europe, if you ask a man to define anything, his definition always moves away from the simple things that he knows perfectly well, it recedes into an unknown region, that is a region of remoter and progressively remoter abstraction.

'Thus if you ask him what red is, he says it is a "colour".

'If you ask him what a colour is, he tells you it is a vibration or a refraction of light, or a division of the spectrum.

'And if you ask him what vibration is, he tells you it is a mode of energy, or something of that sort, until you arrive at a modality of being, or non-being, or at any rate you get in beyond your depth, or his depth.

(pp. 3–4).

The transcriber pauses here again to evoke the schoolroom in *Hard Times*:

' "Bitzer", said Thomas Gradgrind. "Your definition of a horse."

' "Quadruped. Graminivorous. Forty teeth, namely, twenty-four grinders, four eye-teeth, and twelve incisive. Sheds coat in the spring; in marshy countries, sheds hoofs, too. Hoof hard, but requiring to be shod with iron. Age known by marks in mouth." Thus (and much more) Bitzer.

' "Now girl number twenty," said Mr. Gradgrind. "You know what a horse is." '

This is more than a convenient illustration. Dickens' ferocity in *Hard Times* is directed against the current of thought, of which James Mill's education of his son is the best-known instance, running from Descartes through Locke to Bentham, I. A. Richards, and the contemporary pseudo-Aristotelians of Chicago. Addison's naïve struggle to give an account of poetic experience in the terms provided by Locke's epistemology (*Spectator* 420) merely serves to show how intrinsically hostile a dialectical milieu is to the arts, excepting as the latter afford it handy laboratories in which 'problems of communication' can be worked out. In *Human Understanding* II. xi, 3, Locke disposes of the artist as one who provides facile entertainment for the relaxed and infantile mind. Judgment, he tells us, is

'. . . a way of proceeding quite contrary to metaphor and allusion; wherein, for the most part, lies that entertainment and pleasantry of wit, which strikes so lively on the fancy, and is therefore so acceptable to all people; because its beauty appears at first sight, and there is required no labour of thought to examine what truth or reason there is in it. The mind, without looking any further, rests satisfied with the agreeableness of the picture and the gaiety of the fancy; and it is a kind of affront to go about to examine it by the severe rules of truth and good reason: whereby it appears that it consists in something that is not perfectly conformable to them.'

These dichotomies working on a distinguished mind produced the emotional crisis that interrupted John Stuart Mill's education until Wordsworth's poetry saved him from total neurosis; Mill himself in his essay on Bentham describes a mind that found this barbarism congenial:

'He had a phrase, expressive of the view he took of all moral speculations to which his method had not been applied, or (which he considered the same thing) not founded on a recognition of utility as the moral standard; this phrase was 'vague generalities'. Whatever presented itself to him in such a shape he dismissed as unworthy of notice, or dwelt upon only to denounce as absurd. He did not heed, or rather the nature of his mind prevented it from occurring to him, that these generalities contained the whole unanalysed experience of the human race.'

It will hardly be denied that the Locke citation does in fact describe the way most students are taught to read poetry; that the higher study of literature as established in the nineteenth century according to the pattern of the dominant scientific metaphors of the time simply fostered the scholars' contempt for 'that entertainment and pleasantry of wit, which strikes so lively on the fancy, and is therefore so acceptable to all people'; that the recent shift in academic emphasis from historiography to criticism is merely a move from one part of the desert to another, the Ricardian 'semasiology' which dominates the 'scientific' critics being simply an accelerated

Lockeian buzz-saw; and that the fanatical book-keeper who emerges from Mill's portrait of Bentham has much in common with the professional literary historian.

To return to Pound's account of the ideogrammic method:

'By contrast to the method of abstraction, or of defining things in more and still more general terms, Fenollosa emphasizes the method of science, "which is the method of poetry", as distinct from that of "philosophic discussion", and is the way the Chinese go about it in their ideograph or abbreviated picture writing. . . .

'He (the Chinaman) is to define red. How can he do it in a picture that isn't painted in red paint?

'He puts (or his ancestor put) together the abbreviated pictures of

ROSE	CHERRY
IRON RUST	FLAMINGO

That, you see, is very much the kind of thing a biologist does (in a very much more complicated way) when he gets together a few hundred or thousand slides, and picks out what is necessary for his general statement. Something that fits the case, that applies in all of the cases.'

pp. 4, 6, 7.

This can scarcely be further simplified. The mode of making complete and properly qualified statements is to present a selection of EXAMPLES.

The only trouble with the Rose-Cherry-Rust-Flamingo instance is that while perfectly sound in principle, it is perhaps over-simple. There is still room for the reader to draw the wrong deduction of principle. Quasi-mathematical habits of mind die hard, it is too easy to think of the process of extracting a common factor. So a more complicated instance may have virtues.

(1) Anyone who has seen pots boiling on the ungainly black iron wood stove in the back of a farmhouse kitchen will know what is meant by taking it to typify, as distinguished from the enamelled gas-range, a 'way of life'. An attempt to explore his

sense of this way of life further will yield remembered details like the oilcloth on the kitchen table, the beaten path to the root-house, the worn stair-boards, the cupboards filled with preserves, the rocker on the back porch. Even a casual visitor's knowledge of the 'feel' of American farmhouse life is perfectly real, though resistant to propositional formulation and derived from observed particulars that have no syllogistic connection with one another. These data do not lie about inscrutable in odd corners of the mind. The mind works upon them, relates them, draws from them real if not articulate knowledge. Hence the good poet or novelist or movie director knows exactly what glimpses to give us. An attempt to convey such knowledge leads back to the data. The knowledge resides in the particulars.

(2) In the same way, we derive knowledge *of* (not about) a man's tastes from inspection of his bookshelves, extracting an intelligible form from items that have no syllogistic connection. A library registers a concept, as did the tempio of the Malatesta (Canto IX). Joyce's catalogue of Bloom's books in *Ulysses* is the simplest possible application of the ideogrammic method; so is Pound's transcription of the contents of Sigismundo's post-bag. It may be suggested as a helpful analogy for the cohesive principle of the heterogenous *Cantos* that Pound knew what materials belonged in his poem exactly as one knows what books would belong in one's ideal library.

(3) The biologist who has worked out a genetic law doesn't then burn his notes. The 'law', a piece of real knowledge, is a way of bracketing observations for convenient reference. What the biologist has seen, and knows, is the behaviour of plants and animals. He doesn't 'know' his equation. The equation is something to be used. The knowledge is in the particulars.[1]

Try a fourth field of knowledge:

'May I suggest (not to prove anything, but perhaps to open

[1] 'Twenty-five factors in a given case may have NO LOGICAL connection the one with any other. Cf.: A definition of fever which excluded typhoid would be unscientific. Knowledge cannot be limited to a collection of definitions.'—*Polite Essays*, p. 115.

the reader's thought) that I have a certain real knowledge which would enable me to tell a Goya from a Velasquez, a Velasquez from an Ambrogio Praedis, a Praedis from an Ingres or a Moreau

and that this differs from the knowledge you or I would have if I went into the room back of the next one, copied a list of names and maxims from the good Fiorentino's *History of Philosophy*, and committed the names, maxims, and possibly dates to my memory.

'It may or may not matter that the first knowledge is direct, it remains effortlessly as residuum, as part of my total disposition, it affects every perception of form-colour phenomena subsequent to its acquisition.

Culture, p. 28.

The use of poetry as positive nutriment for the affections follows from this last sentence:

'And herein is clue to Confucius' reiterated commendation of such of his students as studied the Odes.

'He demanded or commended a type of perception, a kind of transmission of knowledge obtainable only from such concrete manifestation. Not without reason.'

Let this remain as a pointer to the next stage while we consolidate our position somewhat. There is nothing anti-Aristotelian about these positions. (Homer was to Aristotle's Greece what the Odes were to Confucius' China.) Aristotle on the process of intellection is as particularist as one could wish. The shows of things don't just tickle the keys of a recording and calculating apparatus. The agent intellect (its Greek name, suggestively, is *nous poietikos*) goes to work on the phantasms presented by the senses and extracts 'intelligible species' whose validity is then actively affirmed with the exultation that attends the grasp on the real. The most valuable consequence of the 'Existentialist' movement has been its extraction from M. Maritain of this careful counter-affirmation:

'When the intellect judges, it lives intentionally, by an act

85

proper to itself, this same act of existing which the thing
exercises or is able to exercise outside the mind. Existence
thus affirmed and intentionally experienced by the mind is
the consummation or completion, in the mind, of intelligibility
in act. It corresponds to the act of existing exercised by things.
And this act of existing is itself incomparably more than a mere
positing without intelligible value of its own; it is act or energy
par excellence; and as we know, the more act there is the greater
the intelligibility.'

Existence and the Existent, p. 18.

This liquid is certainly a
         property of the mind
nec accidens est   but an element
              in the mind's make-up
est agens and functions   dust to a fountain-pan otherwise
                               (Canto LXXIV).

Chapter 11

IDEOGRAM: MAKING

that hath the light of the doer, as it were
a form cleaving to it.

The astute reader will have sensed metaphysical implications here which we have not space to go into.
Suffice it to say that as long as the doctrine of substantial form lasted, poetry mattered. Sidney's and Milton's
claims for it as an indispensable means of education are well
known. Such claims could be made because the intelligible
species achieved by intellection were known to be real. The
poet was setting real things in action in such a way as to elicit
from them their non-propositional significance. Aristotle's
encomium of metaphor follows from this:

'But the greatest thing by far is to be a master of metaphor.
It is the one thing that cannot be learnt from others; and it is
also a sign of genius, since a good metaphor implies an intuitive perception of the similarity of dis-similars.'

Poetics, XXII.

Pound has several times cited this statement approvingly.

Metaphor, as Aristotle tells us in another place, affirms that
four things (*not* two) are so related that A is to B as C is to D.
When we say 'The ship ploughs the waves', we aren't calling a
ship a plough. We are intuitively perceiving the similarity in
two dissimilar actions: 'The ship does to the waves what a
plough does to the ground.'

When Shakespeare tells us that 'Night's candles are burnt
out', he affirms that the stars are to the night what the candles

87

are to the salon. On contemplation, this yields a flow of emotional nutriment. The relation includes more than two sets of extinguished lights. The andrenal stimulation of the lovers' night above Capulet's orchard is conveyed through the image of night-long banqueting; the exhilaration of the interdicted lovers becomes for a moment continuous with communal elation and social revelry. But in the same instant Romeo's sudden realization of danger with the departure of night fuses with the death of candle flames and the fading of the stars at the end of a keyed-up action protracted until dawn. The tiptoe posture of jocund day in the following line is simultaneously an ironic icon of the aroused Veronese police, a projection of the alertness enjoined on Romeo by danger, and a counterpoint to the deflated ending of this surreptitious wedding-night.

No perception of the vivid little multiple plot here presented in two lines is possible to a sensibility blinkered by analysis in the fashionable terms of 'tenor' and 'vehicle', for which metaphor, or imagism, becomes simply a circuitous way of saying something else: 'The day has dawned.' The latter is abstraction. The former is the mind feeding on particulars.

In his essay on the Chinese Written Character, Ernest Fenollosa thus glosses the ideograms corresponding to the abstract statement, 'Man sees horse':

'First stands the man on his two legs. Second, his eye moves through space; a bold figure represented by running legs under an eye, a modified picture of an eye, a modified picture of running legs but unforgettable once you have seen it. Third stands the horse on four legs. . . . Legs belong to all three characters; they are *alive*. The group holds something of the character of a continuous motion picture.'

How Aristotle's *mimesis*, which is inseparable from his account of perception, is related to the transfers of force between words in a passage of poetry is well suggested by this example.

Again, Fenollosa tells us that the Chinese writer may refer to himself, or his *persona*, in five distinct ways:

'There is the sign of a 'spear in the hand' = a very emphatic

I; five and a mouth = a weak and defensive I, holding off a crowd by speaking; to conceal = a selfish and private I; self (the cocoon sign) and a mouth = an egoistic I, one who takes pleasure in his own speaking; the self presented is used only when one is speaking to one's self.'

It is easy to see how our analysis of metaphor applies here. Take 'five and a mouth'; we have a threefold proportion. This man's relations with other men are those of a speaker holding off a crowd, the speaker holding off a crowd with his words as an inadequate debater lunges out at a heckler with his (five-fingered) fist.

| | Speaker's | |
This man	mouth	Fist
Other men	Hostile	Enemy
	audience	

This dramatic bit of character analysis is contained in a single ideogram as if in a couplet of Pope; the ingredients of a psychologist's account in terms of anxiety-neuroses and compensatory aggressions are all there.

Pound, it may be recalled, discovered Chinese after translating Anglo-Saxon. The Anglo-Saxon scholar's term for just such a vivid figure is 'kenning': the particulars by which the person or object in question is *known*. 'Whale-road,' 'soul-bearer,' are both ideogram and metaphor.

The Chinese ideograph, like the metaphor, deals in exceedingly condensed juxtapositions. But it should not be thought that it is an overhaul of diction alone that is in question. Otherwise the impact of Fenollosa on Pound would have bred merely picturesque phraseology of the Hopkins order. Poetic method, on the contrary is all of a piece; if the principles that are carried out in detail do not extend to the organization of the whole, the relation of images to poem remains that of plums to cake. Just as, according to Pound, 'any given rhythm implies about it a complete musical form,' so a metaphoric mode of perception of things implies about it the organization of an entire poem.

This is easy to see when the poem is two lines long.

> Swiftly the years beyond recall.
> Solemn the stillness of this spring morning.

Mr. Empson has made a lengthy and subtle analysis of these lines; the essentials may be graphed more rapidly. Two experiences, two concretions of emotion, are juxtaposed to yield the proportion, 'My feelings of transience are held in tension with my desire to linger amid present pleasures, as the flight of time is in tension with the loveliness of this spring morning.' The presence of two purely emotional components among the requisite four does not differentiate this in principle from the entirely 'objective' metaphor, 'The ship ploughs the waves.'

This two-line poem, the Japanese *hokku* with which Pound experimented extensively in his *Lustra* volume, contains the condensed essence of all poetic expression. Juxtaposed things illuminate[1] one another, and gear dramatically with juxtaposed (i.e. complex) emotions.

The rhetoric of a longer poem may be apprehended in exactly the same way.

> A slumber did my spirit seal;
>   I had no human fears:
> She seemed a thing that could not feel
>   The touch of earthly years.
>
> No motion has she now, no force;
>   She neither hears nor sees;
> Rolled round in earth's diurnal course,
>   With rocks, and stones, and trees.

The reader who can feel the invitation to ponder implied in the emotional weight of these lines will not need to be told that a detailed analysis is not feasible in a few words. It is only the relation between the two stanzas that concerns our argument here; it will be found to be identical with that of the two lines

---

[1] This releasing of intelligibility enforces Aristotle's remark that in the best poetic actions peripeteia and 'discovery' are simultaneous (*Poetics*, XI).

in the *hokku* previously quoted. The speaker's insentience to temporal ravages, evoked, like a spell, by the girl's animal vitality, is juxtaposed with the emotions implied by her mortality. The connection is not syllogistic. There is as sharp a break between the two stanzas of this poem as between any of the *Cantos*, or any of the things in the *Cantos*.

As things are set in relation in metaphor, according to an acute intuition of their similarity and dissimilarity, so actions, passions, places, times, blocks of experience are set in relation in a more extended poem. This is as true of the *hokku* as of the epic, of *King Lear* as of the *Cantos*. Six months after reading *King Lear* one's memory, one's sense of its vital reality, consists perhaps in recalling that a storm is followed by a pathetic death. We don't remember the plot as set forth in handbooks: 'An aged and headstrong king, determined to abdicate, called his three daughters before him, etc. etc.' Memory automatically strips any intense experience down to its poetic essentials, a few vivid juxtapositions. Similarly, the relation between Shakespeare's simultaneous high-life and low-life plots is no more *logical* than that between Lucy and earth's diurnal course, between faces in a crowd and petals on a wet, damp bough. And the fact that *Lear* or *Henry IV* survives in the mind as a pattern of major images suggests that (as in fact happens with double-plot) a sequential linkage between successive scenes might as well be scrapped without detriment to poetic logic. This, of course, is what is done in the *Cantos*, as in Ford Madox Ford's device of 'time-shift', or the encyclopaedic ranging of *The Waste Land* and *Ulysses*. The great discovery of the French symbolists was the irrelevance, and hence the possibility of abolition, of paraphrasable plot.

In connection with major form, two ideogrammic principles may with advantage be distinguished. We have quoted Aristotle on the principle of metaphor being the intuition of similarity in dissimilars. It is obvious that for poetic purposes either the likenesses or the differences can receive the greater emphasis. The former emphasis inclines towards *genre*, the latter towards what may be described as syncopation.

These are distinctions of emphasis, not of principle. Poetic organization demands at least some tenuity of connection among discordant items; the mind is helpless before absolute disparity, and indeed probably never encounters it, as the Christian tradition understands in stressing the angelic nature of Satan. On the other hand, some continual admixture of novelty can alone justify an extended presentation of a single theme.

'Real knowledge goes into natural man in tidbits. A scrap here, a scrap there; always pertinent, linked to safety, or nutrition or pleasure.

'Human curiosity survives and is catered for, by the two-penny weeklies, 24 lines on chromosomes, six lines on a three-headed calf. . . .

'A mean might be discovered. No man can contemplate the point of a candle flame for how long is it?? If however an underlying purpose or current cd. be established beneath a series of facts (as is done by Edgar Wallace, even in some of his craziest stories) education might be more rapid. . . .'

Culture, pp. 99–100.

It is of the very nature of metaphor, and so of poetry, that it satisfies simultaneously the appetite for pertinence and the appetite for incongruity; with the possibility of securing large-scale rhythms within a whole work by shifting the emphasis on these elements back and forth.

On the last three pages of Canto LXXX we have an ideogram of specifically English culture, moving from typical point to typical point, the form of the verse varying to match each component, while an over-riding mood is built up, congruous and yet apprehended through discreet images: tilled fields, carriage yards, ballad-jingles, ghosts, the murders surrounding Mary Queen of Scots, the wars with France, the wars of the Roses, murk and fratricide and blood on the gothic stones.

After the famous quatrains that gather up these images into sombre choric assurance, the balance suddenly shifts for the climax of the Canto: we hear, with spices of unexpected epithet, about the lizard at the poet's feet:

as the young lizard extends his leopard spots
   along the grass-blade seeking the green midge half an ant-size
and the Serpentine will look just the same
and the gulls be as neat on the pond
and the sunken garden unchanged
and God knows what else is left of our London
      my London, your London
and if her green elegance
   remains on this side of my rain ditch
   puss lizard will lunch on some other T-bone

sunset grand couturier.

The pace of the verse secures continuity for the elegiac mood of the previous contemplation of declining empire; the sunset against which the red and white roses were glowing recurs in the last line as the melodramatic provider of trappings for faded beauty, and a pathos of mute depopulation inheres in the fragments of London whose survival is assured:

      and the Serpentine will look just the same
      and the gulls be as neat on the pond
      and the sunken garden unchanged

(how resonant is that 'sunken'!) Further inspection reveals a continuance of the Imperial theme in the image of automatic saurian rapacity: the cross-channel wars suddenly diminished to a mechanically cunning stalking of prey along a grass-blade; the consoling T-bone of the beef-eater, ultimate hyperbole for a succulent insect, throws a further witty cross-light on these altering perspectives, as does the odd Henry-Jamesian implication of the lounge-lizard suitor stalking 'her green eminence'. There is no lack of *continuity*. What is functional is the studied *incongruity* of image and language whose tensions both climax and resolve the preceding passage. From the very first imposition of Anglo-Saxon rhythms on a Latin transcription of Homer it is these expansions and contractions of the scale of congruity that keep the *Cantos* alive. Dante's store of similes works to a similar end, Milton's inelastic medium defeats it. This freedom is characteristic of the ideogrammic method in action. Before accusing Pound of incoherence we should turn an eye sharpened for analogies on his sudden contrasts; it is only when we have sensed the connections that the discords can fulfil their role in the harmonic scheme.

It should be noted, finally, that the ideogrammic method as a means of prose exposition permits inter-relation of interests and perceptions drawn from diverse materials in a way impossible to schematic presentation.[1] To understand this the reader need only think of what is meant in college curricula by 'English'. Hamlet's personality, Browning's poems, Milton's theological and Burke's political controversy, Newman's observations on Church history and his account of the development of his religious convictions, Sidney's observations on the practice of popular dramatists and his account of the function of poetry, Dryden's jingoism and Carlyle's Teutonism, are all wrenched into a single ragged line of stylistic mutation and their vital centres of interest and importance relegated to ancillary or 'background' status. The method of a book like *Culture* on the other hand is to present each of a number of foci of interest—Erigena, Aristotle, painting, Chinese history, musical criteria, architectural achievements, in contact with as many others as possible. Topics recur and recur, never twice with the same neighbours. The juxtapositions are precisely calculated, and this is as far as possible from (what it is sometimes supposed to be) the hurling at the reader of block after block of enthusiastically recorded but quite indiscriminate entities. (The latter is after all the method of the *Encyclopaedia Britannica*). Ideogram of course seems chaotic as long as the classification of knowledge into 'subjects' prevents us from drawing upon Frobenius for light on painting, or using music to explain philosophy.

[1] Fenollosa remarks of syllogistic method that 'Even in its own sphere it can not think half of what it wants to think. It has no way of bringing together any two concepts which do not happen to stand one under the other and in the same pyramid.'

Chapter 12

IDEOGRAM: REPRISE

and the news is a long time moving
a long time in arriving
thru the impenetrable
crystalline, indestructible
ignorance of locality.

The reader who is satisfied may skip this chapter. The one who wants more light on the situation of English poetry prior to the Joyce-Eliot-Pound impact may welcome further theoretical axes of reference.

We have already suggested that the linguistic analyses in Fenollosa's essay contain nothing intrinsically novel for the West. Its effectiveness lay in the rhetorical strategy of utterly novel examples drawn from an alien poetic tradition. Whereas the present writer, wishing, for the sake of completer conviction, to lay bare the linkages among familiar philosophic and poetic developments, finds himself hoping against hope that his every reference to Aristotle and Wordsworth will not be totally misunderstood through the inertia of a complex misinformation, Fenollosa was able to use a terminology still un-desensitized and examples which no-one was in a position to dispute. (The objection of Sinologues that the metaphoric life of many Chinese characters has been totally denatured after the analogy of 'buried' metaphors in English and all other languages does not touch the essentials of his argument at all.)

We have said that this terminology—'metaphor;' 'analogy;' 'perception;' 'knowledge;' 'form'—became denatured with the scrapping by Descartes of the idea of substantial form. When the mind no longer lays hold of things, when it does no more than construct its own world according to the hints afforded by sensation, when it knows nothing but its own 'ideas', poetic modes of statement, which work by the juxtaposition of objects, are immediately relegated to the status of day-dream, of interest only to the kind of person, usually a woman, who is 'inclined that way'. The poem affords nothing real. (By contrast, the honour paid poetry before the time of Descartes as an indispensable educational *modus* may again be recalled. A wealth of human experience inhered in any good lyric. Homer was the educator of Greece).

For Descartes, Locke, Kant, and Korzybski, the mind knows essences only. It does not spread its digestive tentacles around things. As Maritain puts it,

'If existence lies outside the field of the intelligence, it is the will alone that can bring them together.'

A poem, that is, becomes a combining operation which some starry-eyed johnny does 'because he feels like it'. Poetic form is *imposed* on conceptual materials; we have no longer to do with a way of seeing rooted in the intrinsic analogy of being. Maritain goes on,

'Si l'essence seule est le terme ultime de l'activité intellec-tuelle, sa réalisation dans une existence indépendante de la pensée devient pour celle-ci problématique, et finalement un non-sens.'

De Bergson à Thomas d'Aquin, p. 207.

When the meaning of the statement 'My love *is*' becomes 'problématique', that of the statement 'My love is a red, red rose', or even '. . . is like a red, red rose', is obviously not far from 'un non-sens'. M. Maritain reminds us of the Cartesian thinkers' hatred of things outside themselves:

'They imagine, or construe the object as a reified idea, as a bit of pure externality, passive and inert, an obstacle to the mind, something interposing itself between the mind and the world of existence, or real subjects. Consequently, they contend that only the actual experience of subjectivity could reach those subjects. They do not see that object and objectivity are the very life and salvation of the intellect.

Existence and the Existent, p. 13.

Such a world is, precisely, the dead grey landscape inhabited by Picasso's lumpy giantesses. Pound has himself characterized the precedent medieval world, which nourished *The Divine Comedy* and lasted long enough to make *Hamlet* possible for a skilled, tough-minded, miraculously sensitized executant who did not need to spend nine-tenths of his time, as Pound, Eliot, and Joyce have had to, unthinking the thought of his time:

'A mediaeval "natural philosopher" would find this modern world full of enchantments, not only the light in the electric bulb, but the thought of the current hidden in air and in wire would give him a mind full of forms, "*Fuor di color*" or having their hyper-colours. The mediaeval philosopher would probably have been unable to think the electric world, and *not* think of it as a world of forms. Perhaps algebra has queered our geometry. . . .'

Make It New, p. 352.

It is interesting to run across the suggestion that Descartes queered geometry just as, in Boileau's phrase, he 'cut the throat of poetry'. Descartes, it will be remembered, holding that the mind knows only essences or diagrams, regarded language, rammed as it was with the cloddered garbage of the senses, as intrinsically treasonable to the pure concepts that had perforce to be entrusted to it. Hence his bias towards mathematics. (A mathematical analogy, $1/2 = 2/4$, far from filling the mind like a poetic analogy, is instantaneously exhaustible. It has no tinge of 'the uncontrollable mystery on the bestial floor'.) Attacks on the intrinsic relation between reason and will, from his time to that of Watson and Kinsey, have always been carried on with a great reliance on mathematical apparatus. The charts in any sociological primer are the post-Cartesian equivalent for the wisdom of St. Augustine. That the artist's social reports might be regarded as data for ethics[1] is held to be laughable.

[1] See 'The Serious Artist', *Pavannes and Divisions*, pp. 219–42.

In his *Principles of Philosophy* (1-30) Descartes remarks,

'Mathematical truths ought now to be above suspicion, since these are of the clearest.'

In 1-74 he laments an inescapable source of error:

'We can scarcely conceive anything with such distinctness as to separate entirely what we conceive from the words that were selected to express it.'

It is easy to sense the presupposition that words are at best a makeshift dress for the transcendent. M. Maritain has remarked brilliantly on Descartes' 'angelism'. Speech has become a mark of man's brutish condition, not, as was held with tireless reiteration from the time of the Stoics to that of Francis Bacon, the sign of his distinction from the brutes. Shakespeare is of the old dispensation. His Prospero taught Caliban to speak instead of giving him a geometrical toy to contemplate.

These citations may help us to see that there can be no *mot juste* unless there can be a real and supple relation between the world consisting of a congeries of intelligible things, and language considered as a structure of directed perceptions. When that sense of language died, the *mot juste* died with it. Hence the nineteenth-century diarrhoea, 'Snowdrops that plead for pardon and pine for fright,' and the rest of it, a rush of verbiage not to be confused with the proportion of bad poetry that has existed in all ages, but profuse and incongruous on principle, occasionally achieving surprising effects on premises of loosely-linked verbal suggestiveness. Mr. Eliot, paying tribute to the 'singular life' of Swinburne's poetic world, adds:

'The poetry is not morbid, it is not erotic, it is not destructive. These are adjectives which can be applied to the material, the human feelings, which in Swinburne's case do not exist. The morbidity is not of human feeling but of language. Language in a healthy state presents the object, is so close to the object that the two are identical.'

Selected Essays.

When, because words are rooted in matter whereas thought deals in essences, no *mot* can be *juste*, a metaphor or a poem, because of its emotional implications or the complexity it introduces among ideas that ought to be 'clear and distinct', is scarcely to be trifled with by an honest man. And as Mill noted of Bentham, what can't be dealt with by subject-predicate postulations is for this mercantile intelligence 'vague generality'; it doesn't exist. It is of paramount importance to see that this state of mind follows from a way of seeing. Metaphor is a 'pestilent cosmetic' if, denying the reality of substantial forms and so the intelligibility of things in relation, we leave all things unrelated so that there are no *real* relations to be perceived, and denying the integrity of the mental act, we separate intuition from execution (as Pound is ludicrously accused of doing) so that the former, the Cartesian diagram, remains the locus of truth while the latter becomes merely a sweaty arena for patching and botching.

We have spoken of the mercantile intelligence, a phrase the applicability of which to Benthamite morals is obvious. More generally, the rise of the dualistic milieu, with its deep-rooted hostility to the artist, is rooted in questions of philosophy which are questions of appetite which are questions affecting commerce. The sociological implications of the rise of the novel with the rise of the mercantile classes furnish a better-known example of this connection. This is one axis of reference for the usury theme in the *Cantos*.

In this way metaphor was transformed from a drama involving four terms to a detour using two ('tenor and vehicle'): an avoidance of barren country by the choice of prettier words. The 'plain sense', which can be extracted by paraphrase, goes as the crow flies. The poet is a man who can make plain sense beguiling; often he overdoes things and simply makes it difficult. In classrooms the poetry is stripped off Shakespeare so that the students, contemplating the skeleton plot and a few sketches of characters, can see 'what the author meant'.

In fact, the use of metaphor as interchangeable ornamentation was perhaps the earliest apprehensible sign of the change of mental habits that was to settle over Europe in the seventeenth century. Pound has discerned it in Petrarch:

'When the late T. E. Hulme was trying to be a philosopher in that milieu, and fussing about Sorel and Bergson and getting them translated into English, I spoke to him one day of the difference between Guido's precise interpretative metaphor, and the Petrarchian fustian and ornament, pointing out that Guido thought in accurate terms; that the phrases correspond to definite sensations undergone. . . .

Hulme took some time over it in silence, and then finally said: "That is very interesting"; and after a pause: "That is more interesting than anything anyone ever said to me. It is more interesting than anything I ever read in a book." '

Make It New, p. 361.

Hulme's accredited status as the philosopher of the 1914 *avant-garde* should gain the implications of this dialogue serious attention.

It should be noted, finally, that the theoretical activities of Wordsworth, Coleridge, and Shelley were directed against an Augustanism utterly infected with Locke's brand of rationality (not to be confused with the earlier Augustan serenity underlying the lively grasp on particulars of Pope at his best) and simultaneously against a mercantile and mechanistic milieu which was also the milieu of official philosophy. They threw up more or less *ad hoc* breastworks against spiritual annihilation. These defences and prefaces had the utility of securing a space within which a few good poems could be written, but because the philosophical terminology had all to be taken from the opposition, with edges rusted and planes warped, the theories that got built with such tools were mostly piles of brush, not concrete emplacements. Shelley begins his *Defence* by postulating the very Lockean distinction which was actually the focus of infection:

'According to one mode of regarding those two classes of mental action, which are called reason and imagination, the former may be considered as mind contemplating the relations borne by one thought to another, however produced; and the latter, as mind acting upon those thoughts so as to colour them with its own light, and composing from them, as from elements, other thoughts, each containing within itself the principle of its own integrity.'

Shelley was offered his choice of weapons only after every available sword had been blunted; so it came about that he was forced into the position of defending a little patch of beautiful unreason against what appear to be all the forces of sanity. 'Reasoners and mechanists' are challenging the 'civic crown': Locke, Hume, Gibbon, and Voltaire, despite their practical achievements, were 'mere reasoners'. This dichotomy was prepared for Shelley by the opposition, and there was nothing for him to do but turn his fever into an energy: if this be reason, away with it! But even the terminology for 'poetic' or 'imaginative' activity comes from the *Essay Concerning Human Understanding.* 'Thoughts' get into the mind (presumably by way of the senses) and are arranged and 'coloured'.

The necessity for throwing out the entire world of reason, morals, practical activity, and to some extent even social intercourse, and then defining the function that was left (imagination) in terms that the mechanists had turned into phrases of contempt, may be likened to amputating a diseased body at the neck. The head continued mouthing for a little space, after which the death of poetry itself set in.

Fifteen years ago Pound wrote,

'Bad writing, or a great deal of it, drips down from an abstract received "idea" or "generality" held with fanaticism (twin beast with personal vanity) by men who NEVER take in concrete detail.

'Men are good or bad in the year 1935 in proportion as they will LOOK AT the facts, new facts, any facts.

That is part of the new FORMA MENTIS. Forma to the great minds of at least one epoch meant something more than dead pattern or fixed opinion. "The light of the DOER, as it were a form cleaving to it" meant an ACTIVE pattern, a pattern that sets things in motion.

Polite Essays, p. 51.

The revitalizers of language have owed nearly everything to minute observation: Flaubert's journey's in search of seen particularity, Joyce's trunkfuls of social documentation, the voluminous notations of Fabre and Frazer and Frobenius as utilized in the *Cantos* and *The Waste Land.* Frazer's collection of folklore gave a clue to the treasure of psychological verity available in Ovid. Criticism is recalled by de Gourmont and Eliot from its monistic obsession with poetry as the automatic writing of the Zeitgeist to a method of 'comparison and analysis', and the chief qualification of the critic, as Mr. Eliot tells us, is 'a very highly developed sense of fact'.

'This is by no means a trifling or frequent gift. And it is not one which easily wins popular commendations. The sense of fact is something very slow to develop, and its complete development means perhaps the very pinnacle of civilization.'

* * *

'To the member of the Browning Study Circle, the discussion of poets about poetry may seem arid, technical, and limited. It is merely that the practitioners have clarified and reduced to a state of fact all the feelings that the member can enjoy only in the most nebulous form; the dry technique implies, for those who have mastered it, all that the member thrills to; only that has been made into something precise, tractable, under control. That, at all events, is one reason for the value of the practitioner's criticism—he is dealing with his facts, and he can help us to do the same.

Selected Essays: 'The Function of Criticism.'

This should be coupled with Eliot's recent remark that Pound's criticism seems irritatingly biased to those 'to whom "literary criticism" means something quite different from the notes of a poet on his craft'.

The word 'periplum', which recurs continually throughout the *Pisan Cantos*, is glossed in Canto LIX:

> periplum, not as land looks on a map
> but as sea bord seen by men sailing.

Victor Brerard discovered that the geography of the *Odyssey*, grotesque when referred to a map, was minutely accurate according to the Phoenician voyagers' *periploi.* The image of successive discoveries breaking upon the consciousness of the voyager is one of Pound's central themes for the New Learning. The voyage of Odysseus to hell is the matter of Canto I. The first half of Canto XL is a periplum through the financial press; 'out of which things seeking an exit,' we take up in the second half of the Canto the narrative of the Carthagenian Hanno's voyage of discovery. Atlantic flights in the same way raise the world of epileptic maggots in Canto XXVIII into a sphere of swift firm-hearted discovery:

> And lest it pass with the day's news
> Thrown out with the daily paper,
> Neither official pet
> Nor Levine with the lucky button
> Went on into the darkness,
> Saw naught above but close dark,
> Weight of ice on the fuselage
> Borne into the tempest, black cloud wrapping their wings,
> The night hollow beneath them
> And fell with dawn into ocean
> But for the night saw neither sky nor ocean
> And found ship . . . why? . . . how? . . . by the Azores.

The periplum, the voyage of dicovery among facts, whose tool is the ideogram, is everywhere contrasted with the conventions and artificialities of the bird's-eye view afforded by the map. Forms grow out of data. They are not to be imposed upon data.

'Academicism is not excess of knowledge. It is the possession of *idées fixes* as to how one shall make use of one's data.'

Antheil, p. 16.

Nor can the poet impose a conceptual strait-jacket upon the flux of memories:

> as the winds veer and the raft is driven
> and the voices   ,   Tiro, Alcmene
> with you is Europa nec casta Pasiphaë

Eurus, Apeliota as the winds veer in periplum

Io son la luna,'   Cunizza

as the winds veer in periplum

and from under the Rupe Tarpeia

drunk with the wine of the Castelli

'in the name of its god' 'Spiritus veni'

adveni / not to a schema

'is not for the young' said Arry, stagirite.

(Canto LXXIV).

'Not to a schema' is Aristotelian advice. Aristotle, as Pound often reminds us, collected 158 constitutions for examination. In *Culture* he concludes his severe criticism of Aristotelian dissective tendencies with this:

'Perhaps the finest thing in this story is that he assembled the collection of state constitutions, seeing clearly that it wd. be *no use unless* someone had the experience and intelligence to know "what to make of it".'

(p. 343.)

The bearings of the periplum-discovery theme in the *Cantos* on the ideogrammic method and the sense of fact should be obvious. 'The great periplum brings in the stars to our shores.'

Fitzgerald's *Omar*, unread,

lay there till Rossetti found it remaindered
at about twopence

(Canto LXXX).

The risks of biological discoverers are analogous with those of Homeric explorers:

Ten million germs in his face,
'That is part of the risk and happens
'About twice a year in tubercular research, Dr. Spahlinger . . .'
'J'ai obtenu' said M. Curie, or some other scientist
'A burn that cost me six months in curing,'
And continued his experiments.

(Canto XXVII).

Cantos LII–LXI, eschewing the map and the epitome, take us on a brilliantly varied tour through the documentary concreteness of Chinese history. The poet personifies himself from the first as intellectual voyager, in one instance counterpointed with a pathetic image of tangible returns:

> so that leaving America I brought with me $80
> and England a letter of Thomas Hardy's
> and Italy one eucalyptus pip
> from the salita that goes up from Rapallo
> (if I go)
> (Canto LXXX).

The sense of intellectual adventure, the sense of fact, the sense of the intelligibility of assembled particulars, 'too necessary a conclusion from all the more intelligent activity of many decades for there to be the least question of its belonging to anyone in particular', comprise the *forma mentis* of ideogram and of the *Cantos*. The *Cantos*, like the best of contemporary anthropology, are filled with records of places visited, things and men seen, books read, ideas hammered out. In shifting his interest, between *Exultations* and *Lustra*, from the articulation of personae to the observation of epiphanic events, Pound was participating in the major intellectual *peripeteia* of the past eighty years, the desertion of the windowless monadic world of pigeonholed 'subjects' for a lively explorer's interest in particulars, that can grasp simultaneously, as from a moving ship, the relative and the continuous. Literary histories will henceforth be meaningless until they can take account of this change. Ironically, it is our rampantly conceptual approach to the arts that constitutes perhaps the rockiest Cartesian-Kantian survival in the world of Einstein, Freud, and Frobenius.

Part Two

Personae

Finding the precise word for the inarticulate heart's tone means not lying to oneself, as in the case of hating a bad smell or loving a beautiful person, also called respecting one's own nose.

On this account the real man has to look his heart in the eye even when he is alone. . . .

You improve the old homestead by material riches and irrigation; you enrich and irrigate the character by the process of looking straight into the heart and then acting on the results. Thus the mind becomes your palace and the body can be at ease; it is for this reason that the great gentleman must find the precise verbal expression for his inarticulate thoughts.
—THE GREAT DIGEST, VI, 1, 4

(This section has reference to the collected edition of Pound's poems up to the *Cantos*, published under the title *Personae* in 1926, and not to be confused with the earlier *Personae* of 1909.)

Chapter 13

RHYTHMS

Once only in Burgos, once in Cortona
was the song firm and well given.

I t is sheer waste of time to seek to contradict Mr. Eliot's
frequent statements concerning the crucial importance
of Pound's early verse (pre-*Cantos*) for the instruction
of young poets: 'There is, in fact, no one else to study.' That
dimension of the *Personae* collection comes within the competence neither of the present commentator nor (fortunately)
of the present book. It may not be irrelevant however to
suggest that at least a nodding acquaintance with this
enchiridion of technical discoveries would make easier for the
present-day reader the evaluation of much new and unfamiliar
work. Not only does the volume abound in sketches of details
for the *Cantos*, but it epitomizes a development of sensibility,
out of the decades of romance and golden hair, which no later
poet need recapitulate from exactly the same premises; and
time after time its author gives rhythmic and melodic articulation to states of consciousness that, once so fixed, need not
again be adumbrated less skilfully.

Too little attention is usually paid to rhythmic discoveries.
'Most so-called prose poetry lacks adequate rhythmic vitality,'
Pound has written; and again,

'In fact I am tempted to put it as a brace of axioms for all
poetry:
'WHEN the metre is bad, the language is apt to be poor.

'WHEN the metre is good *enough* it will almost drive out all other defects of language.'

The Townsman, July, 1938.

In Canto LXXXI we find,

> (to break the pentameter, that was the first heave)
> or as Jo Bard says: they never speak to each other,
> if it is baker and concierge visibly,
>   it is La Rochefoucauld and de Maintenon audibly.

The iambic pentameter has strait-jacketed English verse much longer and more rigidly than the cadres of elegance have eviscerated French conversation. Pound's discovery of ten or so substitutes (one of which, the roughly dactylic metre of the *Cantos*, probably underlies Mr. Eliot's post-Sweeney dramatic verse) has so embarrassed the impressionable with riches as to obscure the status of 'free verse' as anything but a roughly rhythmical speech. When everyone wrote couplets it was easier to spot the ones who handled the instrument badly. The would-be judicious reader who, not wanting to be taken in, acquaints his ear with such cadences as

> Eyes, dreams, lips, and the night goes

or

> See, they return; ah, see the tentative
> Movements, and the slow feet,

or

> Midonz, with the gold of the sun, the leaf of the
>   poplar, by the light of the amber,
> Midonz, daughter of the sun, shaft of the tree,
>   silver of the leaf, light of the yellow of the
>   amber,
> Midonz, gift of the God, gift of the light, gift of
>   the amber of the sun,
>   Give light to the metal

will find much that offers itself to his scrutiny turning at such confrontation into jelly.

Pound's polyphonic endings should also be examined. 'The Alchemist,' from which we have just been quoting, ends,

> Selvaggia, Guiscarda, Mandetta,
> > Rain flakes of gold on the water
> Azure and flaking silver of water,
> Alcyon, Phaetona, Alcmena,
> Pallor of silver, pale lustre of Latona,
> By these, from the malevolence of the dew
> > Guard this alembic.
> Elain, Tireis, Allodetta
> > Quiet this metal.

And 'Na Audiart' ends, with a dying flutter on the strings,

> ... Knowing, I know not how,
> Thou once wert she
> > > Audiart, Audiart
> For whose fairness one forgave
> > > Audiart,
> Audiart
> > Que be-m vols mal.

These and other such 'effects', unique in English, will at least help sensitize the ear to certain aspects of the versification of the *Cantos* (which are too often called 'formless'). Their pattern not wholly apprehensible by the ear, their qualities of sound that do not tempt the reciter and are not to be described as sonorities, are put in the long poem to dramatic uses of endless subtlety. (The end of Canto LVIII is especially striking.) The approach to the justly-celebrated 'libretto' and 'Pull down thy vanity' sequence in Canto LXXXI builds in this way, with indubitable authority but without a trace of jig-stepping emphasis, its form multi-dimensional in the air:

> and my ole man went on hoein' corn
> > while George was a-tellin' him,
> come across a vacant lot
> > > where you'd occasionally see a wild rabbit
> or mebbe only a loose one

AOI!

a leaf in the current

        at my grates no Althea

It will take some readers, accustomed as they are to a 'hefty swat on alternate syllables', considerable acquaintance with the *Personae* volume to persuade themselves that significant rhythms are in many cases present at all.

> Bah! I have sung women in three cities,
> But it is all the same;
> And I will sing of the sun.
> Lips, words, and you snare them,
> Dreams, words, and they are as jewels,
> Strange spells of old deity,
> Ravens, nights, allurement:
> And they are not;
> Having become the souls of song.

With perhaps more than usual risk of insisting on the obvious, it may be pointed out that in this particular case it is the very gentleness of the accents that is functional; and that if no two lines scan alike, it is not because the poet wasn't competent at 'sticking to a pattern'. Donne's rhythmic licenses have gained acceptance, but Donne works in stanzas, i.e. turns his audacities into patterns by repeating them; and in any case his syllabic swat is relatively hefty. It may be well to emphasize that the 'image', that which the poet constructs, is not necessarily a static 'thing' like a pine-tree or a suit of armour, but may be, and in all but the simplest cases will be, a chain of events, an interaction of rhythms (for an accent *is* an event), anything up to the most intricate combinations of visual, tactile, neuro-muscular, and rhythmic to be found in the last phase of Shakespeare. That a rhythm is *part of*, not background music to, a poem, Pound explains in these words:

'. . . I believe in an absolute rhythm. I believe that every emotion and every phase of emotion has some toneless phrase, some rhythm-phrase to express it.

'(This belief leads to *vers libre* and to experiments in quantitative verse.)

'To hold a like belief in some sort of permanent metaphor is, as I understand it, "symbolism" in its profounder sense. It is not necessarily a belief in a permanent world, but it is a belief in that direction.

'Imagisme is not Symbolism. The symbolists dealt in "association", that is, in a sort of allusion, almost of allegory. They degraded the symbol to the status of a word. They made it a form of metonomy. One can be grossly "symbolic", for example, by using the word "cross" to mean "trial". The symbolists' *symbols* have a fixed value, like the numbers in arithmetic, like 1, 2, and 7. The imagiste's images have a variable significance, like the signs a, b, and x in algebra.

'Moreover, one does not want to be called a symbolist, because symbolism has usually been associated with mushy technique.'

Gaudier-Brzeska, p. 97.

It is easy to see that in Donne's

>   ... he that will
> Reach her, about must, and about must go,

the 'reaching' which the reader must enact in passing backwards the length of a line to complete the verb phrase is the fulcrum of the presentation. This is kindergarten material beside the strategic audacities of the later *Cantos*; the principle remains valid, but the later poet has extended and refined its application to correspond to a more discriminating consciousness:

> Here are lynxes   Here are lynxes,
> Is there a sound in the forest
>   of pard or of bassarid
> of crotale   or of leaves moving?
>   (Canto LXXIX.)

Such effects are not to be dismissed as typographic. They are rooted in the scrupulous interplay of consciousness, technique, and material, from moment to moment.[1] Verse is

[1] In *The Film Sense* (p. 63), Sergei Eisenstein has an illuminating comment on an elementary example of this kind:

'inevitable' when the requisite decorums never slacken; this need not contradict the advisability of the rhythm, in calculated stretches, going slack. These remarks should not be received as Sinaitic absolutes, but checked against the reader's continuing experience of *vers libre*. They at least may guard him from the supposition that the essence of metric is a mechanical pattern from which dramatic deviations take place, and hence that *vers libre* is inherently lacking in leverage.

Migratory birds hit their destination year after year by bearing against the circling currents of air. Ocean currents, whose only context is water of another temperature, take directions as chartable as the embanked Mississippi. It requires no stanzaic vehicle to differentiate between the emotional temperature of

Came Mava swimming with light hand lifted in overstroke

and

Oils, beasts, grasses, petrifactions, birds, incrustations

The belief in absolute rhythm, so that 'every emotion and every phase of emotion has some toneless phrase, some rhythm-phrase to express it', leads as Pound saw into deeper issues. It is unnecessary however to posit esoteric webs of correspondences to substantiate it, as Pound saw in dissociating himself from the 'Symbolists'. A rational clue is provided

'Mayakovsky does not work in lines:
            Emptiness. Wing aloft
            Into the stars carving your way.
He works in shots:
            Emptiness.
            Wing aloft,
            Into the stars carving your way.
Here Mayakovsky cuts his line just as an experienced film editor would in constructing a typical sequence of "impact" (the *stars*—and *Yesenin*). First—the one. Then—the other. Followed by the impact of one against the other.'

Eisenstein here indicates the intimate relation between rhythmic and typographic devices and the ideogrammic structure of released intelligibility. In such details as (from Canto LXXX)
            there can be honesty of mind
                        without overwhelming talent
      I have perhaps seen a waning of that tradition
Pound reinforces the theme-countertheme-resolution pattern with a rhythmic pattern of strophe, antistrophe, and full chorus.

by Remy de Gourmont, whose *Le Latin Mystique* makes it plain that the phrase 'absolute rhythm' was used by the Gregorian musicians to refer to the relation of the anterior and posterior morphologies of words and syllables.[1] As a structural relation, not an abstractable quantity, and rooted in basic human gestures (Paget's and Malinowski's celebrated later theory of language as gesture, phatic communion, is an obvious cross-light here), 'absolute rhythm' provides at once a psychological and an objective correlative of emotions and shades of emotion transcending both exegesis and vocabulary. The structural principle of Gregorian chant, the exact and indissoluble union of the music, phrase by phrase and rhythm by rhythm, with the sacred text, is obviously related to *vers libre* as the opposite conception of a tune to which words are fitted is related to the stanza form. So that Eliot's early insistence that 'no *vers* is *libre* to a man who wants to do a good job' connects in a surprising way with the liturgical bearings of his later poetry.

Pound's poetry up to *Mauberley* may be very largely regarded as a series of exercises in rhythmic definition. This is of course only one of its dimensions, but since we are working toward the more obvious stumbling-blocks in the *Cantos*, it is the most fruitful one to consider here. The anecdotal society verse that makes its appearance with the *Lustra* series is illuminated by his gloss on a remark of A. E. Housman's:

'I am unqualified to speak of exalted sentiment, but I should say no idea worth carrying in the mind from one year's end to another, and no story really good enough to make me at least want to tell it, but chafes at the flatness of prose, but suffers from inadequate statement, but leaves me feeling it is but half said, or said in abstraction, or defined in terms so elastic that any god's ape can stretch its definition to meet his own squalor or to fit his own imbecility, until it be conjoined with music, or at least given rhythmic definition even though one does not arrive at defining its total articulation.'

Polite Essays, p. 24.

[1] Analogous examples, discovered by Arnold Dolmetsch in the practices of seventeenth-century musicians, are discussed by Pound in *Pavannes and Divisions*, pp. 151–5.

The anecdotes in the *Cantos* are not fitted into the verse, the verse is fitted to the anecdotes. And the intricate techniques by which this is done in the *Pisan Cantos* (easily the summit of Pound's achievement) depend upon the years of work with speech-tones and rhythms that begins before *Lustra*. Comparison between, for instance, 'Our Contemporaries:'

> When the Taihaitian princess
> Heard that he had decided,
> She rushed out into the sunlight and
>   swarmed up a cocoanut palm tree,
>
> But he returned to this island
> And wrote ninety Petrarchan sonnets.
>
> *Personae.*

and a scrap from Canto LXXIX:

> Which being the case, her holding dear H. J.
>   (Mr. James, Henry) literally by the button-hole ...
> in those so consecrated surroundings
>   (a garden in the Temple, no less)
>   and saying, *for once*, the right thing
> namely: 'Cher maître'
> to his chequered waistcoat, the Princess Bariatinsky,
> as the fish-tails said to Odysseus, ἐνὶ τροίῃ,[1]

reveals that the same unmistakable command of tone and rhythm as means of fixing an irony indelibly have been extended after thirty years not by any alteration of principle but rather by a vastly increased capacity to take account of nuances: half-a-dozen mutually tilted facets in place of a single *peripeteia*.

We have had much to say earlier in justification of the existence of these anecdotes, and shall have occasion to say more when we come to the *Cantos*. Be it noted here that the tensions with which they are alive exist in a three-way pull between author, reader, and social context. An inferior anecdote

---

[1] *Odyssey* XII, 189. The entire clause is quoted in the first section of *Mauberley*. 'Cher maître' as the siren-song best calculated to lure Henry James is an exquisite comic perspective.

cancels two of these tensions, assuming solidarity between author and reader *vis-à-vis* the subject-matter, or else lumping reader and subject as victims of the auctorial brickbat. The antiseptic detachment, and the genial tone, respectively, of the vignettes in *Lustra* persuade us that Pound has neither of these thumbs to his nose. This may best be illustrated by quoting an entire poem:

LES MILLWIN

The little Millwins attend the Russian Ballet.
The mauve and greenish souls of the little Millwins
Were seen lying along the upper seats
Like so many unused boas.
The turbulent and undisciplined host of art students—
The rigorous deputation from 'Slade'—
Was before them.

With arms exalted, with fore-arms
Crossed in great futuristic X's, the art students
Exulted, they beheld the splendours of *Cleopatra*.

And the little Millwins beheld these things;
With their large and anaemic eyes they looked out
    upon this configuration.

Let us therefore mention the fact,
For it seems to us worthy of record.

Personae.

The satiric component here will be conceded. Satire however does not necessarily involve a straight-edge, deviation from which is visited by clamorous hoots. It is not simply the insentience of Les Millwin that is in question, and the reader who expects that his sympathies ought to be invested on the side of the Russian Ballet may be checked by the devaluation 'the splendours of *Cleopatra*' incur in juxtaposition with the ritual enthusiasm of 'the rigorous deputation from "Slade".' The centre in relation to which the components of the poem are balanced is not that of Diaghilev's *bon-ton* 'culture'. It is to be looked for in the ironic impersonality that reduces the writer to a recorder of social contours more autonomously complex than any formulable attitude and locks into semi-comic relation scriptor, lector, Millwins, students, and ballerinas alike.

That *reportage* charges itself with significance when fully articulated, is a fact complementary to the immolation of auctorial personality that has made possible this impersonal *persona*. The author as *personality* would have spoiled the stasis of tensions by having something to say 'about' it. Which brings us to the next chapter.

Chapter 14

PERSONS

O strange face there in the glass!
    O ribald company, O saintly host,
O sorrow-swept my fool,
      what answer? O ye myriad
      that strive and play and pass,
      Jest, challenge, counterlie!
      I? I? I?
          And ye?

S ome distinction between the personality felt in the verse and the man who made love and drank with his friends is as old as the oldest anecdotes about poets. The Homer who begg'd his bread seems to have overawed no one, and whoever invented the tale about his dying of chagrin through failure to guess that the answer to a riddle was 'Fleas' was trying to visit upon the mortal memory his irritation with the serenity of the poetic persona. Mr. Eliot's distinction between the man who suffers and the mind which creates is a twentieth-century formulation of one of the oldest observed poetic facts.

With Pope's elaborate schemes for altering and suppressing correspondence, however, we find the poet adjusting his private image to his public one in a way perhaps new since the Renaissance, and his poetic personality self-consciously achieving definition by elaborate antithesis with certain dominant elements in its age. 'Literature of escape' derives a good deal of its respectability from the attempts of nineteenth-century readers to copy the attitudes of poets who were constantly being NOT city-dwellers or NOT money-makers or NOT in

119

accord with prevalent marital, aesthetic, or other canons. The personality so defined is two-dimensional, unnecessarily obvious, and rapidly obsolescent: Swinburne's survival value would perhaps have been greater had he not invested so much of his energy in such laboured opposition; the same is true of the social observations of Mencken. It is no accident that Flaubert's doctrine of the impersonality of the artist, and its elaboration by Joyce—'invisible, refined out of existence, indifferent, paring his fingernails'—were interlocked with affectionate observation of precisely those social manifestations from which it had been the pride of the preceding generations of artists to flee with horror. The post-Flaubertian artist, deprived, by Flaubert's demonstration of its sterility (Frederic Moreau: cf. Stephen Dedalus), of the easy route to a workable *persona*, is put to the labour of refining his habitual self out of existence and simultaneously building his new voice, tone by tone, from within. He can no longer simply utter oaths in drawing-rooms, or sing loud when the world sings soft. 'Self-expression' is not merely *passé*, it is useless to anyone whose artistic ambitions extend beyond the organized contempt of *The New Yorker* or the Winchell column, where the Romantic artist has found his eventual level of vulgarity.[1]

Hence *Personae*. Pound's explanation of the kinds of poetry in his early collections is a condensed history of his development up to *Cathay*:

'In the "search for oneself", in the search for "sincere self-expression", one gropes, one finds, some seeming verity. One says "I am" this, that, or the other, and with the words scarcely uttered one ceases to be that thing. . . .'

[Cf. Mr. Eliot's lines.

. . . and every attempt
Is a wholly new start, and a different kind of failure

[1] Cf. Pound on Henry James: 'I take it as the supreme reward for an artist; the supreme return that his artistic conscience can make him after years spent in its service, that the momentum of his art, the sheer bulk of his process, the (*si licet*) size of his fly-wheel, should heave him out of himself, out of his personal limitations, out of the tangles of heredity and of environment, out of the bias of early training, of early predilections, whether of Florence, A.D. 1300, or of Back Bay of 1872, and leave him simply the great true recorder.'—*Make It New*, p. 257.

Because one has only learnt to get the better of words
For the thing one no longer has to say . . .

The third section of *East Coker* ('Every moment is a new and shocking/Valuation of all we have been') raises this early perception of Pound's to tragic intensity.] Pound goes on:

'I began this search for the real in a book called *Personae*, casting off, as it were, complete masks of the self in each poem. I continued in a long series of translations, which were but more elaborate masks.

'Secondly, I made poems like "The Return", which is an objective reality and has a complicated sort of significance, like Mr. Epstein's "Sun God" or Mr. Brzeska's "Boy with a Coney". Thirdly, I have written "Heather", which represents a state of consciousness, or implies, or "implicates" it.

'A Russian correspondent, after having called it a symbolist poem, and having been convinced that it was not symbolism, said slowly; "I see, you wish to give people new eyes, not to make them see some particular new thing."

'These two sorts of poems are impersonal, and that fact brings us back to what I said about absolute metaphor. They are Imagisme, and insofar as they are Imagisme, they fall in with the new pictures and the new sculpture.'

Gaudier-Brzeska, p. 98.

This classification of early work into three sorts is extremely valuable. We may take the hint and consider examples. A very simple example of the mask, or experimental personality, is this stanza from Heine:

> I dreamt that I was God Himself
> Whom Heavenly joy immerses,
> And all the angels sat about
> And praised my verses.
>
> *Adaptations from Heine, IV.*

The 'I' which Pound here enters is only superficially Heine, it is in fact an 'I' which Heine in turn was trying on in mimicry of 'Philistia's pomp and Art's pomposities'. It is both a grimace

121

(the poetaster's notion of how it feels to be an artist) and a statement, shielded in advance against Philistine objections by the extravagance of its metaphor, of the adulatory compensations to which the serious artist feels ideally entitled. These two intentions exist at different levels of irony, to which Pound's donning of the whole complex as a mask of his own adds more. His four lines of English thus extend the range of his private voice (this is said to have been the literal function of the masks utilized by Greek and Roman actors, whence the name *personae*) by setting up a series of reverberations among (1) the poetaster-figure whom Heine manipulated, (2) Heine's concomitant 'serious' *persona*, i.e. the manifestation of Heine-as-poet whose inflections debunk the poetaster's postures, (3) the elements of this emotion seriously maintained by Heine, which may be strained out by reading the stanza in quite a different tone and thus deriving yet a third personality from it, (4) Heine himself, with whom Pound 'lives too late to sup', a civilized German sensibility of a given time making use of this three-ply mechanism to write the poem Pound had before him, (5) the 'resultant' of all these tensions as felt behind Pound's English words and in his motives for setting this particular fish loose in English waters. If this analysis sounds over-brittle, the reader is at liberty to test and modify it. Its purpose is to encourage explanation of the web of dramatic tensions that can be set up in twenty-one words by the manipulation of *personae*.

The tensions in this particular example, being ironic and therefore affording ready intellectual handles, can be indicated with relative brevity by the analytic vocabulary. In 'Cino', in 'Marvoil,' in 'Blandula, Tenulla, Vagula,' there is, despite an impalpability which looks like tenuity because we lack mechanisms for discussing it, a web of interrelations no less complex to the suitably sensitized apprehensor. The reader seeking to match its movements with suitable vocal gestures is kept continually alert from line to line.

In the paragraph we have quoted, Pound notes as a second category 'poems like "The Return", which is an objective reality and has a complicated sort of significance, like Mr.

Epstein's "Sun God" or Mr. Brzeska's "Boy with a Coney".'
The analogy, that is, is no longer poet-as-actor but poet-as-
sculptor.

THE RETURN

See, they return; ah, see the tentative
  Movements, and the slow feet,
  The trouble in the pace and the uncertain
  Wavering!

See, they return, one, and by one,
With fear, as half-awakened;
As if the snow should hesitate
And murmur in the wind,
   and half turn back;
These were the 'Wing'd-with-Awe',
  Inviolable.

Gods of the wingèd shoe!
With them the silver hounds,
  sniffing the trace of air!

Haie! Haie!
 These were the swift to harry;
These the keen-scented;
These were the souls of blood.

Slow on the leash,
  pallid the leash-men!

Personae.

  This verse moves slowly and should be read slowly, with
attention to the pointing. It should not be searched for
allusions. There is no *external* answer to the man-with-a-note-
book's question, 'Who are "They"?' (There is nothing to
indicate that these elementary things do not still need saying.
The man who can't enjoy a film that isn't about 'the kind of
people he knows', has his analogies among devotees of the
subtler arts.) While it is not wholly irrelevant to bring to the
poem for clarification one's odds and ends of observation
about the decline of passion in classical study, about the

123

bloodlessness into which some of the Hellenizing Imagists fell, about aesthetic misadventures in general, it should be plain that it is these experiences that get clarified, rather than the poem. It exists primarily in and for itself, a lovely object, a fragment of Greek frieze, the *peripeteia* of impalpable huntsmen too firmly-drawn to be wraiths in a dream, set in verse delicate, clear, and word by word inevitable:

> Form, forms and renewal, gods held in the air, . . .
> 'as the sculptor sees the form in the air . . .
> 'as glass seen under water,
> 'King Otreus, my father . . .
> and saw the waves taking form as crystal,
> notes as facets of air,
> and the mind there, before them, moving,
> so that notes needed not move.
>
> (Canto XXV).

It is the curious positive achievement of such verse that it exists as it were disembodied, with a minimum of reference to circumjacent experiences, tensions, or categories of language. This intangible mode of impersonality is too finely wrought, too far arouses the faculties, to be confounded with 'poetry of escape' or 'incantation', which mean a debauch of familiar emotions rather than the creation of unfamiliar ones. Such depressurized lyrics of hyperaesthetic stasis occur over and over in the *Cantos*, for the sake of their interaction with other material.

'Thirdly, I have written "Heather", which represents a state of consciousness, or implies, or "implicates" it.' This is the other sort of impersonal poem, which the Russian correspondent was persuaded was not 'symbolism', and which he finally agreed gave people new eyes, rather than made them see some particular new thing:

HEATHER

> The black panther treads at my side,
> And above my fingers
> There float the petal-like flames.

The milk-white girls
Unbend from the holly-trees,
And their snow-white leopard
Watches to follow our trace.

Personae.

This, which imports a depersonalized experiencing 'I' into a world similar to the world of 'The Return', will be recognized as the technique of such poems as Canto VII in nucleus. Personality, stripped of contingencies, has become at length a point of light moving through possible worlds, a mode of consciousness capable of being put to an indefinite number of uses.

Chapter 15

PASSION

And the days are not full enough
And the nights are not full enough
And life slips by like a field mouse
Not shaking the grass.

The force of our introductory remarks on the—generally unwelcome—readjustment forced by Pound's verse upon Mr. Eliot's cozier readers will have begun to come out by now. Mr. Eliot's is a poetry of exploration at another level altogether. Its basis is tirelessly psychological; hence the unanswerable authority with which line after line rings into the consciousness of even the half-alert reader. The entire Eliot *œuvre* may be described as a metamorphosis of *personae*. Prufrock passed through the acid of Sweeney's world and unfolded, purified, in time and space, becomes Tiresias; Tiresias not hoping to turn again, dismembered by leopards and climbing certain stairs of the Chapel Perilous (*Ash-Wednesday* is one prolonged ordeal) becomes consecrated, suffers anew as Becket, and now habitually inhabiting the spiritual world is able with utterly impersonal authority to speak the *Quartets*, where in *The Dry Salvages* the ordeal is yet once more and with ultimate multi-dimensional comprehension recollected in tranquillity. From 'Let us go then, you and I' to 'And the fire and the rose are one' we have one long poem of recurring situations, about the length of thirty Cantos, which deserves to be far more adequately read than it is.

The 'hard squares' of Pound's 'intaglio method', however, explore other dimensions of experience altogether. The early work with personae nowhere reaches *Prufrock* levels of intensity because it is a preliminary purification of the artist *qua* artist for an impersonal handling of *things*.

The *Cantos* create the modes of consciousness of a new Paideuma because the things, and the ways of seeing things, are kept before the reader's eyes in a timeless present that corresponds to the continual contemplation of a vision, not to the continual purgation of the voluntary faculty. These phrases are not to be pursued to the false conclusion that *directio voluntatis* occupies an unimportant place in Pound's critical lexicon; but until we come to the Confucian bases of the *Cantos* we are equipped to make only the most rough-and-ready distinction. Put it that the Poundian purgation is not homeopathic, that no identification between the reader and a dramatic spectator or protagonist takes place. Tiresias, Mr. Eliot, and, ideally, the 'hypocrite lecteur' have 'foresuffered all'. Tiresias not only sees but as Mr. Eliot's note implies ultimately *is* all the characters in *The Waste Land*. And the reader, stirred by the psychic reverberations of line after line, undergoes in the grip of the drama continual spiritual metamorphosis. On the other hand, the reader looks into the Inferno of Cantos XIV–XV as one being led past a vision which exists tamed, in an ideal order, behind glass. So that Mr. Eliot's celebrated note that Pound's hells are 'for other people' points not to a defect of contagion but to a radical difference of poetic method. In an important statement about music, where visceral tendencies are familiar, Pound notes an ideal distinction between the studio and the concert-hall, not devoid of poetic application. The studio—

'Have we not all, with the shades of Murger, with the well-known death mask gaping at us, and with the plaster cast of the drowned girl hanging in the other corner, have we not all of us known the charm? . . .

'But what has all this to do with the concert-hall? . . .

'The magnetic theory is invalid. No performer can rely on emotionalizing the audience.

'Music in a concert-hall must rely on itself and the perfection of its execution; it is, as it were, under glass. It exists on the other side of the footlights, apart from the audience. With apologies to the language, the audience are spectators, they watch a thing of which they are not part, and that thing must be complete in itself. They may be moved by the contemplation of its beauty, they are not moved—or at least can be moved only in an inferior and irrelevant way—by being merged into the action of the stage.

'A concert in a concert-hall . . . should be as definitely a presentation or exhibition as if the performer were to bring out a painted picture and hang it before the audience. The music must have as much a separate existence as has the painting.'

Antheil, pp. 56–9.

The relation of all this to the question of *personae* is clinched by one of Antheil's marginalia: 'By the way that reminds me that the emotionalism you speak of is the performer's dramatic disguise.'

A passage from Canto LXXX already quoted in our first chapter could with profit be reconsidered here:

> Prowling night-puss leave my hard squares alone. . . .
>
> 'mi-hine eyes hev'
> > well yes they *have*
> seen a good deal of it
> > there is a good deal to be seen
> fairly tough and unblastable
> > and the hymn . . .
> well in contrast to the *god*-damned crooning
> > put me down for the temporis acti

It had better be repeated that no attack on Mr. Eliot's poetry is here in question. When two kinds of poetry are distinguished it is unnecessary to suppose that one of them is rejected. By putting his 'magnetic' evocation of inarticulate feelings to controlled dramatic use, Mr. Eliot has triumphed with the more dangerous method: ample tribute to his integrity, surely.

We are now in a position to consider 'acquisition of technique', as exhibited in Pound's early translations and dramatic projections, more accurately than heretofore. We can see that demands for irrelevant poetic interests have underlain the habit of writing these pieces off as five-finger exercises of undeniable benefit to Mr. Pound, but interesting now mainly to other poets. An element in the quasi-drama with which we are in fact confronted is isolated by a retrospective remark of Pound's:

'When I translated Guido eighteen years ago [i.e. 1910] I did *not* see Guido at all. . . .

'My perception was not obfuscated by Guido's Italian, difficult as it then was for me to read. I was obfuscated by the Victorian language. . . . the crust of dead English, the sediment present in my own available vocabulary—which I, let us hope, got rid of a few years later. You can't go round this sort of thing. It takes six or eight years to get educated in one's art, and another ten to get rid of that education.

'Neither can anyone learn English, one can only learn a series of Englishes. Rossetti made his own language. I hadn't in 1910 made a language, I don't mean a language to use, but even a language to think in.'

Make It New, pp. 398–9.

We find ourselves, as usual, sorting out a number of related problems. In the first place, there is the technique of pouring an 'original' into a 'medium'. Guido's seventh sonnet begins,

> Chi e questa che vien, ch'ogni uom la mira,
> Che fa di clarita l' aer tremare!
> E mena seco Amor, si che parlare
> Null' nom de puote, ma ciascun sospira. . . .

Trying, as he tells us, simply to preserve 'the fervour of the original' and with only a Rossetti-Swinburne emotional vocabulary at his disposal, Pound in 1910 rendered this as,

> Who is she coming, drawing all men's gaze,
> Who makes the air one trembling clarity
> Till none can speak but each sighs piteously
> Where she leads Love adown her trodden ways?

About 1928, in the course of illustrating a point in an essay, he offers another version in 'pre-Elizabethan English, of a period when writers were still intent on clarity and explicitness', acknowledging parenthetically the disproportionate quaintness inherent in such a strategy:

> Who is she that comes, making turn every man's eye
> And makying the air to tremble with a bright clearenesse
> That leadeth with her Love, in such nearness
> No man may proffer of speech more than a sigh?
>
> *Make It New*, p. 406.

This more precise, if over-leisurely, language enables the translator to get rid of such inert bricks as 'piteously' and 'adown her trodden ways'. The 'fervour' has gone because 'As this fervour simply does not occur in English poetry in those centuries (fourteenth, fifteenth, sixteenth) there is no ready-made verbal pigment for its objectification.'

Taking the language as we receive it, that is, we find that there are certain things, whether discovered within ourselves or in poems of other tongues, that just can't be said. Seeking out former and discarded states of the language may or may not afford solutions to particular problems of constatation in hand, but will bring in 'period' flavours we may or may not want. Which is only to rephrase Mr. Eliot's frequent and little-heeded observation that as sensibility alters from generation to generation, language becomes perpetually littered with

> hints of earlier and other creation:
> The starfish, the horseshoe crab, the whale's backbone.

'Sensibility alters from generation to generation, but expression is only altered by a man of genius.' We are back with Ching Ming. Calling things by their names is an endless task. The names rust. In the *Great Digest* we find,

II.1. In letters of gold on T'ang's bathtub:

> AS THE SUN MAKES IT NEW
> DAY BY DAY MAKE IT NEW
> YET AGAIN MAKE IT NEW.

Pound's footnote to his earlier translation of this is helpful:

'The pictures are: sun renew sun sun renew (like a tree-shoot) again sun renew.

'That is to say a daily organic vegetable and orderly renewal; no hang over.'

It would be useful to carry on with the same example; showing how the new speech, expanding the dimensions of current English, could adequately render Guido's sonnet. Unfortunately the exhibit isn't available. We may shift for our final stage however into a parallel example out of Propertius. Near the beginning of the *Personae* collection we find a very early version of Elegy III-26 (II-28a in the Loeb numbering). The Latin reads,

> Haec tua, Persephone, maneat clementia, nec tu,
>   Persephonae coniunx, saevior esse velis.
> sunt apud infernos tot milia formosarum:
>   pulchra sit in superis, si licet, una locis!
> vobiscum est Iope, vobiscum candida Tyro,
>   vobiscum Europe nec proba Pasiphae,
> et quot Troia tulit vetus et quot Achaia formas,
>   et Phoebi et Priami diruta regna senis:
> et quaecumque erat in numero Romana puella,
>   occidit: has omnes ignis avarus habet.
> nec forma aeternum aut cuiquam est fortuna perennis:
>   longius aut proprius mors sua quemque manet.

Pound's early version (which omitted the last two lines) reads:

> Here let thy clemency, Persephone, hold firm,
> Do thou, Pluto, bring here no greater harshness.
> So many thousand beauties are gone down go Avernus,
> Ye might let one remain above with us.
>
> With you is Iope, with you the white-gleaming Tyro,
> With you is Europa and the shameless Pasiphae,
> And all the fair from Troy and all from Achaia,
> From the sundered realms, of Thebes and of aged Priamus;

And all the maidens of Rome, as many as they were,
They died and the greed of your flame consumes them.
Personae, Prayer for his Lady's Life.

This is one dimension of the Latin: it is Propertius seen through the eyes of Swinburne. But by 1917 Pound had forged a new language; not only the expression, but the sensibility brought to the Latin, is liberated from Victorian emotional cliché. The result is not only a new translation, but a block of speech and perception new to the English poetic tradition, and a use of language that responds to the pressures of perception with (Ching Ming) accuracy and adequacy:

Persephone and Dis, Dis, have mercy upon her,
There are enough women in hell,
            quite enough beautiful women,
Iope, and Tyro, and Pasiphae, and the formal girls of Achaia,
And out of Troad, and from the Campania,
Death has his tooth in the lot,
            Avernus lusts for the lot of them,
Beauty is not eternal, no man has perennial fortune,
Slow foot, or swift foot, death delays but for a season.
Personae, Homage to Sextus Propertius, IX.

That the phrase on which the tone of the whole stanza may be said to turn is derived, by a species of pun, from 'quot Achaia formas', need not distress the Latinist. This is recreation, not transcription. The competent poet is entitled to every toehold.

Pound the specialist in literary history has put it on record that the logopoeia ('the dance of the intellect among words') here performed by Pound the poet is analogous to a quality achieved by and discoverable in Propertius. Having, that is, made himself a language that does not obfuscate his perceptions (it being as we have seen difficult or impossible, given an inertly inherited emotional vocabulary, to apprehend the emotions of foreign poets and distant times, let alone one's personal emotions, otherwise than stained by its clichés) he is prepared to make Propertius' poem anew. And as a corollary, having made a language in which it was possible to write the *Cantos*, he is free to use in the *Cantos* a scrap of translation as an emotional peg, a way of marking out a zone of feeling. The *Donna mi pregha* of Guido is such an absolute; in Canto XXXVI it reprimands the preceding survey of Mitteleuropa by exhibiting a compendium of certain modes of perception brought to maximal development. At the same time its very integrity, in Pound's English, affords it autonomy: we have not to deal with an exercise in a known style; something altogether new has been made to exist in English:

> A lady asks me
>> I speak in season
> She seeks reason for an affect, wild often
> That is so proud he hath Love for a name
> Who denies it can hear the truth now
> Wherefore I speak to the present knowers
> Having no hope that low-hearted
>> Can bring sight to such reason
> Be there not natural demonstration
>> I have no will to try proof-bringing
> Or say where it hath birth
> What is its virtu and power
> Its being and every moving
> Or delight whereby 'tis called 'to love'
> Or if man can show it to sight....

(The lovely but less novel version in *Make It New* should be compared.) It may be said in the same way of all the verse translations in the *Cantos* that they perform this dual function: marking historically a perceptive maximum ('tale of the tribe,' in dimensions missed even, or especially, by self-styled 'historians of ideas'); epistemologically a new quiddity let loose in English ('Make It New;' 'Ching Ming;' 'Donner un sens plus pur aux mots de la tribu.') It is also possible, when technique has become in this way coterminous with perception, to arrange a witty interplay between the classical author and modern phraseology:

> Under the portico Kirké: . . .
> 'I think you must be Odysseus. . . .
>> feel better when you have eaten. . . .

Always with your mind on the past. . . .
Ad Orcum autem quisquam?
nondum nave nigra pervenit. . . .
Been to hell in a boat yet?

(Canto **XXXIX**).

A quarter of a century's work remaking a language underlies such possibilities.

It may now be indicated very briefly that 'acquiring technique' by translation means a more or less dramatistic struggle to win the means of seeing and translating *this* or *that* poem, and so of enriching the English tradition with a wealth of other modes of thinking and feeling; setting new fish loose in English waters. This account may be extended to the early *personae* which are not explicitly translations (e.g. 'Cino;' 'Marvoil'); self-nourishment through exploring the experiences of other men and ages leads to a purgation of the contingencies of a personality partly private (Hailey, Idaho; Hamilton College), partly public (the legacy of Rossetti, the emotional climate of 1900–12) but in any case irrelevant to the fulness of poetic achievement. So it is meaningless to use 'technician' as a term of dismissal, or to suppose that the metaphor of a kit of tools is adequate to cover technical competence (as Pound is often accused of separating technique and sensibility, and so of concentrating on ways of saying while having nothing to say). A way of saying becomes itself a thing said. Pound's translations are not archaeology. He selected his texts because they represented poetic maxima the lack of analogies for which left English the poorer. 'Lordly men are to earth o'ergiven' does not dump matter out of an old book into a medium, it epiphanizes the Anglo-Saxon elegiac sensibility. It was discovered in the process of translating 'The Seafarer' (1912); it endures as a building-stone to be *used* in Canto LXXIV (1945).

'To deal with the surface of life is to deal deliberately.' 'Surface' here may remind us that as the rhythms and images of the translations are handled by the factive intellect, so are the gestures and modalities of the *personae*. The latter are

134

deliberate dramatizations which extend the modes of thinking
and feeling accessible to the quotidian inhabitant of a given
London decade. And the persona is both sympathetic (bringing for example the methods of Heine or Voltaire to bear upon
contemporary society, while at the same time distancing the
latter by making it contemporary with Heine or Voltaire) and
felt as finite (because the limitations of a troubadour's or
Saxon seafarer's *Weltanschauung* are being deliberately explored.) In neither case is the persona a means of escaping the
present. Not even that bright world of ideal beauty maintained, as though by impossible strain, at the end of the fine
early poem, 'The Flame,' is a never-never land:

> Thou hooded opal, thou eternal pearl,
> O thou dark secret with a shimmering floor,
> Through all thy various mood I know thee mine;
> If I have merged my soul, or utterly
> Am solved and bound in, through aught here on earth,
> There canst thou find me, O thou anxious thou
> Who call'st about my gates for some lost me;
> I say my soul flowed back, became translucent.
> Search not my lips, O Love, let go my hands,
> This thing that moves as man is no more mortal.
> If thou hast seen my shade sans character,
> If thou hast seen that mirror of all moments,
> That glass to all things that o'ershadow it,
> Call not that mirror me, for I have slipped
> Your grasp, I have eluded.

The analogies of this kind of experience are with the subtle
reward of strenuous contemplation. It is extension, to invisible apexes, of the ascending contours of a fine and high
Provençal civilization—

> 'Tis not a game that plays at mates and mating,
> Provence knew;
> 'Tis not a game of barter, lands and houses,
> Provence knew.
> We who are wise beyond your dream of wisdom,
> Drink our immortal moments; we 'pass through'.

135

We have gone forth beyond your bonds and borders,
Provence knew;
And all the tales of Oisin say but this:
That man doth pass the net of days and hours.
Where time is shrivelled down to time's seed corn
We of the Ever-living, in that light
Meet through our veils and whisper, and of love.

                    Personae, 'The Flame.'

It is the, so to speak, athletic quality of this aestheticism, its pushing to the uttermost of accessible modes of perception, its existence as, to revert to an indispensable bit of jargon, the 'objective correlative' of an exultant contemplative intensity, that is to be marked in distinguishing it from what have come to seem the evasive daydreams of the generation preceding, from Yeats' account, for instance, of how a Princess Edain wandered 'half awake and half asleep' to where stars walk. We should carry away from *Personae* an image at the very least of intellectual passion antipodal to flopping into this ancient dream or that; a passion that endures to stiffen with radiance the sequence of memories of the older poet looking back at those years from the prison in Pisa:

Time is not, Time is the evil, beloved
Beloved the hours βροδοδάκτυλος
          as against the half-light of the window
          with the sea beyond making horizon
le contre-jour the line of the cameo
profile 'to carve Achaia'
          a dream passing over the face in the half-light
          Venere, Cytherea 'aut Rhodon'
          vento ligure, veni
'beauty is difficult' . . .

                              (Canto LXXIV).

Chapter 16

CATHAY

The fire? always, and the vision always,
Ear dull, perhaps, with the vision, flitting
And fading at will. Weaving with points of gold,
Gold-yellow, saffron.

When the widow of Ernest Fenollosa perceived that the poet of *Lustra* was ideally fitted to work into articulated form the notes and cribs on certain early Chinese poems assembled by her husband, Pound for the first time had the opportunity at once of consolidating his new modes of poetic speech and of penetrating an utterly alien poetic method from which unworn procedures and formulations might be drawn. The importance of Fenollosa's essay on the Chinese Written Character needs no emphasis. The technical importance of the *Cathay* translations, in preparing for the *Cantos*, probably still deserves a page or two.

We are happily spared the pitfalls of praising as translations versions of originals unknown to us, by some notes from an expert, Hsieh Wen Tung, in the April, 1938 *Criterion*. Surveying 'English Translations of Chinese Poetry', he finds Mr. Pound 'the only one who, uninhibited by tradition, moulds his style on the text.' What 'the text', with the Fenollosa notes and the decipherings of the Japanese professors Mori and Ariga, looked like when it first lay in front of Pound we unfortunately do not know. Whatever crutches were provided, however, it cannot be doubted that it was Pound's imagist training in stating the 'image' exactly and then leaving it

137

alone to do its work that permitted the astonishing result. Mr. Hsieh's paragraphs on Pound should be transcribed at length:

'The one translator who makes no such concessions to the reader as to substitute explication for implication or insert extraneous information is Mr. Ezra Pound. How much of this restraint contributes to the excellence of his work, and the degree of that excellence, may be measured by comparing these two versions of Li Po's poem:

ON CLIMBING IN NANKING TO THE TERRACE OF PHOENIXES

Phoenixes that played here once, so that the place was named
    for them,
Have abandoned it now to this desolate river;
The paths of Wu Palace are crooked with weeds;
The garments of Chin are ancient dust.
. . . Like the green horizon halving the Three Peaks,
Like this island of White Egrets dividing the river,
A cloud has arisen between the Light of Heaven and me,
To hide his city from my melancholy heart.

Witter Bynner and Kiang Kang-Hu.

THE CITY OF CHOAN

The phoenix are at play on their terrace.
The phoenix are gone, the river flows on alone.
Flowers and grass
Cover over the dark path
    where lay the dynastic house of the Go.
The bright cloths and bright caps of Shin
Are now the base of old hills.
The Three Mountains fall through the far heaven,
The isle of White Heron
    splits the two streams apart.
Now the high clouds cover the sun
And I can not see Choan afar
And I am sad.

Ezra Pound: Cathay.

'It will be noticed that Mr. Bynner has, in the first line, inserted an explanatory detail; in the second, replaced the Chinese formal articulation (parallelism) with the English grammatical; in the fifth and sixth added the wholly unjustified "like this" for the sake of imaginary poetic articulation; and in the last couplet arbitrarily turned a semi-symbolic statement into a metaphoric. Mr. Pound's version is at once good poetry and faithful translation. His missing out the "half" point in the fifth line (his eighth) and the adding of the two "brights", like the errors in his other translations, may be explained by his having to use the Fenollosa texts from the Japanese. . . .

'While I have not seen the Fenollosa manuscripts, I dare say they were defective, because Mr. Pound's errors are all obvious ones. For what he lacked in lingual access, however, Mr. Pound almost made up in an astonishing interpretative acumen, by which he often penetrated through the veil of an alien text to the significant features of the original: tone, poetic intention, and verbal felicity.'

Mr. Hsieh makes one other remark of the utmost importance to the student of literature: 'Style is as important in translation as in composition. Messrs. Bynner, Waley, and Pound all have it. The drawback lies in the possession of *a* style: a style individual and inflexible, as in the case of Mr. Bynner. Mr. Waley submerges his individuality to re-express the original but compromises with English tradition (especially in the matter of articulation). Mr. Pound is the only one who, uninhibited by tradition, moulds his style on the text.' The bearings of these remarks on materials of the the foregoing chapter should be pondered: depersonalization as a means of making a language adequate to any object or situation. The theme will come up again apropos of the *Cantos*. 'Ching Ming' commands moral discipline.

Mr. Hsieh's essay, which abounds in examples and details, should be looked up. It raises questions of principle that go far beyond the practical exigencies of translating Chinese.

* * *

Pound notes in *ABC of Reading* one exceedingly suggestive

139

fact about Chinese poetry as an arena of practice for the English poet:

'I once got a man to start translating the *Seafarer* into Chinese. It came out almost directly into Chinese verse, with two solid ideograms in each half-line.'

(p. 35).

As translated into English by Pound about 1912, the *Seafarer* ends,

> Waneth the watch, but the world holdeth.
> Tomb hideth trouble. The blade is layed low.
> Earthly glory ageth and scareth.
> No man at all going the earth's gait,
> But age fares against him, his face paleth,
> Grey-haired he groaneth, knows gone companions,
> Lordly men, are to earth o'ergiven,
> Nor may he then the flesh-cover, whose life ceaseth,
> Nor eat the sweet nor feel the sorry,
> Nor stir hand, nor think in mid heart,
> And though he strew the grave with gold,
> His born brothers, their buried bodies
> Be an unlikely treasure-hoard.

Personae.

It is easy to underestimate the sophistication of this verse, to overlook its reliance on juxtaposed *things*, to skim it in search of 'meaning'. Its mode is 'phanapoeia'. Chinese poetics go back to the roots of English in a more than philological way (the 'kenning' is ideogram: flesh-cover, whale-road). Contemporary alliterative verse, like that of the first section of *Little Gidding*, repeats initial sounds not for Swinburnian incantation but as a binding-pin for quasi-nouns. In *Murder in the Cathedral* we read,

> Fare forward, shun two files of shadows:
> Mirth merrymaking, melting strength in sweetness,
> Fiddling to feebleness, doomed to disdain;
> And godlovers' longings, lost in God.

Shall he who held the solid substance
Wander waking with deceitful shadows?
Power is present. Holiness hereafter.

The analogy between the four ideograms or metaphors or key-words per line of Anglo-Saxon and the four-part structure of the couplet of Pope (which simply uses a different binding-device) would detain us too long. Suffice it to say that the poetic principles explored in *Cathay* are far from exotic.

Finally, their solidity of *tone* should not be missed. Every-thing depends upon the alteration of voice that brings off the *peripeteia*, and this the language invariably enforces; nothing is left to the elocutor. (See particularly 'The River-Merchant's Wife', and the ending of 'Poem by the Bridge at Ten-Shin'.) Those who find these poems monotonous should handle the reading voice with more alertness: or rather, the set of per-ceptions that control that voice. The great virtuoso exercises in tone that make up the *Homage to Sextus Propertius* were still in 1915 two years ahead, but the solid basis was ready.

A very simple example of how flexibility of tone can in certain cases contribute almost literally everything to poetic effect is given by the rough translation, in *Culture*, of a bit of Lacharme's Latin version of one of the Confucian Odes. Lacharme:

'Regio quam alluit amnis Fen dictus humida est, et depressa juxta amnem herba Mou decerpitur. Hic vir formosus quidem, sed caret prudentia; praeclara est specie; sed nullo consilio; a regis auriga multum abludit (et regis currum regendo ineptus est).

Pound (after a note on Catullan irony in certain phrases above):

A low damp kingdom, by the river which they call Fen
and they mow Mou grass along the river bank.
This man is handsome, my word! and lacking in prudence,
marvellous in appearance, and null in advising,
a bit off key for a charioteer
and useless for driving king's wagons.

Culture, p. 214.

Apropos of this example, Mr. Hsieh's remarks on explicit vs. implicit comment should once more be considered. The *Cantos* and *Propertius* are as firmly rooted in *Cathay* as in any of the other precedent work. It was not exotica that Pound, with an eye on the deficiencies of English, was all those years gathering.

Chapter 17

PROPERTIUS

Now if ever it is time to cleanse Helicon.

The years 1915 to 1917 saw Europe in turmoil and Pound much occupied with problems of translation. These facts are not unconnected. The war spelled out for the most innocent the water-tightness of national sensibilities; the exigencies of continental alliances set men like Hilaire Belloc and Ford Madox Ford to work against the educational currents of over a century in attempting to convey to the insulated British public some intuition of a western European culture to be defended against Prussia. The emphases provided by the propaganda of the time should not be overlooked by the historian seeking an immediate context for Mr. Eliot's famous formulations of 1917:

'. . . the historical sense involves a perception, not only of the pastness of the past, but of its presence; the historical sense compels a man to write not merely with his own generation in his bones, but with a feeling that the whole of the literature of Europe from Homer and within it the whole of the literature of his own country has a simultaneous existence and composes a simultaneous order. . . .

'. . . He must be quite aware of the obvious fact that art never improves, but that the material of art is never quite the same. He must be aware that the mind of Europe—the mind of his own country—a mind which he learns in time to be much more important than his own private mind—is a mind which changes, and that this change is a development which abandons nothing *en route*, which does not superannuate either Shakespeare, or Homer, or the rock drawing of the Magdalenian draughtsmen. . . .'

   Selected Essays, 'Tradition and the Individual Talent'.

Beyond its obvious function of to some extent filling a gap for the reader who has no Greek or no Italian, a translation of Homer or Dante into current idiom serves to extend, inform, and articulate the preoccupations of the present by bringing the past abreast of it. Pope made Homer an Augustan and sharpened thereby the scholarly Augustan's perception of the Greek. *Cathay* not only gives voice to a previously inarticulate portion of contemporary sensibility, it exhibits a contemporary relevance in the old Chinese poets that most of us would be incapable of discerning in the originals even if we could read them.

At this point a neglected paragraph of Mr. Eliot's comes in pat; having briefly surveyed contemporary anthropology and sociology, he remarks,

'All these events are useful and important in their phase, and they have sensibly affected our attitude towards the Classics; and it is this phase of classical study that Professor Murray—the friend and inspirer of Miss Jane Harrison—represents. The Greek is no longer the awe-inspiring Belvedere of Winckelmann, Goethe, and Schopenhauer, the figure of which Walter Pater and Oscar Wilde offered us a slightly debased re-edition. And we realize better how different—not how much more Olympian—were the conditions of Greek civilization from ours; and at the same time Mr. Zimmern has shown us how the Greek dealt with analogous problems. Incidentally we do not believe that a good English prose style can be modelled upon Cicero, or Tacitus, or Thucydides. If Pindar bores us, we admit it; we are not certain that Sappho was *very* much greater than Catullus; we hold various opinions about Virgil; and we think more highly of Petronius than our grandfathers did.'

   Selected Essays, 'Euripides and Professor Murray.'

We no longer, that is, read Homer as Chapman and Pope read him. We look at Greece with an eye differently sensitized. Our awareness of this fact is not more articulate, probably, than our awareness, when unaided by the artist, that our emotional world is no longer that of Housman. An adequate translation of Homer—adequate to our perception and idiom, not in the chimerical sense of absolute equivalence; Matthew Arnold was deceived with all his generation in supposing Chapman, Pope, and others to have been in competition to produce the 'final' translation—would focus our special sense, different from that of any previous age, of the aliveness and relevance of the *Odyssey,* just as *The Waste Land* and *Ulysses* focus our peculiar emotional climate, our special sense of the quality of quotidian life. In this way tradition is vitalized, and perception is articulated 'not only of the pastness of the past but of its presence'.

Such translation is work for a poet rather than a scholar, in exactly the same way as the interpretation of contemporary life is work for a novelist or poet and not for a sociologist. The valuable data are commonly spaded up by men who can only vaguely sense their relevance. Joyce found Freud's discoveries indispensable, though Freud himself remains hopelessly old-fashioned, a model-T Mephisto smelling of *Trilby.* Frazer remains embedded in naïve Huxleyan Bible-smashing, yet *The Golden Bough* colours our sense of Christian roots in a way that *The Waste Land* makes explicit. Remarking on the paradox that the Swinburnian Euripides translations of Gilbert Murray, 'a very insignificant follower of the pre-Raphaelite movement,' were the work of 'a Hellenist . . . very much of the present day, and a very important figure in the day', Mr. Eliot concluded:

'We need a digestion which can assimilate both Homer and Flaubert. We need a careful study of Renaissance humanists and Translators, such as Mr. Pound has begun. We need an eye which can see the past in its place with its definite differences from the present, and yet so lively that it shall be as present to us as the present. This is the creative eye; and it is because

Professor Murray has no creative instinct that he leaves
Euripides quite dead.'

A contemporary translation is as much a creative feat as a
contemporary poem. These terms are in one way misleading:
a contemporary translation *is* a contemporary poem. While
their explicit materials differ, both involve the same linking,
for creative purposes, of critical sense and technical resource.
Mr. Eliot has not, in the obvious sense, translated; but his
Agon and parts of *The Waste Land* owe much to his study of
Seneca, and may be taken as bearing much the same relation
to the Latin tragedies as Pound's *Homage* bears to Propertius'
Latin elegies. It was a similar application of perception and
skill that derived from

> Rex est timendus.
>
> > Rex meus fuerat pater.
>
> Non metuis arma?
>
> > Sint licet terra edita.

the antiphonal horrors of

> 'What is that noise?'
>
> > The wind under the door.
>
> 'What is that noise now? What is the wind doing?'
>
> > Nothing again nothing.

In the same way, a contemporary mode of interest in

> Moriere.
>
> > Cupio.
>
> > > Profuge.
>
> > > > Paenitunt fugae.
>
> Medea.
>
> > Fiam.
>
> > > Mater es.
>
> > > > Cui sim vides.

went into the see-saw numbness of Doris and Sweeney:

> DORIS: That's not life, that's no life
> > Why I'd just as soon be dead.

146

SWEENEY: That's what life is. Just is.

DORIS: What is?

What's that life is?

SWEENEY: Life is death.

Mr. Eliot read the tragedies of blood through a perceptive apparatus conditioned by jazz automatism and post-war brutality. Mr. Pound in the same way brought to Propertius' Elegies a sensibility alert to elegant cynicism, informed by Laforgue's dealings with pretentious sentiment and pretentious bombast alike. In a passage like:

> deficiunt magico torti sub carmine rhombi,
>   et iacet exstincto laurus adusta foco;
> et iam Luna negat totiens descendere caelo,
>   nigraque funestum concinit omen avis.
> una ratis fati nostros portabit amores
>   caerula ad infernos velificata lacus.
> sed non unius quaeso, miserere duorum!
>   vivam, si vivet: si cadet illa, cadam.
> pro quibus optatis sacro me carmine damno:
>   scribam ego 'Per magnum est salva puella Iovem';
> ante tuosque pedes illa ipsa operata sedebit,
>   narrabitque sedens longa pericla sua.
>
> (II-xxviii, 35–46).

it is impossible, after Laforgue, to be unaware of a calculated excess of atmospherics, to miss risible implications in the locution 'Luna negat', or comic inflections in the tableau of grateful loquacity presented by the last distich. And a fully contemporary awareness of this verse will turn on awareness of these nuances; we cannot give ourselves to these suspiciously elaborated emotions of passion and aspiration with quite the simple-hearted immersion of Arnold's generation; we credit Propertius with a sense of humour. The passage, specifically, reads to us somewhat as follows:

> The twisted rhombs ceased their clamour of accompaniment;
> The scorched laurel lay in the fire-dust;
> The moon still declined to descend out of heaven,
> But the black ominous owl-hoot was audible.

147

And one raft bears our fates
> on the veiled lake toward Avernus

Sails spread on Cerulean waters, I would shed tears for two;
I shall live, if she continue in life,
> If she dies, I shall go with her.

Great Zeus, save the woman,
> or she will sit before your feet in a veil,
> and tell out the long list of her troubles.

This version recreates a quality of speech which, with our eyes thus opened, it is easy to find in the original. It is a rescription, in Pound's term, a *Homage*; it would be, of course, a dangerous, if plausible, crib. 'Cerulean' is a pun on the Latin; 'tears for two' a pun on an English idiom. 'Great Zeus, save the woman' is merely suggested by 'Per magnum est salva puella Iovem'. It is a little late in the day to continue the wrangle with those who, overlooking their wit and scandalized by their levity, have persisted in regarding these poems as attempts at close translation studded with schoolboy howlers. The ghost of the indignant classicist has been laid by Mr. Lawrence Richardson, whose examination of Pound's dealings with Propertius, in the *Yale Poetry Review*, No. 6 (1947), should be looked up as the persuasive last word from a perceptive Latinist.

We may as well inspect a few more details while we are about it. The Loeb text is here used for Propertius; the sources of Pound's patchwork, for the convenience of the student, may be listed as follows:

ONE: III–1, lines 1–11, 14, 15–23, 25–33, 35–8; III–2, lines 1–26.

TWO: III–3, lines 1–52.

THREE: III–16, lines 1–30.

FOUR: III–6, lines 1–19, 25–33, with a few lines omitted and transposed.

FIVE: II–10, lines 1–20; II–1, lines 1–26, 37–50.

SIX: II–13A, line 17; III–5, lines 13–16; III–4, lines 1–6; III–5, lines 13–16; II–13A, lines 19–30, 35–6, 50–8.

SEVEN: II–15, lines 1–16, 23–6, 29–34, 49, 51–4, 50, 35–40.

EIGHT: II–28, lines 1–34.

NINE: II–28, lines 35–46; II–28A, lines 47–62.

TEN: II–29, 1–22; II–29A, lines 23–42.

ELEVEN: II–30, lines 1–8; II–32, lines 17–20, 23–8, 31–4;
II–30, lines 26–30; II–32, line 35.

TWELVE: II–34, lines 1, 3, 5, 6–18, 33, 37–8, 41, 45–6, 51–4,
61–78, 55–60, 81–94.

We have only to look at this list to see how freely Pound has
turned Propertius' pages for suggestions; not without a grin
at the wholesale transpositions attempted by several editors
in quest of rationale for a badly mangled text.

His puns on the Latin[1] are incessant.

> Actia Vergilio custodis litora Phoebi,
> Caesaris et fortes dicere posse rates

('Be it for Vergil to sing the shores of Actium o'er which
Phoebus watches, and Caesar's gallant ships of war') emerges,
at the suggestion of 'custodis', as:

> Upon the Actian marshes Virgil is Phoebus' chief of police,
> He can tabulate Caesar's great ships.

A few lines later Propertius has,

> utque decem possint corrumpere mala puellas

('how ten apples may win the love of a girl'), and Pound,
finding in 'mala' too good an opportunity to be missed,

---

[1] The rationale of these and allied devices is provided by Pound's
contention that elaborate contextual wit is discoverable in the Latin—
'Unless I am right in discovering *logopoeia* [defined below—p. 160,
footnote] in Propertius (which means unless the academic teaching of
Latin displays crass insensitivity, as it probably does), we must almost
say that Laforgue invented logopoeia . . .'—coupled with his expert
dictum that '*Logopoeia* does not translate; though the attitude of mind
it expresses may pass through a paraphrase. Or one might say, you
can*not* translate it "locally", but having determined the original author's
state of mind, you may or may not be able to find a derivative or an
equivalent.' (*Polite Essays*, pp. 181, 170). Hence it is useless to try to
expose the dimensions of the Latin in which he is interested by direct
rendering. Mr. Richardson provides a good example: on Pound's 'de-
virginated young ladies' for *Gaudeat ut solito tacta puella sono* he comments,
'The *tacta* of Propertius is ambiguous; it includes both: touched at heart
and the opposite of *intacta* (virgin); Pound's rendering . . . does violence
to the context, but it is the meaning which will escape a casual reader.'
It escaped the Loeb translator, who has, 'Let the heart of my mistress
be moved with joy at the old familiar music.'

And how ten sins can corrupt young maidens.

On the next page is a truly glorious botch. The Latin looks conventional enough:

> tale facis carmen docta testudine quale
> Cynthius impositis temperat articulis.

('Such music makest thou as the Cynthian god modulates with fingers pressed upon his well-skilled lyre.') To the mind of the unscholarly reader English associations leap unbidden ahead of Latin roots; before being able to construe these lines, were they suddenly shoved in front of him, he would have to brush away the irrelevances of testudine/turtle (via Caesar), impositis/imposition, Cynthius/Cynthia (the imperious lady-love), temperat articulis/temper my articulation. Sticking these irrelevancies together in a vaguely plausible syntax, Pound gives us the superbly impressionistic distich,

> Like a trained and performing tortoise,
> I would make verse in your fashion, if she should command it.

Once launched in this way, the merest hints from Propertius' next four lines enable him to carry on to the climax:

> With her husband asking a remission of sentence.
> And even this infamy would not attract numerous
> readers
> Were there an erudite or violent passion,
> For the nobleness of the populace brooks nothing below
> its own altitude.
> One must have resonance, resonance and sonority ... like a
> goose.

A neglected level among the layer upon layer of irony in Pound's *Homage* is this sort of reflection of the ghosts that dance before schoolboys' eyes. The *raison d'être* of such familiar howlers as 'There stands a litter of puppies' (*stant litore puppes*) and 'They were all County Kerry men' (*conticuere omnes*) lies, as the enjoyment of such puns by scholars testifies, not in blank ignorance but in the uncontrollable instant of irrational impressions that attends the gear-change of the most highly-trained mind into the foreign tongue. Except by the most numbing familiarity with the classic text, such vestigial surrealisms can never be completely cleaned out of our consciousness of a Latin poem; there is in fact a middle stage in learning to read Latin verse, perception of grammatical linkages having gotten beyond the mathematical phase and not yet into the automatic, when the magnetic affinities of random words for sophisticated but irrational English contexts troubles the mind with continual false scents. The deliberate *collage* of poker-faced misreadings performed by Pound in certain portions of this poem should perhaps be connected with the exploration of these zones of consciousness initiated by Joyce five years later.

Of greater importance for our present purposes is the enormous expansion achieved in these pages both of Pound's expressive resources and those of the language. Few more original poems exist in English. There is nothing earlier in Pound's output to prepare us for the full-winded *brio* of the opening strophe:

> Shades of Callimachus, Coan ghosts of Philetas
> It is in your grove I would walk,
> I who come first from the clear font
> Bringing the Grecian orgies into Italy,
> and the dance into Italy.
> Who hath taught you so subtle a measure,
> in what hall have you heard it;
> What foot beat out your time-bar,
> what water has mellowed your whistles?

What an innovation was this extending of the curve of speech beyond the limits of the line may be seen by contrasting an earlier specimen of Poundian *vers libre*:

> At Rochecoart,
> Where the hills part
> in three ways,
> And three valleys, full of winding roads,

Fork out to south and north,
There is a place of trees . . . gray with lichen.
I have walked there
            thinking of old days.
                    Personae, 'Provincia Deserta.'

The suitability of this mode of speech for the uses to which
Pound was putting it is not to be questioned. It is one of the
tests of poetic integrity that the rhythms of speech and of
mood shall coincide, as in Pound they may be said invariably
to do. The corollary is not always noticed. Having perfected
a way of speech, a gamut of characteristic rhythms, the less
inventive artist either never lets his feelings outgrow it and
confines his later work, as has Hemingway, to details and implications obviously present in his earlier; or else as he sees and
feels more, attempts to force his form where it will not go.
Form and content are only separable where they have been
combined by this latter violence; the fact that so many people
suppose them intrinsically separate results from their having
been taught to praise so much bad verse. Artistic integrity
demands developments of form to match every mutation of
sensibility; and the emotional revolutions of the romantic and
post-romantic periods, roughly Shelley to Housman, on which
most taste is still formed, were accompanied by a striking
infertility of expressive means.

The stanza from *Provincia Deserta* has been quoted above
as an example of the extreme tendency of Pound's early
techniques. It is admirably suited to choked reverie; isolated
phrases acquire a maximum of poignancy without adjectival
violations of tact. But it is obvious that we are approaching
the borders of parody; a comic prolongation of these tendencies
would drop little groups of words one by one like glycerine
tears, to the crashing of intermittent minor chords on a baby
grand. Pathetic devices of which a Noel Coward has not been
innocent, like the stock-in-trade of all vulgarisateurs, caricature
the genuine aesthetic developments of his impressionable years.

The limit Pound was approaching before 1917 may be
described in another way, by roughly schematizing the con-

tours of his *vers libre*. All verse is at some remove modelled on the expressive gestures of human speech, and tends, when it is verse meant for speaking, toward a 'normal' line, about the length of the English pentameter, whose pace is related to that of unstudied breathing. The 'heroic' tends to lengthen this unit, the pathetic to shorten it; and these tendencies are especially noticeable in free verse, whose contours, following no *schema*, are modulated only by the systole and diastole of emotional pressure. That the relation between emotion and line-length is obscurely related in part to the pace of the lungs and heart seems probable; in any case, page after page of the *Personae* collection reveals strophic articulation of this order:

> I mate with my free kind upon the crags;
>   the hidden recesses
> Have heard the echo of my heels,
>   in the cool light,
>   in the darkness.
>
>   Tenzone.

> Lady, since you care nothing for me,
> And since you have shut me away from you
> Causelessly,
> I know not where to go seeking,
> For certainly
> I will never again gather
> Joy so rich. . . .
>
>   'Dompa Pois de me no'us Cal'.

> And the glow of youth that she spread about us
>   As she brought us our muffins
> Will be spread about us no longer.
>   She also will turn middle-aged.
>
>   The Tea Shop.

The impact, the ply-back, goes with the short line and the dropped voice:

> Only emotion remains.
> Your emotions?
>
>   Are those of a maître-de-café.
>
>   Epilogue.

153

No, not quite; but the fashionable *maître-de-café* who is waiting in the wings will soon find those gestures useful in concocting bittersweet toffee;

> (Time may lie heavy between
> But what has been
> Is past forgetting)

and it will not be difficult for Wyndham Lewis, his tongue curled in his cheek in a complicated fashion, to scarify plausibly in Pound himself a 'melodramatic, chopped, "bitter" tone' which 'with its sententious pauses is unpleasantly reminiscent of the second-rate actor accustomed to take heavy and emotional parts' (*Time and Western Man*, p. 89). Lewis's accounts of Pound, Joyce, and Eliot are studiously unfair, but the accuracy of his eye for the bathetic destination of any tangent drawn from their surfaces can be tested by inspection of what, since Lewis wrote, vulgarizers of their methods have in fact done.

Cathay is notable, considered as an English rather than a Chinese product, as a remarkable attempt to fill in the emotional air-pockets of the early *vers-libre* method without abandoning its essential procedures. The structural unit is still the single line (each line, that is to say, still calls fairly dramatic attention to its point of ending) but the extreme alternations of line-length which had previously been the vehicle of passion are abandoned in favour of a kaleidoscope of delicate images:

> The sun rises in the south-east corner of things
> To look on the tall house of the Shin
> For they have a daughter named Rafu (pretty girl)
> She made the name for herself: 'Gauze Veil',
> For she feeds mulberries to silkworms.
>
> Ballad of the Mulberry Road.

What sort of advance this marks can be seen by noticing that it is possible to shift from the delicate to the bravura with little metrical alteration,[1] by changing the key of the images themselves:

[1] That is to say, without recourse to abrupt rhythmic shifts *within* the passage. The lines of course are longer and more exuberant.

... To the dynastic temple, with water about it clear as
        blue jade,
With boats floating, and the sound of mouth-organs and
        drums,
With ripples like dragon-scales, going grass-green on the
        water,
Pleasure lasting, with courtezans, going and coming without
        hindrance,
With the willow flakes falling like snow....

                                 Exile's Letter.

This is subtly articulated, and not short-winded. Surprising
volume is being compelled from a delicate instrument, though
we still have not the orchestral texture for an epic. The
tendency of free-verse lines to end-stop has still the look
of an intrinsic limitation, however skilfully the sutures are
stitched, or however flamboyant the tapestry of images
superimposed.

The verse of *Cathay* has not been successfully imitated. It
remains the most flexible development from the earlier pre-
misses of free verse ever achieved. It brings Pound's pre-war
procedures to a very high degree of expressiveness indeed; it
might have been thought a dead end. It might have seemed, in
1916, as though only a change of basis to a weightier medium,
some adaptation perhaps of the Miltonic 'paragraph', could
carry the new poetry further.

At that point there occurred the unpredictable fusion that
ultimately made possible the *Cantos*. The elegiac couplet of
Propertius blended with the *hokku* techniques of the *Lustra*
epigrams to give not merely lines of alternate lengths, but an
actual current of movement forward and back; the sophisticated tone of the 'Mœurs Contemporaines' vignettes left off
belabouring the dead to discover its own affinities with
choreographic dignity and with Laforguian hot-and-cold;
Seafarer intensity and Latin 'carpe diem' poetry of love
united in a context of multiple irony that brisked every mode
of passion with freshened alertness. A new momentum was
given to Pound and a new elaboration to English verse:

Shades of Callimachus, Coan ghosts of Philetas
It is in your grove I would walk,
I who come first from the clear font
Bringing the Grecian orgies into Italy,
                and the dance into Italy.
Who hath taught you so subtle a measure,
          in what hall have you heard it;
What foot beat out your time-bar,
          what water has mellowed your whistles?

This is nothing less than a new way of articulating extended passages of English verse: a new form, a positive *trouvaille* to be set beside the fourteener, the heroic couplet, and the Miltonic paragraph; as copious as the first, as urbane as the second, capable of as extended a syntactic line as the third but with infinitely greater inflective possibilities. Milton's blank verse, punctuated almost entirely by enjambed or caesural thumps, is largely remarkable for what it excludes; communications from Jonson, Marvell, Chaucer, do not pass beyond that 'Chinese wall', as we are reminded by the novelty of Pound's modulation from the opening cymbal-clashes of exotic names to the Jacobean geniality of 'what water has mellowed your whistles?' Such flexibility of tone has not been brought off in English since the *Coy Mistress*.

To this returned prodigal Pound offers up a succession of fatted calves:

Outweariers of Apollo will, as we know, continue
    their Martian generalities,
        We have kept our erasers in order.

                ★   ★   ★

Annalists will continue to record Roman reputations,
Celebrities from the Trans-Caucasus will belaud Roman
        celebrities
And expound the distentions of Empire,
But for something to read in normal circumstances?
For a few pages brought down from the forked hill unsullied?
I ask a wreath which will not crush my head.

And there is no hurry about it;
I shall have, doubtless, a boom after my funeral,
Seeing that long standing increases all things
     regardless of quality.

This is not archaeology. Kipling was still in 1917 the belauded laureate of Empire; the press was full of the perorations of Lloyd George; Rupert Brooke was being compared to Keats.

And you will not leave off imitating Aeschylus.
   Though you make a hash of Antimachus,
You think you are going to do Homer.
    ★ ★ ★
Make way, ye Roman authors,
       clear the street, O ye Greeks,
For a much larger Iliad is in the course of construction
(and to Imperial order)
Clear the streets, O ye Greeks!
    ★ ★ ★
And behold me, small fortune left in my house.
Me, who had no general for a grandfather!
I shall triumph among young ladies of indeterminate character,
My talent acclaimed in their banquets,
   I shall be honoured with yesterday's wreaths.
And the god strikes to the marrow.

This wry reflection of the wartime *situation de la poésie* goes with an unembarrassed defence of the less strenuous aesthetic modes:

The primitive ages sang Venus,
    the last sings of a tumult,
And I also will sing war when this matter of a girl is exhausted.
    ★ ★ ★
If she with ivory fingers drive a tune through the lyre,
  We look at the process.
How easy the moving fingers; if hair is mussed on her forehead,
If she goes in a gleam of Cos, in a slither of dyed stuff,
There is a volume in the matter; if her eyelids sink into sleep,
There are new jobs for the author;

And if she plays with me with her shirt off,
    We shall construct many Iliads.
And whatever she does or says
    We shall spin long yarns out of nothing.

The scholar of Provençal tunes, the translator of the leisurely
sophistications of Cathay, wittily deprecates 'current exacerbations' with a glee that refutes imputations of deficient
vitality. To a generation brought up to think of poetry
in terms of Shelley's open collar and flowing locks, this
assertion of the masculinity of lyric preoccupations has an
air of swagger, of rakish paradox, whose tensions are part and
parcel of the poem. (Three years later these identical antitheses were to find their sculptured definition in the very
different tone of *Mauberley*; 'The age demanded . . .

    Not, at any rate, an Attic grace;

    Not, not certainly, the obscure reveries
    Of the inward gaze;
    Better mendacities
    Than the classics in paraphrase!

    The 'age demanded' chiefly a mould in plaster,
    Made with no loss of time,
    A prose kinema, not, not assuredly, alabaster
    Or the 'sculpture' of rhyme.

This evidence of continuity of theme with the Propertius
rescriptions may help us not to be taken in by the motif of
loss and regret, the pretended foreswearing of Pound's previous, disengaged, 'aesthetic' career, that too many critics
have emphasized in the *Mauberley* sequence.)
    It is impossible to represent by quotation the enormous
freedom and range of tone, the ironic weight, the multiple
levels of tongue-in-cheek self-deprecation everywhere present
in the *Propertius*. Suffice it to isolate one device, adumbrated
in *Lustra,* here brought to perfection, and basic to the organization of the most apparently chaotic of the *Cantos*. This is the
ironic use of Latinate diction.

The Parthians shall get used to our statuary
and *acquire* a Roman religion.

★   ★   ★

Jove be merciful to that *unfortunate* woman
Or an *ornamental* death will be held to your *debit*.

The formality of 'acquire', 'unfortunate', 'debit', in the second
example the formality of the passive construction ('will be
held to your debit') are played against the colloquial ('get
used to') and the passionate ('Jove, be merciful') to secure a
co-presence of contradictory feelings in a way that will later be
used to organize, by setting it in tension with an urbane
observer, the utmost flop and muddle:

             . . . that lousy old
bewhiskered sonovabitch Francoise Giuseppe of whom nothing
good is recorded—in fact with the most patient research—
nothing good is recorded . . . and so forth . . .
this is Mitteleuropa
             and Tsievitz
has explained to me the warmth of affections,
the intramural, the almost intravaginal warmth of
hebrew affections, in the family and nearly everything else. . . .
pointing out that Mr. Lewinesholme has suffered by deprivation
of same and exposure to American snobbery . . . 'I am a
     product,'
said the young lady, 'of Mitteleuropa,'
but she seemed to have been able to mobilize
and the fine thing was that the family did not
wire about papa's death for fear of disturbing the concert
which might seem to contradict the general indefinite wobble.
It must be rather like some internal organ,
some communal life of the pancreas . . . sensitivity
without direction . . . . this is . . .

                                        (Canto **XXXV**).

This is the *Propertius* tone carried to still greater subtlety and
flexibility. If the reader, by frequenting the Propertius
sequence, will acquire a sensitivity to the weight of Latin

abstract definition in unexpected contexts, he will find it easier to see how large stretches of the *Cantos*, in which for reasons of decorum rhythmic definition is diminished to contrapuntal status, are organized as it were from the centre out, by stiffening and relaxing the texture of the vocabulary.[1] We should not be so utterly hypnotized by rhythms as to be baffled by their suppression. When we read,

> ... The small lamps drift out with the tide,
> sea's claw has gathered them outward,
> Four banners to every flower
> The sea's claw draws the lamps outward,
>
> (Canto XLVII).

and in another place,

> and il Gran Maestro
> Mr. Liszt had come to the home of her parents
> And taken her on his prevalent knee and
> She held that a sonnet was a sonnet
> And ought never be destroyed,
> And had taken a number of courses
> And continued with hope of degrees and
> Ended in a Baptist learnery
> Somewhere near the Rio Grande,
>
> (Canto XXVIII).

—we are probably willing, despite the disparity of materials, to call both 'poetic'. The rhythms of the second passage, though a bit looser, are perfectly definite. We recognize too the altera- tion of texture: the irony of the elegant 'prevalent', the diarrhoeic succession of 'And . . . And . . . And . . . And'. But when we read,

[1] 'LOGOPOEIA, "the dance of the intellect among words," that is to say, it employs words not only for their direct meaning, but it takes count in a special way of habits of usage, of the context we *expect* to find with the word, its usual concomitants, of its known acceptances, and of ironical play. It holds the aesthetic content which is peculiarly the domain of verbal manifestation, and cannot possibly be contained in plastic or in music. It is the latest come, and perhaps most tricky and undependable mode.'—*Polite Essays*, p. 170.

> . . . is that moral considerations seldom
> appear to have much weight in
> the minds of statesmen
> unless connected with popular feelings
> (Canto **XXXIV**).

or

> the army vocabulary contains almost 48 words
> one verb and participle one substantive   ὕλη
> one adjective and one phrase sexless that is
> used as a sort of pronoun
> from a watchman's club to a vamp or fair lady
> (Canto **LXXVII**).

or

> Died Mahomet VIth Yahid Eddin Han
> 'by profession ex-sultan'
> 65 years of age in San Remo (1926)
> begotten of Abdul Mejid. At beatification
> 80 loud speakers were used.
> (Canto **XLVIII**).

we are apt to imagine ourselves confronted with three pieces of cut-up prose. These are in fact examples of unusual but highly sophisticated verse. The rhythm is not a means of beating time but of grouping words; the division into lines sometimes suggests the phrasing of colloquial speech—

> the army vocabulary contains almost 48 words//

sometimes avoids the normal speech-pause—

> . . . one verb and participle⌒one substantive . . .

and sometimes syncopates with it:

> . . . and one phrase sexless that is//
> used as a sort of pronoun . . .

These notational equivalents for lifted eyebrows detach the poet as civilized consciousness from his role as narrator and transcriber; they refine upon the similar functions performed by inverted commas in *Mauberley* and *Propertius*:

The 'age demanded' chiefly a mould in plaster ...

      ★   ★   ★

Died some, pro patria,
      non 'dulce' non 'et decor' ...

      ★   ★   ★

'Of' royal Aemilia, drawn on the memorial raft,
'Of' the victorious delay of Fabius, and the left-
      handed battle at Cannae,
Of lares fleeing the 'Roman seat' ...
      I had sung of all these
And of Hannibal,
      and of Jove protected by geese.

In the last example we see both inverted commas and line-
endings used as instruments of irony. In the *Cantos* the former,
as indicating perhaps too heavy an ironic stress, are virtually
abandoned.

It will have been noted that the shards of Latin diction in
the examples from the 'prosaic' Cantos above:

    ... moral considerations seldom
appear to have much weight in
      the minds of statesmen ...

      ... At beatification
80 loud speakers were used ...

—the formal words in '-ation', the deliberative framing
('seldom appear to have much weight'), the passive voice as a
means to impersonal dignity—function in much the same way
as the rhythmic devices just outlined, and as the parallel
Latinizations in *Propertius*. They too import the distancing,
balancing, savouring sensibility into passages of transcription
and enumeration, as in the *Propertius* sequence into passages
that would otherwise be composed of unabashed lyric cliché.
(It is as cliché that Propertius emerges in the usual translations). The devices by which Pound gleefully riddled the
affairs of Cynthia with irony are employed in the *Cantos* to
frame and distance and epiphanize tag-ends of governmental

intrigue and financial malpractice: the clichés of journalism handled with forceps devised for the clichés of passion. A close study of the techniques of *Homage to Sextus Propertius* is recommended to anyone who finds undifferentiated muddle in large blobs of the *Cantos*. These devices for organizing verse by shifts of texture and tone are central to Pound's mature poetic practice.

Chapter 18

MAUBERLEY

Firmness,
Not the full smile,
His art, but an art
In profile.

With the partial exception of the *Cathay* sequence, the *Personae* volume up to page 183 may be said to be implicit in the *Cantos*. The early poems are deficient in finality; they supplement and correct one another; they stand up individually as renderings of moods, but not as manifestations of mature self-knowledge; they try out poses. They are leading their author somewhere; the reader may be excused if his interests are not wholly engaged, if he finds himself separating the technique from the value of the presented state. This may be said without unsaying anything in the preceding survey, the object of which has been to suggest considerable profit in what may not appear of compelling interest at first glance in 1951. Not only is the history of the purification of our post-Victorian speech contained in those pages, but a right perception of the kinds of achievement there contained will make the *Cantos* easier reading. And in isolating principles of apprehension it has been an advantage to have relatively uncomplicated texts to explicate.

The volume ends, however, with two great self-justifying poems. *Homage to Sextus Propertius* (1917) and *Hugh Selwyn Mauberley* (1920) would, had not a single Canto been finished, dispel any doubt of Pound's being a major poet.

It will be convenient to shorten our discussion by referring the reader to Dr. Leavis' tributes to *Mauberley* in *New Bearings in English Poetry*. That the poem moves him as it does, and that he registers his admiration so adequately and with such economical power of inciting others to comprehension, may, considering the intrinsic resistance of the Bloomsbury-Cambridge milieu to all but certain types of subtly-discriminated moral fervours, be taken as some gauge of the emotional weight, the momentum of essential seriousness, massed in these seventeen pages of disrupted quatrains.

Yet the reader will infer correctly from this way of describing Dr. Leavis' dealings with *Mauberley* that the highly selective vision of that honest and irascible critic has screened out certain essential elements. Pound emerges from his account as a man of one poem; the early work is uninteresting, the *Cantos* a monument of elegant dilettantism. In *Mauberley*, for a few pages, under urgent and unhappily transient personal pressures, he found himself with precision and sincerity. Dr. Leavis' view of Pound's career is introduced here as representative of the most respectable critical thought. Setting aside journalistic opportunism of the kind that has no real concern for letters, attacks on Pound are generally attacks on the *Cantos*. The isolated success of *Mauberley* is generally conceded. The dispraise even of Mr. Winters is qualified somewhat at this point.

Mauberley, that is, is a tricky poem. It is difficult for men of a certain training not to misread it subtly, to select from its elements certain strings that reverberate to an Eliotic tuning fork. A taste for contemporary poetry that has shaped itself almost entirely on Mr. Eliot's resonant introspections has no difficulty in catching what it has come to regard as the sole note of contemporary poetic sincerity in:

> For three years, out of key with his time,
> He strove to resuscitate the dead art
> Of poetry: to maintain 'the sublime'
> In the old sense. Wrong from the start—

It is easy to see how this chimes with such passages as:

So here I am, in the middle way, having had
    twenty years—
Twenty years largely wasted, the years of *l'entre deux*
    guerres—
Trying to learn to use words, and every attempt
Is a wholly new start, and a different kind of failure
Because one has only learnt to get the better of words
For the thing one no longer has to say, or the way in which
One is no longer disposed to say it . . .

                                  East Coker, V.

It may briefly be said that there has been a muddle about
'impersonality'. Mr. Eliot's impersonality is Augustinian; a
dispassionate contemplation of the self which permits without
romantic impurities a poetic corpus of metamorphosed
personae. Pound's impersonality is Flaubertian: an effacement
of the personal accidents of the perceiving medium in the interests of accurate registration of *mœurs contemporaines*. As
we have said, the adoption of various personae is for such an
artist merely a means to ultimate depersonalization, ancillary
and not substantial to his major work. J. Alfred Prufrock is
not Mr. Eliot, but he speaks with Mr. Eliot's voice and bears
intricate analogical relations with the later Eliot persona who
is the speaker of *Four Quartets*. Hugh Selwyn Mauberley, on
the other hand, does not speak with Mr. Pound's voice, and is
more antithetically than intimately related to the poet of the
Cantos. It would be misleading to say that he is a portion of
Mr. Pound's self whom Mr. Pound is externalizing in order to
get rid of him (like Stephen Dedalus); it would be a more
accurate exaggeration to say that he is a parody of Pound the
poet with whom Mr. Pound is anxious not to be confounded.

The sort of critic we have been mentioning, the one who
finds the note of sincerity in *Mauberley* as nowhere else in
Pound, pays unconscious tribute to the accuracy with which
Pound, in quest of devices for articulating this quasi-
Prufrockian figure, has echoed the intonations and gestures of
a characteristic Eliot poem.[1] Such a critic has been known to

[1] The primary echo is as a matter of fact with Corbière.

quote in confirmation of his view of Pound Mr. Eliot's remark, 'I am sure of *Mauberley*, whatever else I am sure of.' Mr. Eliot has not, however, the perceptive limitations of his disciples; in the same essay he insists that the entire *Personae* collection is to be read as a process of exploration leading up to the *Cantos*, 'which are wholly himself.'

It may be helpful to remark that Joyce is in this respect like Pound, an artist of the Flaubertian kind; his Stephen Dedalus is a parody of himself, not an artist but an aesthete, at length mercilessly ridiculed in *Finnegans Wake*. The analogy is reasonably exact; Stephen is partly an aspect of Joyce himself which Joyce is trying to purify; his horror of bourgeois civilization echoes Joyce's much as *Mauberley's* 'sense of graduations',

> Quite out of place amid
> Resistance of current exacerbations,

echoes Pound's. But Joyce refrains from unambiguous sympathy with Stephen's desire for Shelleyan sunward flight; he involves Stephen in an Icarian fall into the sea of matter just as Pound reduces Mauberley to

> Nothing, in brief, but maudlin confession,
> Irresponse to human aggression,
> Amid the precipitation, down-float
> Of insubstantial manna,
> Lifting the faint susurrus
> Of his subjective hosannah.

This cannot be taken as an account of the poet of the *Cantos* any more than Stephen's fastidious shrinking away from common noises can be regarded as characteristic of the author of *Ulysses*. Both men channelled their disgust into patient sifting of immense sottisiers; Pound has been, significantly, almost alone in perceiving the continuity between *Ulysses* and *Bouvard et Pécuchet*. In *Ulysses* Stephen is the focus of spectacular technical sonorities, sympathized with and rejected; the same is true of the Lotus-eaters in the *Cantos*.

It may be remarked that the critic who thinks of *Mauberley* as Pound's one successful poem commonly sees Stephen Dedalus as the hero of *Ulysses*, perceives in both figures elements of failure, and takes as dim a view of Joyce as of the author of the *Cantos*.

Against what may be mistaken for the drift of the above paragraphs, it should be insisted that the process of creating and disowning Hugh Selwyn Mauberley had not the personal importance for Pound that the purgation of the Dedalian aspects of himself had for Joyce. No such trauma was involved in the Idaho poet's flight from America as in the Irish novelist's disentanglement from Church and Motherland. It is not true, on the other hand, to say that Joyce could do nothing until he had focused and gotten rid of Stephen: the bulk of *Dubliners* was written in 1904, in Joyce's twenty-third year. But even when we have balanced *Dubliners* with the social observations in *Lustra*, and *Chamber Music* with the first volume of *Personae*, the excernment of Stephen Dedalus remains of crucial importance to Joyce's future achievement in a way that the writing of *Mauberley* probably was not to Pound. It was probably necessary that he focus in some such oblique way the tension between popular demands and his earlier poetic activities before embarking on the *Cantos*; but the process need not be thought to have coincided with a spiritual crisis from which, as it suits the critic, he emerged either crippled or annealed.

Mauberley does not mark in that way a hurt awakening from aesthetic playgrounds into thin cruel daylight. Its postures and conflicts continue, as we have indicated, those of *Propertius*, the *robustezza* of which could scarcely be confounded with hurt awakening.[1] If a decisive point of maturation must be found, it is to be found in *Propertius*, the earlier poem, it is not always remembered, by some three years. It is easy, for that matter, to over-estimate the reorientation there involved *vis-à-vis* the earlier work. There need be nothing traumatic about supervening maturity; the bulk of *Personae*

[1] Since writing this I find in Pound's recently published *Letters* a reference to *Mauberley* as essentially a popularization of *Propertius*; though the context indicates Pound's awareness that this is not the whole story.

is the work of a young man in his twenties. Pound was born in 1885. The earliest *Personae*, dated 1908, belong therefore to *œtat*. 23. He published the *Seafarer* translation at 27; *Lustra* at 30, *Cathay* at 31. The next year saw *Propertius* and the first drafts of the earliest *Cantos*. He published *Mauberley* at 35. The *Pisan Cantos* are the work of a man of 60. Emotional maturation may be seen going on in the *Lustra* volume; and there is enough difference between the monolinear intensity of 'The Needle' (*Ripostes*, 1912):

> Come, or the stellar tide will slip away,
> Eastward avoid the hour of its decline,
> Now! for the needle trembles in my soul! . . .

and the calm detached emotion of 'Gentildonna' (*Lustra*, 1915):

> She passed and left no quiver in the veins, who now
> Moving among the trees, and clinging
> in the air she severed,
> Fanning the grass she walked on then, endures:
> Grey olive leaves beneath a rain-cold sky.

to preclude any suggestion of a cataclysmic reorientation a few years later.

These pages will have performed their function if they can arm the reader against the too-easy supposition that Pound found in *Mauberley* an eloquence of disillusion. The subtle balance of diverse strong emotions in that poem will be utterly destroyed by too ready a response to one or two elements. We may now look, belatedly, at the text.

The subtitle ('Life and Contacts') and the title-page footnote ('. . . distinctly a farewell to London') furnish a perspective on the title of the first of the eighteen poems: 'E. P. Ode Pour L'Election de son Sepulchre.[1]' This is largely Pound's

[1] A line of Ronsard, connected by Pound with the *Epitaphe* of Corbière, to whose procedures *Mauberley* is related as early Eliot is related to Laforgue. At the time when *Mauberley* was written, Eliot was getting rid of Laforgue and in collaboration with Pound assimilating Corbière and Gautier. The Corbière reverberations are functional in Pound's poem, relating it to still more complex modes of self-knowledge than we have opportunity to go into here. At its deepest levels the poem is still virtually unread.

career in London seen through the eyes of uncomprehending
but not unsympathetic conservers of the 'better tradition':
a strenuous but ineffectual angel, his subtleties of passion
'wrong from the start', accorded the patronizing excuse of
having been born 'in a half savage country, out of date', and
given to Yankee intensities ('bent resolutely on wringing
lilies from the acorn') of an unclubbable sort. The epitaph
modulates into grudging admiration for the pertinacity of this
dedicated spirit—

> His true Penelope was Flaubert,
> He fished by obstinate isles;
> Observed the elegance of Circe's hair
> Rather than the mottoes on sun-dials.

The first line of this stanza renders with astonishing concision
an intricate set of cultural perspectives. Pound's voyages to
China, to Tuscany, to Provence, his battles with Polyphemic
editors and his dallyings with pre-Raphaelite Sirens, are
transformed, as in the *Cantos*, into an Odyssey of discovery
and frustration, imposed, for jealous and irrelevant reasons,
by the ruler of the seas (a neat fusion of the chaotic state of
letters with English mercantile smugness; the 'obstinate isles'
are both the British Isles and recalcitrant aesthetic objectives.)
The irony with which the British mortician of reputations is
made to utter unambiguous truths about artistic effort (cf.
the 'Beauty is difficult' motif of the *Pisan Cantos*) at the
same time as he vaunts his national obstinacy and imper-
ception, is carried on with the mention of Flaubert, the 'true
Penelope' of this voyage. For Pound, Flaubert is the true
(=faithful) counterpart, entangling crowds of suitors (superficial 'realists') in their own self-deceit while she awaits the
dedicated partner whose arm can bend the hard bow of the
'mot juste'. Flaubert represents the ideal of disciplined self-
immolation from which English poetry has been too long
estranged, only to be rejoined by apparently circuitous
voyaging. For the writer of the epitaph, on the other hand,
Flaubert is conceded to be E. P.'s 'true' (=equivalent)
Penelope only in deprecation: Flaubert being for the English

literary mind of the first quarter of the present century a foreign, feminine, rather comically earnest indulger in quite un-British preciosity; 'wrong from the start,' surrounded by mistaken admirers, and very possibly a whore; a suitable Penelope for this energetic American. England was at that time preparing to burn and ban *Ulysses* exactly as France had sixty years before subjected *Madame Bovary* to juridical process; it was the complaint of the tribunal against Flaubert that he had spent pains on the elegance of his Circe's hair that might better have been diverted to honester causes.

The implications of line after line, irony upon irony, might be expanded in this way; the epitaph concludes with a superbly categorical dismissal of this *impetuus juventus* from the cadres of responsible literary position:

> Unaffected by 'the march of events',
> He passed from men's memory in *l'an trentiesme*
> *De son eage*; the case presents
> No adjunct to the Muse's diadem.

The echo of Villon is of course the crowning irony. *His* passage from the memory of his contemporaries has if anything augmented his place in the history of poetry.

As soon as we see that this epitaph is not (except at the level at which it transposes Corbière) being written by Pound, the entire sequence falls into focus. The eleven succeeding poems (II–XII) present an ideogrammic survey of the cultural state of post-war England: of the culture which we have just heard pronouncing upon the futility of Pound's effort to 'resuscitate the dead art of poetry'. The artist who was 'unaffected by the march of events' offers his version of this criterion:

> The age demanded an image
> Of its accelerated grimace;

the third poem, with its audacious closing counterpoint from Pindar's *Second Olympic* (of which there is a readily accessible translation in the *Biographia Literaria*, ch. xviii), generalizes with a more austere bitterness:

> All things are a flowing,
> Sage Heracleitus says;
> But a tawdry cheapness
> Shall outlast our days.

Poems IV and V are similarly paired. IV surveys with compassion the moral dilemmas of the war:

> These fought in any case,
> and some believing,
>   pro domo, in any case . . .

poises sacrifice against domestic cheapness:

> walked eye-deep in hell
> believing in old men's lies, then unbelieving
> came home, home to a lie,
> home to many deceits,
> home to old lies and new infamy;
> usury age-old and age-thick
> and liars in public places.

and closes with a quick evocation of the pullulating new artistic soil, entrapping the artist in an opportunity for defined and significant passions that all but swamp his Flaubertian criteria:

> frankness as never before,
> disillusions as never told in the old days,
> hysterias, trench confessions,
> laughter out of dead bellies.

Poem V intensifies the antithesis between sacrifice and gain:

> Charm, smiling at the good mouth,
> Quick eyes gone under earth's lid,
>
> For two gross of broken statues,
> For a few thousand battered books.

The cultural heritage has been reduced to the status of a junkman's inventory by the conservators of tradition mobilized behind the epitaph of poem I; the superimposed tension of the apparent incommensurability, at best, of human lives and civilized achievements brings the sequence to a preliminary climax that prepares for the change of the next six sections into a retrospective key.

'Yeux Glauques' poises the pre-Raphaelite purity,

> Thin like brook water,
> With a vacant gaze

against the bustle of Gladstone and Buchanan (whose attack on 'The Fleshly School of Poetry' was answered by Rossetti and Swinburne). The painted woman of the poem contains in her 'questing and passive' gaze the complex qualities of passion, between the poles of Swinburne and Burne-Jones, which the aesthetic movement of the nineteenth century mobilized against a world in which 'The English Rubaiyat was still-born'. The picturesque reminiscences of the nineties in the next poem intensify the personal tragedies of the inheritors of that movement; 'Dowson found harlots cheaper than hotels.' This struggle and rebuttal is, we see, still being carried on; a new dimension of tradition and conflict is added to the efforts of the epitaphed E. P. of the first poem. The success of official literary history in discrediting the vitality of the century of Rossetti, Swinburne, and Fitzgerald and turning it instead into the century of Ruskin, Carlyle, and Tennyson is epitomized in the final stanza:

> M. Verog, out of step with the decade,
> Detached from his contemporaries,
> Neglected by the young,
> Because of these reveries.

M. Verog, 'author of *The Dorian Mood*', is a pseudonym for Victor Plarr, who appears in Canto LXXIV 'talking of mathematics'.

The next three poems are vignettes of three contrasting literary careers. 'Brennbaum' (? Max Beerbohm) embodies what passes for the cult of 'style':

> The stiffness from spats to collar
> Never relaxing into grace.

173

This style is neo-classical, not that of the leaping arch; Brenn-baum's motive is simply to prepare a face to meet the faces that he meets; such emotional intensity as he knows is not only repressed almost to imperceptibility, its dynamic is private, alien, and accidental to the traditions of Latin Europe: 'The heavy memories of Horeb, Sinai, and the forty years.'

Mr. Nixon, exhibit number two, is the successful public man of letters (? Arnold Bennett). The forced rhymes (reviewer/ you are) enact his hearty grimaces; his drawled climactic maxim,

> ... as for literature
> It gives no man a sinecure,

unites the pretentious popular philosophy of a Wells, a Shaw, a Bennett with the smug generalizations of commercial success and the hard-boiled saws of *Poor Richard's Almanac*.

> 'And give up verse, my boy,
> 'There's nothing in it.'

The third exhibit is the genuine stylist in hiding, an anti-climactic redaction of the Lake Isle of Innisfree:

> The haven from sophistications and contentions
> Leaks through its thatch;
> He offers succulent cooking;
> The door has a creaking latch.

These are not *poèmes à clef*; but the post-war fortunes of Ford Madox Ford are entirely apropos. Ford, the collaborator of Conrad and in the decade pre-war the lone enunciator of the Flaubertian gospel in England, on his discharge from the army retired in disgust to Sussex to raise pigs, and ultimately, at about the same time as Pound, left England. His detailed account of the cultural state of post-war London in the first third of *It Was the Nightingale* can be made to document *Mauberley* line by line. The reviewing synod hastened to write his epitaph, so effectively that his reputation is only beginning to quicken a quarter of a century after the publication of his best work. Pound has never made a secret of his respect for

Ford, and Ford has testified that Pound alone of the young writers he could claim to have 'discovered' about 1908 did not amid his later misfortunes disown and castigate him. It pleases at least one reader to suppose that it is the spectacle of Ford's disillusion that animates these three extraordinary stanzas.

Poems XI and XII present a post-war contrast to the intricate contemplative passion of 'Yeux Glauques'. The twelfth closes the survey of the London situation with an image of grotesquely effusive aristocratic patronage; 'Daphne with her thighs in bark' dwindles to the Lady Valentine in her stuffed-satin drawing-room, dispensing 'well-gowned approbation of literary effort' in sublime assurance of her vocation for a career of taste and discrimination:

> Poetry, her border of ideas,
> The edge, uncertain, but a means of blending
> With other strata
> Where the lower and higher have ending;
>
> A hook to catch the Lady Jane's attention,
> A modulation toward the theatre,
> Also, in the case of revolution,
> A possible friend and comforter.

Dr. Johnson's letter to Lord Chesterfield stands as the archtypal repudiation of the vague, vain, and irrelevant claims of patronage; but the street of literary commerce to which Johnson turned has also lost its power to support the artist:

> Beside this thoroughfare
> The sale of half-hose has
> Long since superseded the cultivation
> Of Pierian roses.

The *Envoi* which follows is a consummate ironic climax; against these squalors is asserted the audacious Shakespearean vocation of preserving transient beauty against the tooth of time (cf. the end of the first *Propertius* poem); against the halting and adroitly short-winded quatrains of the 'dumb-born book' is set a magnificently sustained melodic line:

Go, dumb-born book,
Tell her that sang me once that song of Lawes:
Hadst thou but song
As thou hast subjects known,
Then were there cause in thee that should condone
Even my faults that heavy upon me lie,
And build her glories their longevity....

Seventeenth-century music, the union of poetry with song, immortal beauty, vocalic melody, treasure shed on the air, transcend for a single page the fogs and squabbles of the preceding sections in a poem that ironically yearns for the freedom and power which it displays in every turn of phrase, in triumphant vindication of those years of fishing by obstinate isles. The poet who was buried in the first section amid such deprecation rises a Phoenix to confront his immolators, asserting the survival of at least this song

When our two dusts with Waller's shall be laid,
Siftings on siftings in oblivion,
Till change hath broken down
All things save Beauty alone.

There follows a five-part coda in which the Mauberley *persona* comes to the fore; gathering up the motifs of the earlier sections, the enigmatic stanzas mount from intensity to intensity to chronicle the death of the Jamesian hero who might have been Pound. Part two is practically a précis of the flirtation with passionate illusion of Lambert Strether in *The Ambassadors*. 'Of course I moved among miracles,' said Strether. 'It was all phantasmagoric.' The third part contains the essential action; having postulated Mauberley's 'fundamental passion':

This urge to convey the relation
Of eye-lid and cheek-bone
By verbal manifestations;

To present the series
Of curious heads in medallion,

and implied a context of opportunities missed—

> Which anaesthesis, noted a year late,
> And weighed, revealed his great affect,
> (Orchid), mandate
> Of Eros, a retrospect.

—Pound particularizes on the Propertian conflict between the aesthetic martyr and the demands of the age.

Contemplation is weighed against Shavian strenuousness:

> The glow of porcelain
> Brought no reforming sense
> To his perception
> Of the social inconsequence.
>
> Thus if her colour
> Came against his gaze,
> Tempered as if
> It were through a perfect glaze
>
> He made no immediate application
> Of this to relation of the state
> To the individual, the month was more temperate
> Because this beauty had been.

In Canto XIII Confucius provides a cross-light:

> And Kung raised his cane against Yuan Jang,
> > Yuan Jang being his elder,
> For Yuan Jang sat by the roadside pretending to
> > be receiving wisdom.
> And Kung said
> > 'You old fool, come out of it,
> Get up and do something useful.'

The serious artist does not 'pretend to be receiving wisdom'; we have heard Pound dilating on his quasi-automatic social functions. It is the essence of the artist's cruel dilemma that his just reaction against politicians' and journalists' canons of usefulness drives him so perilously close to

... an Olympian *apathein*
In the presence of selected perceptions.[1]

The descent into this Nirvana of the fastidious moth with the preciously-cadenced name is chronicled with elaborate subtlety. The validity of his perceptions is played off against 'neo-Nietzschean clatter'; but meanwhile the directness of the opening images, the red-beaked steeds, the glow of porcelain, is being gradually overlaid by a crescendo of abstractions: 'isolation,' 'examination,' 'elimination,' 'consternation,' 'undulation,' 'concentration.' The tone shifts from the sympathetic to the clinical:

> Invitation, mere invitation to perceptivity
> Gradually led him to the isolation
> Which these presents place
> Under a more tolerant, perhaps, examination.

The preservation of a critical distance both from the inadequacies of Mauberley and from the irrelevantly active world of Mr. Nixon, Nietzsche, and Bishop Bloughram, with its 'discouraging doctrine of chances', the realization of an impersonality that extracts strength from both of the antithetical cadres of the first twelve poems, is the major achievement of these final pages. Mauberley's disappearance into his dream-world is related without approbation and without scorn:

> A pale gold, in the aforesaid pattern,
> The unexpected palms
> Destroying, certainly, the artist's urge,
> Left him delighted with the imaginary
> Audition of the phantasmal sea-surge,

[1] It should be noted that the *Pisan Cantos* derive their extraordinary vitality from the fact that an *apathein* among memorably-rendered 'selected perceptions' is not being crudely opposed, in H. S. Mauberley's fashion, to the 'current exacerbations' of the prison-camp. The moon-nymph, the lynxes, the Chinese sages, the healing rain, unite with the gun-roosts and the dialogue of murderers to form new perceptive wholes. Pound's 'armor against utter consternation' is not gotten 'by constant elimination' but by vigorous fusion. *The Pisan Cantos* comment on *Mauberley* in a way Pound furthered by incorporating plangent scraps of the earlier poem into Canto LXXIV.

and we are warned by inverted commas in the next stanza against adopting too readily the standpoint of pontifical criticism:

> Incapable of the least utterance or composition,
> Emendation, conservation of the 'better tradition',
> Refinement of medium, elimination of superfluities,
> August attraction or concentration.

That 'better tradition' interjects the accent of a Buchanan or an Edmund Gosse; the other canons are Flaubertian. Mauberley is not simply a failure by Mr. Nixon's standards of success, he is a failure *tout court*; he is the man to whom that initial epitaph might with justice be applied; the man for whom the writer of the epitaph has mistaken 'E. P.' It is the focusing of this that guarantees the closing irony:

> Ultimate affronts to
> Human redundancies;
>
> Non-esteem of self-styled 'his betters'
> Leading, as he well knew,
> To his final
> Exclusion from the world of letters.

The irrelevancy of the canons of 'the world of letters', for once right but from utterly wrong reasons, very efficient in guillotining the already defunct, could not be more subtly indicated.

As a technical marvel this poem cannot be too highly praised. Only Pound's economical means were sufficiently delicate for the discriminations he sought to effect: 'perhaps' and 'we admit' belong to one mode of perception, 'the month was more temperate because this beauty had been' to another, the concessive 'certainly' and the clinical 'incapable' and 'in brief' to a third. The technique of distinguishing motivations and qualities of insight solely by scrupulous groupings of notes on the connotative or etymological keyboard has never been brought to greater refinement. One cannot think of another poet who could have brought it off.

179

The sequence is re-focused by a vignette of hedonistic drift protracting the coral island imagery that had troubled Mauberley's reverie, ending with an epitaph scrawled on an oar,

> 'I was
> And I no more exist;
> Here drifted
> An hedonist.'

pathetic echo of the elaborate opening 'Ode Pour L'Election de son Sepulchre'. The final 'Medallion', to be balanced against the 'Envoi' of the first part, recurs in witty disenchantment to the singing lady. Neither the Envoi's passion:

> Tell her that sheds
> Such treasure on the air,
> Recking naught else but that her graces give
> Life to the moment . . .

nor Mauberley's 'porcelain reverie':

> Thus if her colour
> Came against his gaze,
> Tempered as if
> It were through a perfect glaze

is denied by the paradoxical dispassion of the final picture:

> Luini in porcelain!
> The grand piano
> Utters a profane
> Protest with her clear soprano.

But the tone is 'objective' in a way that detaches the 'Medallion' from the claims of the various worlds of perception projected in earlier parts of the poem. There are witty echoes of those worlds: the 'profane protest' of heavy-fingered clubbably professional letters;[1] an ambrosial Mauberleian dream of braids

---

[1] Cf. 'as the young horse whinnies against the tubas' (Canto LXXIX) and the comments in chapter 23 below.

> Spun in King Minos' hall
> From metal, or intractable amber;

but the closing stanza is pitched to a key of quasi-scientific meticulousness that delivers with Flaubertian inscrutability a last voiceless verdict of inadequacy on all the human squint-ing, interpreting, and colouring that has preceded: fact revenging itself on art and the artists—

> The face-oval beneath the glaze,
> Bright in its suave bounding-line, as,
> Beneath half-watt rays,
> The eyes turn topaz.

Beauty? Irony? Geometrical and optical fact?

And this last poem yields a final irony. 'To present the series / Of curious heads in medallion' was, we remember, Mauberley's ambition, and this sample Medallion in its very scrupulousness exemplifies his sterility. His imagination falls back upon pre-cedents; his visual particularity comes out of an art-gallery and his Venus Anadyomene out of a book. The 'true Penelope' of both poets was Flaubert, but Pound's contrasting *Envoi* moves with authority of another order. Mauberley cringed before the age's demands; he wrote one poem and collapsed. Pound with sardonic compliance presents the age with its desiderated 'image' (poems 3–12); then proves he was *right* from the start by offering as indisputable climax the 'sculpture of rhyme' and the 'sublime in the old sense' which the epitaph-writer had dismissed as a foolish quest. And he adds a sympathetic obituary and epitaph of his own for the *alter ego*.

This thin-line tracing of the action of *Mauberley* is offered with no pretence to fulness. It is possible, as we have seen, to spend a page meditating on a line. The writer professes two objectives in proceeding as above. First, it seemed profitable to trace the 'intaglio method' through an entire work, with a detail which will be impossible when we come to the *Cantos*. Secondly, it seemed important to guide the reader towards an apprehension of *Mauberley* in terms that will not falsify his notion of Pound's later or earlier work. The poem has com-

mended itself too readily as a memorable confession of failure
to those whom it comforts to decide that Pound has failed.
Anyone to whom the above pages are persuasive will perhaps
agree that a less obvious perspective augments, if anything,
the stature of this astonishing poem.

Part Three
The Cantos

De libro CHI-KING sic censeo
    wrote the young MANCHU, CHUN TCHI,
less a work of the mind than of affects
brought forth from the inner nature
here sung in these odes.
Urbanity in externals, virtu in internals
    some in a high style for the rites
some in humble;
for Emperors; for the people
all things are here brought to precisions...

all order comes into such norm
igitur meis encomiis, therefor this preface.

Chapter 19

ONCE-OVER

Eternal watcher of things,
Of things, of men, of passions.

I
t is no longer easy, with the Pisan sequence carrying the work to within sixteen cantos of the end and the large design all but revealed, to dismiss the *Cantos* as either formless or irrelevant. As to their form, even those readers who had grasped the principle of construction could hardly have deduced the major structure from the first thirty cantos alone, on the basis of which, since their collected appearance in 1933, most of the extant critical generalizations have been made (Eliot remarks of Jonson, in an essay that remains the best possible introduction to Pound, that his immediate appeal is to the mind; 'his emotional tone is not in the single verse, but in the design of the whole.') And as to their relevance (though relation to contemporary exigencies is not in Pound's view necessarily a merit in verse, and he has at least once indicated his feeling that the *Cantos* are somewhat deformed thereby), it is important to see that Pound impinges on the citizen of A.D. 1950 or whenever, not via his psychological tensions (which is the one kind of relevance we have been taught to respect), but through a rational, though not syllogistic, amalgam of morals and politics. 'There is no mystery about the Cantos', he writes in *Culture*. 'They are the tale of the tribe.' So they are. And the *Pisan Cantos*, which for some time are likely to be the most frequented entry to the work, should be approached through the preceding seventy-one

185

sections, though they are perhaps unusually rich in passages of immediate lyrical appeal to the casual or uninstructed reader.

Pound's structural unit in the *Cantos* is not unlike the Joycean epiphany: a highly concentrated manifestation of a moral, cultural, or political quiddity. Joyce once epiphanized a whole sermon, audience, theme, and preacher, in nine words: 'Pilate! Wy don't you old back that owlin mob?' Pound's method, like that of *Finnegans Wake*, is the studied juxtaposition of such revelations, presenting through the convention (to be explained later) of a plotless epic detailed, graspable ideograms of entire cultures, motivations, and sensibilities. The reader should beware of mistaking the casual look of the page for evidence of sloppiness or low intensity (a major mistake underlying the failure of Pound's prose to connect with a wide audience). Pound has attained during his thirty-odd years of work on the *Cantos* increasing rhetorical skill, reaching new heights in the most recent sequences in which the spatial disposition of every word is functional:

> Here are lynxes   Here are lynxes,
> Is there a sound in the forest
>   of pard or of bassarid
> of crotale   or of leaves moving?
>
>   Cythera, here are lynxes
> Will the scrub-oak burst into flower?
> There is a rose vine in this underbrush
> Red? White? No, but a colour between them
>   When the pomegranate is open and the light falls
> half thru it
>
>   (Canto LXXIX).

In such a passage (more representative than it seems) the rhetoric of the indentations, in enacting the tension between ecstatic arrest and rhythmic chant, should escape no one. A variation on this device is the interruption of lyric passages by the symbols of commerce found on every typewriter keyboard: a subtle and ironic instrument of tension:

in principio verbum
paraclete or the verbum perfectum: sinceritas
from the death cells in sight of Mt. Taishan @ Pisa
(Canto LXXIV).

Other details of notation, of a kind that have exasperated many a reader's sense of poetic decorum, are not unconnected with the motifs of the work: for example this apparently slap-dash syncopation of Chun Tchi's preface to the *Chi King* (Odes):

> ... for Emperors; for the people
> all things are here brought to precisions
> that we shd/ learn our integrity
> that we shd/ attain our integrity
> Ut animum nostrum purget, Confucius ait, dirigatque
> ad lumen rationis
>   perpetuale effecto/
> That this book keep us in due bounds of office
>   the morn
> show what we shd/ take into action;
>   what follow within and persistently
> CHI KING ostendit incitatque. . . .

(Canto LIX).

With this one should compare Pound's remark that the manuscript facsimiles in his Cavalcanti edition serve to distinguish the transcriber who was all on fire to get the poem down from the one who wanted to produce a pretty page with something nice written on it. There is no reason to suppose such a passage less highly wrought by the poet than the 'Tudor indeed is gone . . .' quatrains. Its underlying strophic dignity is alive with 'plain talk' and pungent ellipses that convey without comment Chun Tchi's quick-eyed absorption in, as distinguished from antiquarian piety towards, the Confucian text. Pound's handling of the epigrammatic-colloquial is a study in itself; its function will be generally found to be of this kind.

The reader should also beware, as the last quotation may serve to remind us, of supposing that the Chinese or Jeffersonian or Adamic cantos are the running by-products of

187

successive splurges of interest in Chinese history or Jefferson
or Adams, or that the *Pisan Cantos* are to be taken as inextri-
cably involved in the accident of Pound's imprisonment in an
open-air cage in Pisa. The cage and the later prison-camp are
explicitly present throughout:

> 'When every hollow is full
> it moves forward'
> to the phantom mountain above the cloud
> But in the caged panther's eyes:
> 'Nothing. Nothing that you can do . . .'
> green pool, under green of the jungle,
> caged: 'Nothing, nothing that you can do.'

(Canto **LXXXIII**).

But the integration of these prisoner's reminiscences into the
growing whole, the cunning with which Pound has taken
advantage of an external (and damnable) situation to reinforce the structure of his epic with a time-capsule of contemporary Europe in juxtaposition to the immediately preceding
sections on Adams and Confucius, should not escape the
reader of the entire work. It is a tribute as much to his
technique as to his integrity that Cantos **LII** to **LXXI**, with
the new material to counterpoint them, function with much
more inevitability than during the years when they temporarily concluded the work. Mr. Eliot's classic statement,
'For order to persist after the supervention of novelty, the
whole existing order must be, if ever so slightly, altered,'
applies to the unrolling of a short lyric or the Poundian epic,
as much as to 'the mind of Europe': as indeed Mr. Eliot implies
in saying elsewhere that we must know all of Shakespeare's
work in order to know any of it.

Here we have the key to the recurrent questions about the
plan of the *Cantos*. It will be suggested later that the demand
for a diagram is as irrelevant as would be a demand for a story.
Joyce's well-known practice of inserting words and sentences
into appropriate parts of *Finnegans Wake* as they occurred to
him is perhaps not strictly parallel, since Joyce worked with,
as it were, his entire canvas in front of him, whereas Pound,

after a false start or two at the very outset, has moved straight ahead through later matter without recasting his earlier sections. But both men have understood that a sufficiently comprehensive vortex of perception could assimilate, could be realized in, any sort of material. Anything at all could be utilized as it turned up. The *Cantos* are 'so and not otherwise' not because at a certain date a parcel of books on Chinese history chanced to arrive in Rapallo, but because of what Pound was able to make of these texts. Nor does the fact that Pound happened to get locked up in an internment camp 'explain' the form taken by Cantos LXXIV to LXXXIV. They took that form because the poet was working with a set of motifs, guided by a set of preoccupations, that enabled him to make use of his Pisan experiences. He might equally well have used pigments of another manufacture.

Brushwork and arrangement of line deliver the painter's meaning exactly as much as his grasp of the psychology of a pair of eyes. Holbein's meaning is independent of his sitter; yet it is on the particular face before him that he brings all his perception to bear. The poetic act consists in so contemplating and manipulating concrete irreducible existences as to release their intelligibility without doing violence to their autonomous 'thusness'. Poets who 'seek sentiments that can be accommodated to their vocabularies' correspond to readers who equate art with self-expression and so seek to be put in touch with an intransigent personality that has arrived on the page either by riding roughshod over what ought to be engaging its slow elaborative attention, or else by slyly selecting materials that answer to its pre-arranged schemes, its wants, or its vanities. Mr. Eliot's remarks on the 'omnivorousness' of the undissociated sensibility, along with his own creative achievement and that of Joyce and Pound, should long ago have put these matters into perspective. Personality and experience are equally contingent. The merest, slightest accident might have made a given poet any one of a million other 'persons', or subjected him to any one of a million patterns of external buffeting. That in him which makes poetry is that faculty of the soul which manipulates the personality and orders the experience. So it is irrelevant to object that the materials of the *Cantos* do not occur in the poem in an order which we can meaningfully diagram. Such a diagram is *ipso facto* meaningless, or else its coincidence with the contours of a denser poetic reality is fortuitous or illusory. It is obvious that the poet like anyone else moves year by year through a *continuum* of experience of infinite breadth, only a selection of which is *recognizably* incorporated in his work. Pound must have had countless interests when he wrote the first ten cantos, which he then chose not to use. During his incarceration he chose to make explicit use of the counterpoint afforded by the Detention Camp. He might, had his mind been shaping his poem in another direction, have written instead during those months cantos of Alpine skiing or London publishing. This is not seriously overstated.

Pound had arrived at an initial formulation of these distinctions when he wrote, in 1910,

'Many have attempted to follow Villon, mistaking a pose for his reality. These searchers for sensation, selfconscious sensualists and experimenters, have, I think, proved that the 'taverns and the whores' are no more capable of producing poetry than are philosophy, culture, art, philology, noble character, conscientious effort, or any other panacea.'

The Spirit of Romance, p. 181.

In a well-known essay on *Ulysses* Mr. Eliot says quite unequivocally,

'. . . in creation you are responsible for what you can do with material which you must simply accept. And in this material I include the emotions and feelings of the writer himself, which, for that writer, are simply material which he must accept—not virtues to be enlarged or vices to be diminished.'

Personality and overt materials alike are material, not efficient, causes of poetry. To call this aesthetic determinism is as silly as to imagine that it does away with any possibility of significant order. Mr. Eliot goes on:

'The question, then, about Mr. Joyce, is: how much living material does he deal with, and how does he deal with it: deal with, not as a legislator or exhorter, but as an artist?'

So much, at this juncture, for the quest of a plan. Commentators have hitherto been too much obsessed with identifying Pound's materials: a certain passage of the *Odyssey* translated by way of a certain Renaissance Latin crib; a certain Metamorphosis of Ovid; a certain slice of Italian history approached via certain chroniclers; and so on. This labour is in one sense ancillary and in another quite unnecessary. The results, when written out and printed, make the poem look more bewildering than ever. The focus of poetic meaning does not lie *there*, any more than that of *Ulysses* is to be excavated from Thom's *Directory of Dublin*.

It remains, before considering these matters in more detail, to offer a few introductory hints for the beginning reader. The *Pisan Cantos* may be recommended as a volume for him to browse in. He may do well to whet his appetite on such sustained magnificence as the lynx-chorus beginning on page 68,[1] or the *libretto* and consequent fugue,

> The ant's a centaur in his dragon world.
> Pull down thy vanity, it is not man
> Made courage, or made order, or made grace,
>   Pull down thy vanity, I say pull down.
> Learn of the green world what can be thy place
> In scaled invention or true artistry,
> Pull down thy artistry,
>   Paquin pull down!
> The green casque has outdone your elegance . . .

on pages 97 to 100. He might then savour the ideogram of specifically English culture beginning on page 92 (' Oh to be in England now that Winston's out') running through the superb quatrains that mark one of the peaks of Pound's lyric achievement:

[1] American edition. In the British edition these passages are located on pp. 76, 111–13, 104.

Tudor indeed is gone and every rose,
Blood-red, blanch-white that in the sunset glows
Cries: 'Blood, Blood, Blood!' against the gothic stone
Of England, as the Howard or Boleyn knows.

Having delayed until he can sense the relation of the items on these three pages, he could pass without difficulty to the superb eighty-third Canto, taking perhaps *Gerontion* as a point of reference; after which, and after such further dipping as arrests him, and fortified by as much as possible of Pound's prose (especially *Culture* and the crucial translation of *The Unwobbling Pivot* of Confucius), he should begin at Canto I and progress through the whole work. There may be then some hope of his perceiving the rationale (*res*, not *verba*; and intellectual, not psychological) of the *Cantos*. He may also perceive how the author of

Evening is like a curtain of cloud,
a blurr above ripples; and through it
sharp long spikes of cinnamon,
a cold tune amid reeds.

is also the author of

Usura rusteth the chisel
It rusteth the craft and the craftsman
It gnaweth the thread in the loom
None learneth to weave gold in her pattern;

and even, and within the same poem, of

An' the fuzzy bloke sez (legs no pants ever wd. fit) 'IF
that is so, any government worth a damn can
pay dividends?'
The major chewed a bit and sez: 'Y—es, eh ...
You mean instead of collectin' taxes?'

And he may finally perceive that author's alignment ('Radix malorum est cupiditas') with the author of *Volpone* or the author of *The Pardoner's Tale*.

Chapter 20

OBSCURITY

and the light became so bright and so blindin'
in this layer of paradise
that the mind of man was bewildered.

The *Cantos* have been found intolerably obscure. Their façade, even more than that of, say, the later Joyce (whose sonorities charm and whose very impertinences may prove seductive) is of a kind impenetrable to the casual browser. It was a pastime of editorial-page wits after the Bollingen award to cite a few snatches and quip about paper dolls from the loony-bin. Beside this cheerful malice (taunting the poet has been a popular sport at least since Gilbert's *Patience*) may be set the howls of protest of the upper-middlebrow literary press on the same occasion. Every so often it became inadvertently obvious that the robes of political righteousness had been seized in an endeavour to transform into some hieratic ritual what was actually a dance of rage in the face of the uncomprehended.

There is some point in recalling these miserable events at this stage, so much light do they throw on the sources of much literary incomprehension. The concern for literature of Pound's detractors has generally been less than pure. (Mr. Eliot in his 1916 pamphlet cited an example, now over forty years old, from *Punch*, cocking the snoot of cracker-barrel shrewdness at Mr. Ezekiel Ton.) And the accidental notoriety of the *Pisan Cantos* exhibited in a peculiarly dramatic light the determination of the self-conscious to feel insulted by whatever resists the cow-at-a-billboard gaze attuned to neon signs

and headlines, and by contrast the singular purity of motive
that underlies the comprehension of *any* poetry. The salience
of this latter statement is obscured by the amount of poetry
most people are prepared to believe they understand; education and journalism mutually adulterated have now for nearly
a century produced the illusion of understanding the pre-
digested, and what does not readily predigest drifts towards
the edge of the curriculum and drops out of sight. There is no
one to-day who is not so much a victim of this situation that
he has not had or will not have to find out by himself against
great odds, by heroic concentration or aided by exceptional
fortune, what paying attention to poetry as poetry feels like.

Probably very few graduate students enjoy a confident,
other than habitual, assurance of the presence of connection
between the two stanzas of the familiar 'Lucy' poem quoted
in an earlier chapter. One can imagine that cryptic bit of
emotional registration striking a contemporary with at least
a Poundian obscurity: the first line, laid under demands for
relevance of the usual kind, becomes especially obscure: 'A
slumber did my spirit seal.' It seems not to have been noticed
that Pound has recommended 'as much of Wordsworth as
does not seem too unutterably dull' to the study of young
poets. Wordsworth's great technical discovery or rediscovery
was of the electric force of startling juxtapositions silhouetted
by limpid diction (though as Ford Madox Ford pointed out,
he often dissipated voltage by mistaking the 'natural' word
for the right one). His 'slumber', 'spirit,' 'seal,' and 'she,'
connected by the simplest of technical devices, seem from one
point of view hardly to belong in the same poem: 'earth's
diurnal course' is merely the most vivid *peripeteia* of many in
those eight lines. Mr. Eliot has said that hostile critics of
Wordsworth and the later nineteenth century innovators
'found them difficult but called them silly'. The analogy is
suggestive. And the difficulty has remained. If we do not to-
day regard Wordsworth as a difficult poet, it is not entirely
because we have outgrown his sensibility. We are systemati-
cally anaesthetized against such jutting edges as familiar
poetry presents. The detailed workings of the 'Lucy' series and

of *Resolution and Independence* remain to this day a blur in the handbooks.

Much of Pound's poetic organization, questions of erudition aside, is essentially similar to Wordsworth's. The reason we do not notice this is simply that tradition has provided us with a cliché version of Wordsworth's poetic objectives ('Leave off thy books;' 'Language of everyday life;' 'One impulse from the vernal wood,' etc.) knowledge of which enables us to suppose that we have arrived without having travelled. The frantic search of commentators for an analogous Poundian cliché (social credit, anti-semitism) may convince us that a prior grasp of the 'meaning' is widely regarded as a *sine qua non* for the reading of poetry. The approach to language of Descartes, Locke, and Kant, which makes the poet at best an embroiderer of familiar sentiments with suitable emotive accessories ('What oft was thought but ne'er so well expressed') has still a powerful grip on our interpretative procedures.

Here we have the explanation of the widespread impression that the *Cantos* are a very uneven mixture. When from time to time a passage turns up whose drift appears to accord with some line of thought already vaguely familiar, we are satisfied. The same is true whenever we encounter a passage we can recognize as translation. The rest is chaos. It is only to be expected, then, that Pound should be widely regarded as an incomparable executant who in ignorance of his own limitations is constantly trying, with ludicrous results, to play without his sheet music before him.

These points can be readily illustrated. Nobody is likely to have difficulty with the wonderful chant at the end of Canto XXXIX. The reason is simple. We have not read ten lines—

> Sumus in fide
> Puellaeque canamus
> sub nocte....
> there in the glade
> To Flora's night, with hyacinthus,
> With the crocus (spring
> sharp in the grass,)

Fifty and forty together
ERI MEN AI DE KUDONIAI
Betuene Aprile and Merche
with sap new in the bough . . .

—before light breaks. We are on known ground; the fertility festival. The replacement, within a familiar circle of ideas, of statement by image gives us no trouble; with Frazer's familiar hypothesis of the continuity between modern religions and the Eleusinian cults of the spirits of grain to guide our apprehension, we relax at last to enjoy Pound's ever-marvellous technical resource. His shifts from language to language no longer baffle: three lines of Latin, a line of Greek, a line of Chaucer, drive the central motif like a spike through divers young and clear-spoken civilizations; the dance-rhythms make their own comment; and in a passage like the following—

> white toward the sea
> With one measure, unceasing:
> 'Fac deum!' 'Est factus.'
> Ver novum!
> ver novum!
> Thus made the spring,
> Can see but their eyes in the dark
> not the bough that he walked on.
> Beaten from flesh into light
> Hath swallowed the fire-ball
> A traverso le foglie
> His rod hath made god in my belly
> Sic loquitur nupta
> Cantat sic nupta
>
> Dark shoulders have stirred the lightning
> A girl's arms have nested the fire,
> Not I but the handmaid kindled
> Cantat sic nupta
> I have eaten the flame.

—the suggested contexts of various phrases, the Eucharistic sacrifice, the impregnation of the Virgin, fire-dances, the rites of spring, the eating of the god, the handmaid of the Lord, and the fire of Heaven folded in His mother's arms, all grow as natural overtones out of the presented and enacted ritual under the familiar auspices of *The Golden Bough.*

It can be said of the passages most widely enjoyed in the *Cantos* that they are either translations apprehended via the original or at least in confidence that an original exists, or anecdotes and adaptations approached via their sources, like the song of the Lotus-eaters in Canto XX (the identification of sources is for this reason the major labour of commentators), or passages like the one above which utilize Pound's most complained-of devices but which give no trouble because their line of development is equated with some *idée reçue.* The reader who finds the poem brilliant and dull by turns is probably unaware of his intermittent reliance on such crutches. He blames for unevenness a poem that is, despite the extraordinary range of materials it employs, of a piece throughout.

The parts of the *Cantos,* then, that a given reader finds difficult deal with modes of experience totally unfamiliar to him. Here Pound's prose provides some useful pointers:

'A gain in narrative sense from 1600 to 1900, but the tones that went out of English verse? The truth having been Eleusis? and a modern Eleusis being possible in the wilds of a man's mind only? . . .

'I admit that the foregoing pp. are as obscure as anything in my poetry. I mean or imply that certain truth exists. Certain colours exist in nature though great painters have striven vainly, and though the colour film is not yet perfected. Truth is not untrue'd by reason of our failure to fix it on paper. Certain objects are communicable to a man or woman only "with proper lighting", they are perceptible in our own minds only with proper "lighting", fitfully and by instants.'

Culture, pp. 294–5.

Pound's observation that the elimination of certain tones from English verse has gone with a gain in narrative sense is thoroughly relevant to the preceding discussion. A narrative provides just such a thread as the schematizing intellect lays hold of eagerly. Aristotle's statement that it is by its action rather than its diction or characters that the poem is primarily to be judged holds good; the pitfall of narrative is that it is *paraphrasable* action. Consideration solely of Milton's handling of the familiar story, to which the handling of language was regarded as accessory, has obstructed the consideration of *Paradise Lost* as poetry until our own time.[1]

We have remarked that the ideogrammic method belongs to a scientific climate that no longer considers it safe to disregard exceptions, intransigent observations, in the interests of formulable normalcy. ('The method of science', wrote Fenollosa, 'which is the method of poetry . . .'). The *Cantos*, similarly, inhabit a world, first entered by the French symbolists, in which it is no longer necessary to twist incidents and persons into a schema or plot. (We are in fact growing used to a novel in which the plot is not a simple line of action, but the process of rendering the data intelligible. This is as true of *The Great Gatsby* and *What Makes Sammy Run?* as of *The Good Soldier*, *Heart of Darkness*, *Ulysses*, *A Passage to India*. The detective story simply reflects the characteristic devices of these novels in a schematic and rationalistic way.) Of the obsolescence of familiar kinds of paraphrasable 'meaning', Mr. Eliot remarks:

'The chief use of the "meaning" of a poem, in the ordinary sense, may be (for here again I am speaking of some kinds of poetry and not all) to satisfy one habit of the reader, to keep his mind diverted and quiet, while the poem does its work upon him; much as the imaginary burglar is always provided with a bit of nice meat for the house-dog. This is a normal situation of which I approve. But the minds of all poets do not work that way; some of them, assuming that there are other minds like their own, become impatient of this "meaning" which seems superfluous, and perceive possibilities of intensity through its elimination. . . . I believe there must be many people who feel, as I do, that the effect of some of the greater nineteenth-century poets is diminished by their bulk. . . . I by no means

[1] Landor's application to *Paradise Lost* of strictly *poetic* criteria in his remarkable Imaginary Conversation with Southey seems to have been read only by Landor's distressed editor.

believe that the "long poem" is a thing of the past; but at least there must be more in it for the length than our grandparents seemed to demand; and for us, anything that can be said as well in prose can be said better in prose. And a great deal, in the way of meaning, belongs to prose rather than to poetry.'

The Use of Poetry, pp. 151–2.

Donne's *Ecstasy* might be adduced as an accepted poem presenting difficulties of the kind encountered in the *Cantos*. To a note on the *Ecstasy* Pound appends this remark on the intrinsic rarefaction of certain valid orders of thought:

'It might be well to emphasize the difference between an expert and an inexpert metaphysician. For centuries a series of men thought very thoroughly and intently about certain problems which we find unsusceptible to laboratory proof and experiment. . . .

'Equations of psychology worked out by knowers of Avicenna may not be wholly convincing, but a number of such equations exist, and cannot be disproved by experience, even though belief and predilection must depend on the introspective analysis of highly sensitized persons.

'Between 1250 and the renaissance, people did manage to communicate with each other in respect to such perceptions and such modalities of feeling and perception.'

ABC of Reading, p. 127.

The business of the poet is to fix for recurrent contemplation such rare accesses of insight and emotion. (It will be recalled that Pound was over a year finding the exact image to evoke his emotion on emerging into the crowd from a Paris subway.) The size and position of the invisible sphere can be indicated by a few tangents. The invisible fields of force surrounding the magnet can be apprehended through the behaviour of multitudinous particles of iron. The usual enquiry into the sources of poetic images throws about as much light on the verse as analysis of the graphite in pencilled tangents does on the undrawn circle. When we have seen that the tangents are not stray lines, that the filings were not

199

disposed by random scatter, we are in a position to intuit
the controlling mystery. There is no incoherence in the
following:

> At Ephesus she had compassion on silversmiths
>> revealing the paraclete
> standing in the cusp
>> of the moon et in Monte Gioiosa
>> as the larks rise at Allegre
>>>> Cythera egoista
>> But for Actaeon
>> of the eternal moods has fallen away
> in Fano Caesaris for the long room over the arches
> olim de Malatestis
>
>>> wan   caritas   *ΧΑΡΙΤΕΣ*
>
> and when bad government prevailed, like an arrow,
> fog rose from the marshland
>>> bringing claustrophobia of the mist
> beyond the stockade there is chaos and nothingness
>>>> (Canto LXXX).

The unique emotional tonality of these rhythms and images,
artificially excerpted from a much more elaborate context,
will scarcely be missed. Such feelings as are aroused in him on
slow reading the reader should encourage toward a degree of
definition that will assist in elucidating the verse, the sense of
which, while all but unformulable in conceptual terms (hence
the tangential images) will be found to be perfectly definite:
apprehensible, not explicable.

We have here a new inflection of the *femme fatale* theme that
runs through the entire poem. Certain transient benisons—
the favours of Diana of the Ephesians to the craftsmen who
worked in her metal, the revelation of the moon-goddess'
paraclete, the vision attended by the rising of larks—receive
from the phrase 'Cythera egoista' an intonation of favours
coldly granted and wilfully withdrawn; the disaster that
befell Actaeon's passion for Diana (Canto IV), the expropria-

tion of the glories of the Malatesta (Canto XI),[1] these carefully
selected calamities transpose the fickleness of Cythera
successively into terms of the personal hopelessness of pur-
suing cruel Beauty and into terms of the generic frustration
the effort to register an enduring concept encounters at the
hands of official power. The last four lines bind these feelings
together, connecting by means of the catalytic magic of a flying hostile arrow the prevalence of bad government with the
marshland mist that conceals the moon. This complex of
figures should be closely examined. 'Prevailed' carries a sense
of omnipresent smothering force, which the trim speed of the
arrow inflects with a somewhat contrary tonality of instan-
taneous disaster. The curious tensions of the entire passage
are registered in the odd irrational logic of the passing arrow
calling up the fog: then the cloak of the moon-nymph (mentioned on the previous page) is transformed, with the final
blackout of her Gioconda strip-tease, into 'claustrophobia of
the mist', and the tenuous vision of Diana who had compassion
on silversmiths is dissolved into 'chaos and nothingness'.

Pound's early epigram to το καλόν:

> Even in my dreams you have denied yourself to me
> And sent me only your handmaids,

may be regarded as a seed-pearl of these metamorphoses,
which contain in their sober progression the plight of the
artist, the struggle to lay hold on beauty, the struggle to
maintain fleeting intuitions of loveliness, the struggle to maintain a civilization at stretch; and contain them not in a mood
of thwarted volition but in a special quality of remote and
impersonal sadness. The manifestations of beauty are far in
time and space (distant and ancient Ephesus), the journeying
and hiding and at long intervals compassionate moon is out of
reach and inexorable, the Actaeon myth is at the same time
too clear-cut to evoke indiscriminate emotions and too remote

---

[1] And the writs run in Fano,
For the long room over the arches
Sub annulo piscatoris, palatium seu curiam OLIM *de Malatestis.*
Gone, and Cesena, Zezena *d'''e b'''e colonne,*
And the big diamond pawned in Venice ...)

201

in its terms from usual experience to involve our active sense of frustration (we do not participate in it as we do, for example, in a Beethoven symphony), the Malatesta debacle is contained in old and unconjurable documents, the spectator is powerless against the closing mist. It is this quality of emotional contemplation without emotional involvement that gives the passage its unique timbre.

Perhaps this kind of talking around the verse will help the reader explore it for himself. It should not be mistaken for a prose equivalent. There is no prose equivalent. There is always the danger of demanding from poetry the wrong kind of coherence. This language of exploration, this music whose silences are filled with the elaborative spinning of invisible filaments, is infinitely closer to Donne's *Ecstasy* (though Donne availed himself of the connective apparatus of scholastic disputation) than to the evocation of mood by a description of the woods beyond Tintern Abbey, or to our being informed, with appropriate orchestration, concerning the names and pedigrees of Satan's captains or the length of his spear.

Chapter 21

GISTS AND PITHS

Invention-d'entités-plus-ou-moins-abstraits-
en-nombre-égal-aux-choses-à-expliquer . . .
La Science ne peut pas y consister.

I n the *ABC of Reading* Pound quotes a Japanese student
on the difference between poetry and prose: 'Poetry consists of gists and piths.' Contemporary poetry owes its
vitality as well as its superficial queerness to the rediscovery
of this truth.

Probably the most difficult readjustment to be made in
starting to take poetry seriously is the extirpation of the
received idea that only prose writing really gets down to
business, while the poet culls superficial flowers and hangs the
sculptured results of prosateurs' hard thinking with daisy-
chains.

The poet works not from the superficies inward but from
the essential action outward. Pope's party-writers and falsifiers
of history compete at polluting the Thames (*Dunciad* II–275
ff.), a transposition into fabulous terms of their characteristic
activity. Such an image is worth a volume of history, and
carries a higher potential than any quantity of invective.
Notes covering seven-eights of the page in the latest scholarly
edition tell us nothing to the point that isn't *in* the poem, that
we won't readily find if we keep our eyes on what happens on
the page, on the diving contest and not on the identity of
Oldmixon or Smedley.

> In naked majesty Oldmixon stands,
> And Milo-like surveys his arms and hands;

Then, sighing thus, 'And am I now three-score?
Ah why, ye Gods, should two and two make four?'
He said, and climbed a stranded lighter's height,
Shot to the black abyss, and plunged downright.
The Senior's judgment all the crowd admire,
Who but to sink the deeper, rose the higher.

The eye doesn't willingly wander from this to a note on Oldmixon's censures of Addison, or his scandalous history of the
Stuarts in folio; doesn't, that is, unless guided by hopeless
misconceptions of how to read a poem. The verse sets Oldmixon characteristically in action in, it is true, a surprising
material context. It is of little further interest to be told into
what controversial waters he generally dived. The action is
everything; the material indifferent.

'Gists and piths' turn out to be actions. We have already
indicated that 'The ship ploughs the waves' doesn't call a ship
a plough (which it would really require a commentator to
unscramble) but compares an action to an action. A metaphor
pegs out the limits of an action with four terms, only two of
which need to be named. The same is true of ideogram. From
seeing things set in relation we intuit, or at least learn to
intuit, the dynamics of that relation.

'The poet imitates men in action'—Aristotle. Pope's eight
lines imitate Oldmixon's action, in a more dramatic material
(Thames mud) than that in which Oldmixon generally dealt.
A metaphor also imitates an action: Pope's lines may be taken
as expansion of the metaphor, 'The party-writer pollutes the
public mind.' The Chinese ideogram imitates an action: it is a
picture of a metaphor. On p. 35 of his *Unwobbling Pivot*
pamphlet Pound reproduces an ideogram showing, literally,
'a man standing by his word.' That this lies in the province
of 'gists and piths' may be seen by contrasting the vaguer
ambience of an abstract noun like 'fidelity' or 'honesty'. The
ideogram is not a makeshift. It is more specific, not less. It
defines by imitation a particular mode of honesty, adherence
to the word previously given. The poetic is in the same way an
exacter speech than the prosaic, whether the material be

passion or economics. Audible song is not of the essence of poetry. The poem sings—the *Cantos* sing—when precision requires a melodic mode of definition.

Ideogram and metaphor, then, are sharply focused as to action, relatively indifferent as to material. The essential action of 'maintaining one's defined intention' is the same whether the 'given word' relate to marriage vows, rates of taxation, or acceptance of responsibility for a bundle of laundry. Hence the suitability of the ideogrammic method for the use to which it is put in the *Cantos*, that of establishing 'a hierarchy of values' by isolating either volitional dynamics or persistent emotional currents from hundreds of different material contexts.

The ideogrammic method consists in using concatenations of metaphor to isolate, define, and compare qualities of action and passion.

It may be noted in passing that the term 'ideogram' has one connotative advantage over the term 'metaphor'. The latter, which for Aristotle meant the intuitive perception of likeness among dissimilars, has been warped toward implying a step into abstraction: a new and exotic 'vehicle' chosen to dress up a humdrum 'tenor'. Such transfer of terms may or may not take place. Pope, in the passage we have quoted, defined Oldmixon's action in a more vivid context, not to dress it up but to isolate its essentials. There is in practice no reason why the terms provided by fact may not be vivid enough: as in the story, recurring throughout the *Cantos*, of Cunizza da Romano freeing her slaves:

> In the house of the Cavalcanti
> > anno 1265:
>
> Free go they all as by full manumission
> All serfs of Eccelin my father da Romano
> Save those who were with Alberic at Castro San Zeno
> And let them go also
> The devils of hell in their body.
> > (Canto **XXIX**; cf. also **VI**).

Pound's remark in *Culture*,

'There was nothing in Crestien de Troyes' narratives, nothing in Rimini or in the tales of the antients to surpass the facts of Cunizza, with, in her old age, great kindness, thought for her slaves,'

(p. 108).

indicates the relation of this example to the present discussion. In many parts of the *Cantos* the transfer of energy doesn't take place so much at the time the matter in hand is rendered (as Pope transfers the activity of Oldmixon from writing hired pamphlets to muddying London's stream) as at the points where it touches other rendered actions in the poem. Light comes from juxtaposition: one might pursue the analogies provided by the chain reactions of the modern physicist. Thus an entire Canto may consist of fragmentary actions set side by side in continuous proportion:

$$\frac{A}{B}:\frac{C}{D}:\frac{E}{F}:\frac{G}{H}:\frac{I}{J}:\frac{K}{L},$$

the archetypal action emerging more and more clearly, and the Canto consisting, as Mr. Eliot says of Dante's *Commedia*, of an extended metaphor with no room for metaphoric expressions in the details. It will be recalled that metaphor takes the form

$$\frac{A}{B}:\frac{C}{D}; \qquad \frac{ship}{waves}:\frac{plough}{ground}.$$

It is convenient to use the term 'ideogram' to describe this means of definition by way of juxtaposed but unaltered facts; and it is convenient to recall that ideogram and metaphor function identically, so that there is nothing 'unpoetic' about this reliance on anecdotes and history-books. The essential distinction between the *Cantos* and *Culture* lies in the infinite increase in emotional range and intellectual precision available through rhythmic definition and through long pondering on the exact disposition of the recurrent components.

The *Cantos* are at one level a notebook of insights. Over and over again during forty years and more, events have arranged themselves in an intelligible posture before the eyes of this indefatigable spectator; his habit of tagging these epiphanies with their addresses and dates testifies anew to his respect for the 'given'. Notation of insights and affirmation of values are for Pound inseparable phases of the creative act; the values are contained nowhere but in the insights.

Facts, fables, and anecdotes have their intrinsic emotional impact, definable through rhythmic and melopoeic means; but structurally what counts is the invisible chain of common or contrasting actions and passions; the curve, to revert to a former figure, to which they are tangent. Only so much of the material context is given as touches that curve. Hence the bewilderment with which these fragmentary allusions strike us when we fail to bring to the verse that energy of perception that discerns the analogies and contrasts running down the page. When we are alert for the connections commentary is superfluous.

Having possibly removed some of the mystery from our former talk of rarefied air and invisible filaments, we quote in exemplification the entire opening movement of the eighty-third Canto:

ὔδωρ
HUDOR et Pax
Gemisto stemmed all from Neptune
     hence the Rimini bas reliefs
Sd Mr Yeats (W. B.) 'Nothing affects these people
       Except our conversation'
lux enim
     ignis est accidens   and,
wrote the prete in his edition of Scotus:
Hilaritas   the virtue *hilaritas*

the queen stitched King Carolus' shirts or whatever
while Erigena put greek tags in his excellent verses
      in fact an excellent poet, Paris
        toujours Pari'
                (Charles le Chauve)

     and you might find a bit of enamel
     a bit of true blue enamel

on a metal pyx or whatever
omnia, quae sunt, lumina sunt, or whatever

so they dug up his bones in the time of De Montfort
     (Simone)
          Le Paradis n'est pas artificiel
and Uncle William dawdling around Notre Dame
in search of whatever
          paused to admire the symbol
with Notre Dame standing inside it
Whereas in St Etienne
         or why not Dei Miracoli:
mermaids, that carving,

    in the drenched tent there is quiet
         sered eyes are at rest
   the rain beat as with colour of feldspar
   blue as the flying fish off Zoagli
pax, ὔδωρ   ΎΔΩΡ
     the sage
delighteth in water
   the humane man has amity with the hills

The tranquillity of spirit that came with the descent of rain on the Pisan stockade—

    in the drenched tent there is quiet
        sered eyes are at rest

—is engaged, in quiet verse whose ictus is rather the heart-beat than the foot-stamp, with a wide variety of analogous rectifications. The opening is keyed by Pound's usual notation for the permanent and ubiquitous: terms drawn indifferently from Greek and Latin:

   ὔδωρ

—the motif of the meditation;

   HUDOR et pax

—the thematic ideogram.

The hydrogenesis of the gods expounded by Gemisthus Plethon is recalled from Canto VIII:

Gemisto stemmed all from Neptune

followed by the assertion of Gemisto's fertilizing power:

hence the Rimini bas reliefs

The next image shifts intellectual fertilization into a new context:

> Sd Mr Yeats (W. B.) 'Nothing affects these people
>   Except our conversation'

It becomes clear that we are contemplating a world of concepts going into action, of operative virtu capable, like Gemisto's water which as in Thales is the source of all being, of ubiquitous material realization. This priority of principle to matter is re-enforced in the next phrases:

> lux enim
>   ignis est accidens

Grammatically, this says that light is an accidental manifestation of fire (hence e.g. the heat of conversation generating public light); but the phrasing suggests 'lux enim' as an elliptical pondering on Grosseteste's and Erigena's generative principle, with 'ignis (nom.) est accidens' as a separate and corollary sentence. The Latin, in any case, transfers us from the Renaissance Platonists to the schoolmen, and

> Hilaritas   the virtue *hilaritas*

slips into place as a generative principle in the moral and social order (risus est accidens).

Hilaritas achieves cultural realization in the charming image of the versifying philosopher in company with the admirably domestic queen. Two minor echoes of the main theme allude in passing to Erigena's theophanic doctrine of divine realization in created diversity, and to the perennial role of Paris as nurse of poetry. The philosopher's *omnia, quae sunt, lumina sunt* is connected, once more genetically, with the shining bits of 'true blue enamel' a few fragments of which, along with a good deal of stone work, survive from that age of argumentative acuteness, just before Dante's (*Culture*, p. 108).

The quietness of the verse, the ease with which it slips from connection to connection, emphasize a *natural* generative and rectificative process, inevitable as the freshness that comes with the rain. It is this element that is underlined by the echo from the deep resignation of Canto LXXXVI that is struck in the next line:

> Le Paradis n'est pas artificiel[1]

with its appended parable:

> and Uncle William dawdling around Notre Dame
> in search of whatever
> > paused to admire the symbol
> with Notre Dame standing inside it

Yeats' incorrigibly symbologizing mind infected much of his verse with significance imposed on materials by an effort of will ('artificiel'); the grotesquerie of Notre Dame is itself perhaps 'artificiel' in contrast with the less strenuous autochthonous richness of other architectural achievements;

> Whereas in St Etienne
> > or why not Dei Miracoli
> mermaids, that carving.

The consonance of carved mermaids (not gargoyles) with a still mythopoeic Christianity and with the Neoplatonic fluidity and fertility of pre-Dantean imaginative thought brings all these chords to their resolution in the quiet of the 'drenched tent' and the tranquil, quasi-Confucian generalization,

> the sage
> delighteth in water
> > the humane man has amity with the hills.

With the sole exception of the contrapuntal anecdote of 'Uncle William', everything here contributes to the vivid definition of a concept, fused with emotion, according to interrelations so exact they can be noted in tabular form:

[1] Baudelaire's *paradis artificiel* was an opium dream.

HUDOR	Pax
Neptune	all things
Gemisto's concept	Rimini bas reliefs
'our conversation'	'these people' affected
lux ⎫	⎧ ignis
ignis ⎭	⎩ lux
Hilaritas	fertile social order
(Erigena's universe	all particular things)
(Paris	art)
'omnia sunt lumina'	enamelled pyxes
Pisan rain	quiet and rest

This is the simplest mode of Poundian verse; its simplicity of
organization harmonizes with the mood of tranquil contemplation. There is no need of commentary on the derivation, from
these constellated particulars, of the middle part of the
Canto:

Plura diafana
      Heliads lift the mist from the young willows
there is no base seen under Taishan
      but the brightness of '*udor*   ὕδωρ
the poplar tips float in brightness
only the stockade posts stand

And now the ants seem to stagger
        as the dawn sun has trapped their shadows,
this breath wholly covers the mountains
      it shines and divides
it nourishes by its rectitude
does no injury
overstanding the earth it fills the nine fields
          to heaven

Boon companion to equity
    it joins with the process
      lacking it, there is inanition

When the equities are gathered together
as birds alighting
it springeth up vital

If deeds be not ensheaved and garnered in the heart
there is inanition

It should be impossible to suppose that we have here to do with odds and ends of reflection strung together by free association. The elements of this canto, of the *Cantos*, were brought together by an alert contemplative energy. They are held together by the fields of force their proximity generates.

It will perhaps be safe now to transcribe three passages from *Culture* which, had they been given earlier, might have short-circuited apprehension of the verse by their attractiveness to the cautious mind as lower-powered substitutes. They are appended here as illustrating (1) the inferior intensity, as compared with verse, of prose, even Pound's prose; (2) the extent to which the liveliest prose 'talks around' its matter, as compared with the concreteness of poetic treatment; (3) the fact that it requires more rather than less grip on one's materials to arrange ideogrammic instances into a meaningful pattern than to process such 'sources' into a set of arguments and conclusions; a requirement over and above the rhythmic and other disciplines the poet must undergo; (4) that prose digestion tends to make the data disappear while poetic organization respects their integrity: this despite what we may have been taught about prose and verse procedures.

I

'The history of a culture is the history of ideas going into action. Whatever the platonists or other mystics have felt, they have been possessed sporadically and spasmodically of energies measurable in speech and in action, long before modern physicians were measuring the electric waves of the brains of pathological subjects.

'They also evolved terminologies and communicated one with another. And there is no field where the careful historian is more likely to make an ass of himself than in trying to deal with such phenomena either to magnify or to deny them.

'There is also no doubt that Platonists, all platonists, every Platonist disturb or disturbs people of cautious and orderly mind.

'Gemisto brought a brand of Platonism into Italy and is supposed to have set off a renaissance.'

Culture, pp. 44–5.

II

'Of his age, that just before Dante's, we have concurrently a fineness in argument, we have the thought of Grosseteste, and of Albertus. We have a few fragments of enamel, and a great deal of stone work. . . .

'Those of us who remember the beginning of the new Westminster Cathedral recall a beauty of stone and brick structure, before the shamrocks (mother of pearl) and the various gibblets of marble had been set there to distract one.'

Culture, pp. 108–9.

III

'. . . And they say Gemisto found no one to talk to, or more generally he did the talking. He was not a proper polytheist, in this sense: His gods come from Neptune, so that there is a single source of being, aquatic (udor, Thales, etc. as you like, or what is the difference). And Gemisto had distinct aims, regeneration of greek people so they wd. keep out the new wave of barbarism (Turkish) etc.

'At any rate, he had a nailed boot for Aristotle, and his conversation must have been lively. Hence (at a guess) Ficino's sinecure, at old Cosimo's expense, trained to translate the Greek neoplatonists. Porphyry, Psellos, Iamblichus, Hermes Trismegistus. . . .

'What remains, and remains undeniable to and by the most hardened objectivist, is that a great number of men have had certain kinds of emotion and, *magari*, of ecstasy.

'They have left indelible records of ideas born of, or conjoined with, this ecstasy.

'*Se non e vero e ben trovato.* No one has complained that this kind of joy is fallacious, that it leads to excess, that its enjoyers have need of detoxication. It has done no man any harm. I doubt if it has even distracted men from useful social efforts.

'I shd. be inclined to give fairly heavy odds to the contrary. An inner harmony seldom leads to active perturbing of public affairs. . . .

Culture, pp. 224–5.

Chapter 22

MINOR TROUBLES

Criminals have no intellectual interests?
'Hey, Snag, wot are the books ov th' bibl' '
'name 'em, etc.
'Latin? I studied latin.'
     said the nigger murderer to his cage-mate.

We are now in a position to dispose summarily of a few of the superficial difficulties presented by the *Cantos*. A paralysis arising from the very look of the page, its Greek types, its unfamiliar names, has probably kept most hit-and-run curiosity from even coming to initial grips with the more resistant problems we have just been canvassing. The difficulties here in question need no anatomizing, they are of the kind a good teacher removes in an informal chat.

LANGUAGES

Latin, Greek, French, German, Italian, Chinese, Spanish, Provençal. One need *not* know them all, though in this as in other matters the more one knows, the sharper one's apprehension. Much-repeated key-words—$\ddot{v}\delta\omega\rho$ (water), $\chi\theta\text{o}\nu\text{o}\varsigma$ (earth)—can be looked up. Beyond that, one need not know the meaning of a phrase to apprehend its function—

1. As music.
2. The special tonalities of national sensibility (Latin aptitude for definition, French precision and colloquial contact with 'highbrow' values) used as elements in the mosaic. Anyone can feel the play of silent cryptic finality in a Chinese

215

ideogram against adjacent fluidity or muddle or struggle after a word, without knowing what the ideogram means.

3. As irreducible formulations; Cavalcanti's 'dove sta memoria', Homer's 'brododaktulos Eos',[1] Dante's 'selva oscura', interest Pound as much by their finality as by their content. Even when we can't read them, their very inscrutability performs half their poetic function. Analogy: stones with inscriptions on them being put into a building. Contrast: Mr. Eliot's habit of engaging in his poems so much of the contextual corpus of allusions that the reader who doesn't know the sources is, while not bewildered, innocent of whole dimensions of the poem.

4. As rendering not the uniqueness of certain modes of perception but their ubiquity; e.g. the juxtaposition of Latin 'humanitas' and Chinese 'jen' (Canto LXXXII) which raises the concept of the full human nature to the status of a permanent perception informing eastern and western cultures alike.

5. As evidence of the relative antiquity of various conceptions. Thus the phrase about altering currency, 'Metathemenon te ton kruson', indicates that this idea had been focused in Greece two millennia before the 'new economics'.

ALLUSIONS

One of the most fateful accidents in literary history was the publishers' demand for a few more pages that led to notes being appended to *The Waste Land*. Nothing has done more to jeopardize poet-audience relations in the present century, largely by spreading abroad the impression that the reader is either playing a hunt-the-source game or is utterly debarred if he can't instantly detect an allusion to any book on an esoteric and polyglot reading-list.

Pound is within his rights in expecting a knowledge of Homer, Dante, the mythology in Ovid. The rest, for the

[1] The celebrated 'rosy-fingered dawn', properly 'hrodo-' or 'rhododaktulos'. But 'brodos' exists as an Aeloic form, and suits Pound's metric much better. To rescue colloquial diversity from the schematizing of grammarians is one of the minor aims of the *Cantos*.

careful reader, is *there on the page*; enough, that is, to keep
whole passages from going utterly blank. The encyclopaedia
will clear up small points; but it is much more important to
sharpen one's ear for nuances of tone and implications of
rhythm. The man who has to be supplied with the denotations
of *all* the words on the page before he can make a start is
making no distinction between a poem and a cross-word
puzzle.

When we read the lines,

> in contending for certain values
> (Janequin per esempio, and Orazio Vechii or Bronzino)

we can see, without knowing whether Janequin is a composer
or an art-gallery, what kind of thing the second line presents.

It happens that Pound attaches peculiar value to Janequin's
bird-chorale (reproduced in Canto LXXXV), an archetype
of indestructible form the birdsongs in which have survived
successive arrangements for chorus, lute, piano and violin.
To know this sharpens the relevance of the line, and no
encyclopaedia would lay the stress thus. But (*a*) the point
occurs several times in Pound's prose; (*b*) without knowing it
we can in any case read on without utter bewilderment.

The 'privacy' of such allusions can be over-stressed. They
are irreducible elements in the poet's vision of the mind of
Europe. Not many teachers have spent as much time as has
Pound in seeking out the indispensable elements of a subject.
The things that went into the *Cantos* impinged as unique and
relevant on a highly-developed historical and critical sense.

It is seldom helpful to know more about the poet's personal
encounters than we are told. Just such elements are given us
as enter the peculiar savour of the passage in question.

> when the cat walked the top bar of the railing
> and the water was still on the west side
> flowing toward the Villa Catullo
> where with sound ever moving
> in diminutive poluphloisboios
> in the stillness outlasting all wars

'La Donna' said Nicoletti

'la donna,

la donna!'

(Canto LXXIV).

The blend of tranquillity and passion that functions at this
point in the structure of the Canto is quite independent of a
footnote identifying Nicoletti.

PERSONS

Mr. Eliot has told of complaining to Pound about an article
on Gesell's economics written by him for the *Criterion*: 'I asked
you to write an article which would explain this subject to
people who had never heard of it; yet you write as if your
readers knew about it already, but had failed to understand
it.' This may have been a demand for more tact rather than
more information; even when he is haranguing the informed
but uncomprehending, Pound generally tucks the essential
data into odd corners of his diatribe. The most puzzling parts
of the *Cantos* for many readers are those that deal with persons
like Van Buren or Nicholas Este. Recourse to the encyclopaedia may or may not be helpful; this puzzlement is generally
due to asking the wrong questions. When we read,

Said one of the wool-buyers:
'Able speech by Van Buren
'Yes, very able.'
'Ye-es, Mr Knower, an' on wich side ov the tariff was it?
'Point I was in the act of considering'
replied Mr Knower
In the mirror of memory: have been told I rendered
the truth a great service by that speech on the tariff
but directness on all points wd. seem not
to have been its conspicuous feature.

(Canto XXXVII).

we are apt to be distracted by our desire to know more about
the speech. What is being held up to our contemplation is a
two-fold epiphany—of the deviousness of practical politics,
and of the rigours of Van Buren's *post facto* self-scrutiny.

In general, Pound's multiple foci of interest deprive us of the dramatic satisfaction of seeing a person engaged in a characteristic action with a beginning, middle, and end. Rather he presents the mind in a succession of characteristic postures. People like the Adamses exist in the *Cantos* in a peculiar modality, as concatenated gists and piths which from one point of view may be taken as commentaries and underlinings of what Pound assumes to be a body of general knowledge, from another point of view as specimens of ideas held, responses given, modes of attack on difficulty, revelations of self-knowledge. When we read in Canto LXII,

> Routledge was elegant
> 'said nothing not hackneyed six months before'
> wrote J. A. to his wife,

it is less important to know who Routledge was and what he talked about on what occasion, than to apprehend the quality and energy of John Adams' critical mind. Impatience of platitude and exact knowledge of what *was* hackneyed six months before are qualities sufficiently rare in statesmen to justify the chisel-cut effected by these lines. The structural units in the Adams Cantos are generally very small, brief intellectual manifestations of this kind. The intended analogy is with the Confucian Analects, of which Pound, remarking 'Points define a periphery', has noted that they 'should be considered rather as definitions of words', as the Adams' quotation defines one aspect of 'elegance'. They are selected stills from an elaborate cinema: an application to character of the method devised in *Mauberley* for rendering the sensibility of an age. If we read rapidly in search of a narrative we shall be very badly baffled indeed.

Chapter 23

MIDDLE STYLE

'Jap'nese dance all time overcoat' he remarked
with perfect precision.

The principle of the ideogrammic method is simply that things explain themselves by the company they keep. Individual opacities reach upward towards an intelligible point of union. The delights of poetry are not all of one kind; the pleasure to be had in many parts of the *Cantos* consists in delight at the witty play of congruence and incongruence; before our eyes details reach forward and backward towards unexpected connections, developing in some cases three or four patterns of intelligibility at once. The principles of organization exemplified by the descant on 'Hudor et Pax' are present in such passages in a much more complicated form, the full enjoyment of which probably demands purgation of romantic dregs to a still unusual degree.

Guard's cap quattrocento passes *a cavallo*
    on horseback thru landscape Cosimo Tura
        or, as some think, Del Cossa;
up stream to delouse and down stream for the same purpose
seaward
different lice live in different waters
some minds take pleasure in counterpoint
       pleasure in counterpoint
and the later Beethoven on the new Bechstein,
or in the Piazza S. Marco for example

finds a certain concordance of size
        not in the concert hall;
can that be the papal major sweatin' it out to the bumm drum?
what castrum romanum, what
        'went into winter quarters'
is under us?
as the young horse whinnies against the tubas
        in contending for certain values
(Janequin per esempio, and Orazio Vechii or Bronzino)
Greek rascality against Hagoromo
        Kumasaka vs/ vulgarity
            no sooner out of Troas
than the damn fools attacked Ismarus of the Cicones
               (Canto LXXIX).

This bewildering variety of items is grouped around three more or less defined 'themes', principles of organization the witty interplay of whose particularizations provides the life of the passage. Thus in comment on the opening double-exposure of chivalric epochs, we have:

(1)   some minds take pleasure in counterpoint
          pleasure in counterpoint

Examples of counterpoint leap to the eye: Beethoven on the electric reproducer, the papal major 'sweatin' it out', the whinny against the sound of the tubas. There lurks however in these contrasts the irony of

(2)   . . . a certain concordance . . .

and the oddly ironic politeness of formulation, an irony deepened by the incongruous materials—lice, sweat, over-blown music—which they are made to illuminate, consorts with the third, aesthetic-pedagogical motif:

(3)   in contending for certain values.

The context of this last phrase fixes the elegantly ironic tonality of the passage:

     as the young horse whinnies against the tubas
          in contending for certain values.

Counterpoint, of course, is still with us: equine self-assertion
contends with the blaring monotones of 'Kulchur'. This sort
of bray has punctuated the *Cantos* before:

> 'Je suis . . .
> (across the bare planks of a diningroom in the Pyrenees)
> . . . plus fort que . . .
> . . . le Boud-hah!'
> (No contradiction)
>
> (Canto **XXVIII**).

The *young* horse, however. A whinny is sometimes excusable.
The vital, 'bohemian', contends with the keyed wind-
mechanism of mobilized *idées reçues*. At this level the young
horse and the tubas furnish a comic transposition of the contention of poets with elderly men of letters, *Blast* with
bourgeois Britain, in a mode that has also turned up before:

> And he looked from the planks to heaven,
> Said Juventus: 'Immortal . . .
> He said: 'Ten thousand years before now . . .
> Or he said: 'Passing into the point of the cone
> You begin by making the replica.'
> Thus Lusty Juventus, in September,
> In cool air, under sky,
> Before the residence of the funeral director
> Whose daughters' conduct caused comment.
> But the old man did not know how he felt
> Nor could remember what prompted the utterance.
>
> (Canto **XXIX**).

The young horse and the tubas; Lusty Juventus speculating
grandly and the morticians' house pullulating with scandalous
daughters. There are gradations of zest.

There are gradations; the young horse is 'contending *for
certain values*'. The subsequent lines, contending for the
admission of certain Japanese qualities alongside certain
Greek ones, not debunking the Odyssey but seeking to supplement it, counterpointing the austere chivalry of the Noh
dramas with the impetuous romance or romantic vulgarity

that is an indubitable Homeric dimension, lift us out of the multiple ironies of conflicting equine and brazen tonalities into an analogously organized world of serious dissociations.

'Certain virtues are established, and the neglect of them by later writers and artists is an impoverishment of their art. The stupidity of Rubens, the asinine nature of French court life from Henry IV to the end of it, the insistence on two dimensional treatment of life by certain modernists, do not constitute a progress. A dogma builds on vacuum, and is ultimately killed or modified by, or accommodated to knowledge, but values stay, and ignorant neglect of them answers no purpose.

'Loss of values is usually due to lumping, and to lack of dissociation.'

Make It New, p. 350.

It is lack of dissociation that commends us for emulation the whole even of Odysseus, whose facet of sheer devilment, exhibited in the utterly unprovoked attack on the Cicones (Pound has elsewhere called attention to this incident: *Polite Essays*, p. 45) comes off badly by comparison with the exquisite shadings of scrupulosity in the Hagoromo drama (translated by Fenollosa and Pound in *Noh: or Accomplishment*).

On the next page, via Pound's characteristic ethical integrity, the conservation of discrete aesthetic values becomes coterminous with the saving of the Constitution and the Theory of the Just Price:

> God bless the Constitution
and *save* it
> 'the value thereof'
> that is the crux of the matter
and god damn the perverters
> and if Attlee attempts a Ramsey
'Leave the Duke, go for the gold'
> 'in less than a geological epoch'
and the Fleet that triumphed at Salamis
> and Wilkes's fixed the price per loaf

ἦθος

The 'perverters' are moral, aesthetic, political, economic. Ramsey Macdonald was the reformer who modulated into Toryism. The 'geological epoch' was Mencken's suggested limit for the achievement of some reforms. The Fleet at Salamis illustrated the principle that the State might lend money instead of collecting it; not yet a grasped idea, but a geological epoch has not yet elapsed since 480 B.C. The price fixed per loaf is one value at least conserved, though from Pound's economic viewpoint mistakenly. These filings from other parts of the poem arrange themselves here within the fields of force liberated on the previous page: counterpoint concordance, contention for certain values. With the Greek term 'ethos' (the active *virtu*, the field of moral force), applied ambivalently to the savers and the perverters, the whole comes to rest and is comprehended.

In thus finding in one of the, by conventional standards, less 'poetic' parts of the *Cantos* more order and intensity than appears to casual inspection, we have far from exhausted the passage with which we started. It is full of witty action. 'Different lice live in different waters' begins as a practical statement (with an overtone of casual invective) and ends by being a wry illustration of the dissociation of values later urged. The opening superimposition of military epochs,

Guard's cap quattrocento passes *a cavallo*
    on horseback through landscape Cosimo Tura

(the locus of this visual impression is of course twentieth-century Pisa) is echoed in the later invocation of archaeological strata reaching down and back to the camps of the Legions:

what castrum romanum, what
            'went into winter quarters'
is under us?

This is both counterpoint and concordance; the persistence of function beneath shifting phenomena gives us one bridge from the *now* of horses and tubas into the world of *formae mentium* and conservable values, which both unites the phenomena and shames them. This multi-dimensionality is everywhere. The massiveness of 'later Beethoven' makes contact both with the Piazza S. Marco and with a freakish electric piano, a double-edged decorum suiting the tone of the passage.

This tone deserves further definition. It depends here, as often elsewhere, on the incongruity of low matter and Latin sophistication, a device by which Pound achieves effects ranging from the genial—

> present Mr G. Scott whistling Lili Marlene
> with positively less musical talent
> than that of any other man of colour
> whom I have ever encountered

through the farcical—

> I wonder what Tsu Tsze's calligraphy looked like
> they say she could draw down birds from the trees,
> that indeed was imperial; but made hell in
> the palace[1]

the comic-elegiac—

> And three small boys on three bicycles
> smacked her young fanny in passing
> before she recovered from the surprise of the first swat
> ce sont les mœurs de Lutèce

and the elegant-ironic—

> Gaudier's eye on the telluric mass of Miss Lowell

to the openly sarcastic—

> and Mr Beard in his admirable condensation
> (Mr Chas. Beard) has given one line to the currency
> at about page 426 'The Republic'

In every case the irony turns on a Latin word or French phrase set in the midst of a more or less strained politeness. This technique, consolidated by Pound on a large scale in his *Propertius* transcriptions (to the organization of which it is basic throughout) is a major device for articulating, often with great subtlety, the material of the later *Cantos*. The peri-

[1] Note the play on the etymology of 'Imperial'.

phrasis, the euphemism, suggesting ironically that directer treatment would be tactless, but redeemed from the evasiveness proper to euphemism by sudden Latin clarity, is the vehicle of our central lines:

as the young horse whinnies against the tubas
in contending for certain values.

'Certain:' well, yes, values; though they may not bear discussion. But 'certain': *certus*: unshakeable.

This tone of flexible urbanity, which can generate tension in contact with almost any material from whinnying horses to the conventionally poetical ('The moon has a swollen cheek'), which can depersonalize exasperation into a reified scrutable marmoreality ('tempora, tempora and as to mores'), and which makes contact at one end with lyric movement and at the other end with didactic, is a major integrating force throughout the poem. It corresponds psychologically to the humorous toughness that sustained the poet in his imprisonment. More important, it is the medium in which all kinds of unexpected conjunctions take place without stark incongruity, to exhibit the unity of the world the *Cantos* project for us: a world of sculptured hierarchic values present even at their own denial.

The scabrous and the idyllic come easily within the almost simultaneous compass of a wit that can scrutinize for gradations even a secular dark night of the soul:

nox animae magna from the tent under Taishan
amid what was termed the a.h. of the army
the guards holding opinion. As it were to dream of
mortician's daughters raddled but amorous
To study with the white wings of time passing
is not that our delight
to have friends come from far countries
is not that pleasure
nor to care that we are untrumpeted?
filial, fraternal affection is the root of humaneness
the root of the process
nor are elaborate speeches and slick alacrity.

employ men in proper season
   not when they are at harvest
   E al Triedro, Cunizza
  e l'altra: 'Io son' la Luna.'
dry friable earth going from dust to more dust
  grass worn from its root-hold
  is it blacker? was it blacker? *Νύξ* animae?
  is there a blacker or was it merely San Juan with a belly ache
     writing ad posteros
  in short shall we look for a deeper or is this the bottom?
        (Canto LXXIV).

Chapter 24

LUCID INTERVALS

And the passion endures.
Against their action, aromas. Rooms, against chronicles.

'**B**ut you can't call it *poetry*.'
The reader should ask himself what he actually enjoys as poetry. Chaucer? Ben Jonson? Pope? Or is his approach to these merely archaeological? Rupert Brooke and the Shropshire Lad are for a surprising number of people the touchstones of 'real poetry a man can enjoy'. Erle Stanley Gardner holds a comparable place in the affections of many who in public know exactly how to converse about Joyce and Kafka. We have spoken above of the extraordinary purity of motive with which, for enjoyment, any poetry must be approached. The conventionally poetical—

> If I should die, think only this of me . . .
>
>   *   *   *
>
> About the orchards I will go
> To see the hedges hung with snow . . .
>
>   *   *   *
>
> Shoulder the sky, my lad, and drink your ale . . .

—invites the reader's immolation from motives of necrophily, mother-hunger, and adolescent heroics.

It is equally true, as Professor Richards found in the series of experiments recorded in *Practical Criticism*, that the effort of continuous attention required by the poet is beyond most readers' habits. This has not been without its influence on taste. A grape, ten lines of sawdust, another grape, becomes

228

the most comfortable structural norm. The bad poems which Richards found his students enjoying had generally a plangent line or two of which the rest was uninspected reverberation. It is this expectation of something which demands attention only in snatches, and affords a moony repose in the intervals, that underlies the frequent complaint that Pound in the *Cantos* exhibits an astonishing lyric gift which unfortunately manifests itself only in in tantalizing flashes. (The rest, therefore, is churned out by will-power, or is crankiness, or 'uninspired') What is really being lamented here is the absence of the sawdust or the moony repose. Pound's lyric moments exist not for indulgence but for definition: they are surveyor's pegs or records of emotional absolutes. When they are over, they stop. Their relationship with 'prosy' or colloquial or technical material, or with other lyric items, obeys definite but invisible laws, which laws it is the first business of the reader of the *Cantos* to apprehend. The metaphor of iron filings exhibiting magnetic fields of force is again strictly appropriate:

> nothing matters but the quality
> of the affection—
> in the end—that has carved the trace in the mind
> dove sta memoria
>
> (Canto LXXVI).

This may be exhibited in a passage with a fairly uncomplicated didactic line of action:

Les hommes ont je ne sais quelle peur étrange,
> said Monsieur Whoosis, de la beauté

La beauté, 'Beauty is difficult, Yeats', said Aubrey Beardsley
> when Yeats asked why he drew horrors
> or at least not Burne-Jones
> and Beardsley knew he was dying and had to
> make his hit quickly

Hence no more B-J in his product.

> So very difficult, Yeats, beauty so difficult.

'I am the torch' wrote Arthur, 'she saith'
in the moon barge βροδοδάκτυλος Ἠώς

with the veil of faint cloud before her
κύθηρα δεινὰ as a leaf borne in the current
pale eyes as if without fire
all that Sandro knew, and Jacopo
        and that Velásquez never suspected
lost in the brown meat of Rembrandt
        and the raw meat of Rubens and Jordaens

'This alone, leather and bones between you and τὸ πᾶν,'
                [*toh pan*, the all]
       (Chu Hsi's comment)
            (Canto LXXX).

Men's 'peur étrange de la beauté' is a motif introduced on the previous page—

    'Here! none of that mathematical music!'
Said the Kommandant when Münch offered Bach to the regiment.

The colloquy between Yeats and Beardsley, with its overtones of irascible earnest innocence on one side—

    When Yeats asked why he drew horrors
    or at least not Burne-Jones

and of irreducible mortal fact on the other—

    and Beardsley knew he was dying and had to
    make his hit quickly

—exhibits the essential equivocalness of human relations with beauty in another light: Beardsley's truth unsuspected by Yeats, liquid Burne-Jones beauty on the other hand both poignantly difficult and for heartbreaking personal reasons ('Beardsley knew he was dying') impractical. The quantity and degree of feeling and complex truth in these six lines surpasses that of most novels. (The novel, for that matter, may be defined, dynamically, as an expanded poem).
    Another motif from the previous page—

(Cythera, in the moon's barge whither?
    how hast thou the crescent for car?)

—is now picked up, and fused with the implacable Damosel of Arthur Symon's poem 'Modern Beauty' (which as a representative document of the nineties leads off Pound's *Profile* anthology):

    'I am the torch' wrote Arthur 'she saith'
    in the moon barge *brododaktylos Eos*—

Homer's 'rosy-fingered dawn' joining hands with the pre-Raphaelite sensibility (Burne-Jones) as united with the French symbolists (their propagandist, Symons).

The following three lines make a complex fusion of lovely austerities, *la beauté* which is difficult, virginal, and of which men have so strange a fear:[1]

    with the veil of faint cloud before her
        Kythera deina as a leaf borne in the current
    pale eyes as if without fire.

The moon, austere, implacable; the leaf fragile and passive, yet *deina*, terrible; the pale eyes uniting the fireless radiance of moonlight with the limpidities of Sandro Botticelli's Venus; the absence of fire in one sense actual (feminine—passive—reflected sunlight—'eye of the beholder'), in another sense apparent only (Symon's torch appealing, as she does at the end of his poem, for moths). Beauty is difficult, and the fading of men's grasp on the world of light and form is epitomized in the history of painting: 'lost in the brown meat of Rembrandt,' whose interest in muscles, shadows, opacities, and the mere accidental occlusions of luminosity marks a certain kind of intellectual death and foreruns a Leopold Bloom's absorption in accidental matter.

The tension of the artist's wrestle with 'meat' is caught up in a last wry paradox of the human state: it is the very con-

---

[1] This motif penetrates every page of the Pisan sequence. For instance, the distich quoted in Canto LXXXI,
    Your eyen two wol sleye me sodenly
    I may the beauté of hem nat susteyne;
is from a poem, attributed to Chaucer, entitled 'Merciless Beaute'.

dition of human existence that precludes *full* existence—so little (yet everything!) stands in the way of the artist's straining towards the world of the fully intelligible, and that little preserves the moth from automatic absorption by the flame: 'Human kind cannot bear very much reality.'

'This alone, leather and bones between you and τὸ πᾶν.'

This statement, in its context, draws on the wisdom of three civilizations: the lesson of Renaissance art and Greek terminology underwritten by a Chinese sage.

It will be seen from this that the five lines to Cythera, far from recording a momentary gasp of inspiration amidst querulous drool, are, with the Yeats-Beardsley conversation and the dictum of Monsieur Whoosis, documents of particular kinds and degrees of perception, points denoting a curve, foci of intersection in an invisible but intelligible multi-dimensional construction. The demand that this spare structure of radiant tensions be 'filled in' with rhetorical suet corresponds in the mind of the reader of poetry to the obsession of Rubens with bodily meat. More than thirty years before these lines were written, Pound had observed, apropos of Gaudier-Brzeska, that the scaffolding of modern buildings was beautiful *until* its enclosure in the mindless rhetoric of brick.

Chapter 25

FIELDS OF FORCE

And thought then, the deathless,
Form, forms and renewal, gods held in the air,
Forms seen, and then clearness,
Bright void, without image, Napishtim,
Casting his gods back into the *νοῦς*.

T here are, if the reader must be presented with a bunch of keys, three or four that will help him unlock most of the *Cantos*. One is a remark of Pound's that out of the three main classes of themes, permanent, recurrent, and haphazard or casual, a hierarchy of values should emerge. Another is the essay, 'Mediaevalism,' written for his edition of Cavalcanti and reprinted in *Make It New*, pp. 345–52. A third, applicable to the *Cantos* by a legitimate extension from musical into poetic organization of analogical aesthetic principles, is the 'Treatise on Harmony' in his 1924 study of George Antheil. A fourth is his 1947 pamphlet of Confucian translations, completed at about the same time as the *Pisan Cantos*: *The Unwobbling Pivot* and *Great Digest*. The latter should be read less for direct elucidation of the Chinese motifs in the *Cantos* than for initiation into the world of ordered perceptions that contains, like a field of force, the materials of the hugely miscellaneous poem.

This is our fifth or sixth recourse to electromagnetic imagery. It is difficult to conduct the present discussion without it. The behaviour of particles of metal in a magnetic field is used by Pound several times as an image of the poetic act:

'I made it out of a mouthful of air' wrote Bill Yeats in his heyday. The *forma,* the immortal *concetto,* the concept, the dynamic form which is like the rose-pattern driven into the dead iron-filings by the magnet, not by material contact with the magnet itself, but separate from the magnet. Cut off by the layer of glass, the dust and filings rise and spring into order. Thus the *forma,* the concept rises from death

> The bust outlasts the throne
> The coin Tiberius.

Culture, p. 152.

The magnet should be compared with Mr. Eliot's analogy of the poet as catalyst, the sheet of glass with his separation between the man who suffers and the mind which creates.

Pound's next paragraph, a gloss on the phrase 'the concept rises from death', glosses also the 'Make It New' injunction in the *Great Digest.* The example is Gerhart Münch's violin transcription of Clement Janequin's bird-song chorale (this is the music reproduced in Canto LXXV):

'Janequin's concept takes a third life in our time, for catgut or patent silver, its first was choral, its second on the wires of Francesco Milano's lute. And its ancestry I think goes back to Arnaut Daniel and to god knows what "hidden antiquity".'

'One of the rights of masterwork is the right of rebirth and recurrence.' Here we have the link between 'Make it New', Pound's translating activities, and the sense of historical recurrence that informs the *Cantos*: not a bulldozed 'All this has happened before', but a lively sense of forms asserting their immortality in successive material opportunities.

The poetic act, the electrification of mute experiential filings into a manifestation of form, is, as we have implied in our account of ideogram, not distinct from the act of intellection itself, as Aristotle implies in referring to the 'active intellect' as the *nous poietikos.*

Serenely in the crystal jet
        as the bright ball that the fountain tosses
(Verlaine) as diamond clearness

How soft the wind under Taishan
        where the sea is remembered
out of hell, the pit
out of the dust and glare evil
Zephyrus / Apeliota
This liquid is certainly a
      property of the mind
nec accidens est   but an element
                in the mind's make-up
est agens and functions   dust to a fountain pan otherwise
    Hast 'ou seen the rose in the steel-dust
                  (or swansdown ever?)
so light is the urging, so ordered the dark petals of iron
we who have passed over Lethe.
                         (Canto LXXIV.)

This passage follows several pages of memories:

or a fellow throwing a knife in the market
past baskets and bushels of peaches
             at $1. the bushel
and the cool of the 42nd St. tunnel   (periplum)
white-wash and horse-cars, the Lexington Avenue cable
refinement, pride of tradition, alabaster. . . .

which emerge in retrospect with diamond clearness, luminous
with social and moral quiddities, to undergo the play of the
active and caressing mind

Serenely in the crystal jet
      as the bright ball that the fountain tosses.

The sea, generically,

                  is remembered
    out of hell, the pit
    out of the dust and glare evil

And clear memories are integral with mental functions ('est

235

agens');[1] otherwise the fountain is stilled and dust-filled, grimy with the accumulated detritus of a lifetime of contacts. But the functioning mind pulls the 'dust and glare evil' itself into forms, as dead iron around the poles of the magnet groups itself into a rose. Dante, whose intellect brought to a focus unimaginable splendours, is our poet's explicit exemplar; the sombre rose of the Detention Camp mocks the white blossom in the form of which the 'sacred soldiery' displayed themselves to Dante (*Paradiso* XXXI) but is scarcely less an imaginative achievement. The 'dark petals of iron': the minor-keyed poetry of the *Pisan Cantos*.

The ellipses of this passage have been thus clumsily expanded in the hope of directing attention on a central Poundian image: art as the process of compelling out of otherwise mute particulars, by their electric juxtaposition, traces, intelligible patterns, of an intense, clear, luminous intellective world. The 'Mediaevalism' essay provides for this conception the clearest gloss one could wish.

'. . . harmony in the sentience, harmony *of* the sentient, where the thought has its demarcation, the substance its *virtu*, where stupid men have not reduced all "energy" to unbounded undistinguished abstraction.

'For the modern scientist energy has no borders, it is a shapeless "mass" of force; even his capacity to differentiate it to a degree never dreamed by the ancients has not led him to think of its shape or even its loci. The rose that his magnet makes in the iron filings, does not lead him to think of the force in botanic terms, or wish to visualize that force as floral and extant (*ex stare*).

'A mediaeval "natural philosopher" would find this modern electric world full of enchantments, not only the light in the electric bulb, but the thought of the current hidden in air and

---

[1] The rising water, that is, is the fountain, not something pushed by the fountain. Cf. Yeats: 'How can we know the dancer from the dance?' In the same way, the Confucian 'process', the realization of the inborn nature, is act, not the railway track along which act travels. Hence 'what you depart from is not the process' (*Unwobbling Pivot* I-i-2; cf. the opening of Canto LXXIV). For the Verlaine allusion, see his 'Clair de Lune' in the *Fêtes Galantes* volume.

in wire would give him a mind full of forms, "*Fuor di color*" or having their hyper-colours. The mediaeval philosopher would probably have been unable to think the electric world and *not* think of it as a world of forms. . . .'

If this is not clear enough, there is more:

'We appear to have lost the radiant world where one thought cuts through another with a clean edge, a world of moving energies, "*mezzo oscuro rade,*" "*risplende in se perpetuale effecto,*" magnetisms that take form, that are seen, or that border the visible, the matter of Dante's *paradiso*, the glass under water, the form that seems a form seen in a mirror, these realities perceptible to the sense, interacting, "*a lui si tiri*" . . .'

We appear to have lost this world; its loss has been referred to in our previous chapter apropos of 'the brown meat of Rubens and Jordaens'. In the 'Mediaevalism' essay the same parallel from painting makes its appearance:

'Durch Rafael ist das Madonnenideal Fleisch geworden', says Herr Springer, with perhaps an unintentional rhyme. Certainly the metamorphosis into carnal tissue becomes frequent and general somewhere around 1527. The people are corpus, corpuscular, but not in the strict sense "animate", it is no longer the body of air clothed in the body of fire; it no longer radiates, light no longer moves from the eye, there is a great deal of meat, shock-absorbing, perhaps—at any rate absorbent. It has not even Greek marmoreal plastic to restrain it. The dinner scene is more frequently introduced, we have the characters in definite act of absorption; later they will be but stuffing for expensive upholsteries.'

(A pertinent contrast is with Walter Pater's account of Botticelli's colouring, 'no mere delightful quality of natural things, but a spirit upon them by which they become expressive to the spirit.' The reader of the *Cantos* could do worse than study Pater's *Renaissance*).

The corresponding change in poetry is exemplified in Cavalcanti and Petrarch, a contrast not of degree but of kind:

'In Guido the "figure", the strong metamorphic or "pic-

turesque" expression is there with purpose to convey or inter-
pret a definite meaning. In Petrarch it is ornament, the
prettiest ornament he could find, but not an irreplaceable
ornament, or one that he couldn't have used just about as
well somewhere else. In fact he very often does use it, and
them, somewhere, and nearly everywhere, else, all over the
place.'

We have remarked on these matters before in connection with
ideogram and metaphor. And it will be seen that in contrasting
the language of exploration with the language of convention
we have gotten from the magnetic fields back to the familiar
Imagist principles: 'Use no unnecessary word.' It was Pound's
knowledge of Provençal and Tuscan poetry that gave Imagism
a useful direction. The collapse of the movement into frigid
Hellenism and utter insipidity was merely an early instance
of the recurrent incomprehension, on the part of alleged allies,
of where Pound's particular technical concerns pointed. His
technical interests have always been connected with qualities
of perception and of civilization.

'Mediaevalism' (*circa* 1931) is simply the most elaborated
expression of what has been a controlling interest of Pound's
ever since *The Spirit of Romance* (1910). That perception of
what is Mediterranean and (apart from Chaucer[1]) not English
has, in one sense, governed his entire subsequent thirty-odd
years of writing. In *The Spirit of Romance*, for example, we
find:

'The cult of Provence was, as we have said, a cult of the
emotions; that of Tuscany a cult of the harmonies of the mind.
The cult of the Renaissance was a cult of culture.

'It is probably true that the Renaissance brought in rhetoric,
and all the attendant horrors.'

(p. 235).

'In architecture, mediaeval work means line; line, composition and design: Renaissance work means mass. The

---

[1] Pound is the first English poet since Pope who has been able to learn
from Chaucer. He has also written (in the *ABC of Reading*) the finest
appreciation of Chaucer extant.

mediaeval architect envied the spider his cobweb. The Renaissance architect sought to rival the mountain. They raised successively the temple of the spirit and the temple of the body.'

(p. 176).

Finally, there is this comment on a poem by Guinicelli:

' "There is no man whose evil thoughts do not cease a little while before she appears."

'Rossetti renders the last line beautifully:

' "No man could think base thoughts who looked on her."

'But *finche la vede* seems to imply that her spiritual influence would reach somewhat beyond her visible presence.

'The distinction may seem over precise, but it is the spirit of this period to be precise . . .'

(p. 93).

The absence of this precision (which is at home, Pound suggests, in 'a decent climate where a man leaves his nerve-set open, or allows it to tune with its ambience, rather than struggling, as a northern race has to, for self-preservation to guard the body from assaults of weather') has made for a thickness in English sensibility incarnate in the characteristic joining of sounds in English verse; once again we find that we have been moving at only a short distance from what appear to be the merest pedantries of vowel-and-consonant technique:

'I don't know how far I succeeded in convincing him [Yeats] that English verse wasn't CUT. Yeats himself in his early work produced marvellous rhythmic effects "legato", verse, that is, very fine to murmur and that may be understood if whispered in drawing-rooms, even though the better readers may gradually pull the words out of shape (by excessive lengthening of the vowel sounds) . . .

'The Elizabethan "iambic" verse was largely made to bawl in theatres, and has considerable affinity with barocco.'

Polite Essays, p. 34.

Finally, this key-essay, 'Mediaevalism,' makes contact with the economic and moral themes of the *Cantos*. The Greek aesthetic, Pound notes, 'would seem to consist wholly in plastic, or in plastic moving toward coitus, and limited by incest, which is the sole Greek taboo. . . . Plastic plus immediate satisfaction.' (This hot and heavy side of the Greek world, it may be noted parenthetically, is most easily accessible to English-reading inspection in the young Keats. The breathing and panting that infects even the *Odes* goes with what were in his own day called Keats' 'Cockney' affiliations, with his passion for a clutter of *objets d'art*, with the fashionable *nouveau-riche* feeling, shortly after the industrial Revolution, that passion was fleeting and fading, and that 'culture' must be hurriedly purchased from dealers in great shipments, urns and statues, and stuck up around the garden. Much nineteenth-century Hellenism was related to the Romantic fever in this way.)

'. . . Plastic plus immediate satisfaction. The whole break of Provence with this world, and indeed the central theme of the troubadours, is the dogma that there is some proportion between the fine thing held in the mind, and the inferior thing ready for instant consumption.'

This is more than a satisfying exegesis of the cult of idealized and unattainable mistresses. It has bearings of a more than 'aesthetic', more than historical kind:

> with usura . . .
> no picture is made to endure nor to live with
> but it is made to sell and sell quickly
> with usura, sin against nature,
> is thy bread ever more of stale rags
> is thy bread dry as paper,
> with no mountain wheat, no strong flour
> with usura the line grows thick
> with usura is no clear demarcation . . .
>   (Canto XLV).

Instant consumption, absence of demarcation, usura. Against this,

Shines
in the mind of heaven God
who made it
more than the sun
in our eye

(Canto LI).

One cannot insist too often on the unified direction of Pound's interests. It is the slow establishment of these linkages in seventy cantos that underlies the exceedingly rapid shifts in the Pisan series. In the later cantos the same lines of force control an infinitely vaster flood of materials in a given brief space. There persists the large dichotomy between what lumps and muddles and abstracts, and what purifies, dissociates, renders in terms of concrete manifestation. 'To have gathered from the air a live tradition' consists largely in his having recovered the latter from its several centuries of burial beneath the former.

. 'For example two centuries of Provençal life devoted a good deal of energy to *motz el son*, to the union of word and music.

'You can connect that fine demarcation with demarcations in architecture and re usury, or you can trace it alone, from Arnaut and his crew down to Janequin, where a different susceptibility has replaced it.

'But the one thing you shd. not do is to suppose that when something is wrong with the arts, it is wrong with the arts ONLY.

'When a given hormone defects, it will defect throughout the whole system.'

Culture, p. 60.

To revert to the list of keys at the beginning of this chapter, it is now perhaps easier to see how Pound expects a hierarchy of values to emerge from the *Cantos*, and where 'Mediaevalism' comes in. How the Great Bass theory underlies the poetic organization, and how the Confucian translations confer fuller articulation upon the world of intelligibles will be hinted at later. It will be expedient first to relate the above material more closely to the verse.

Chapter 26

MUD AND LIGHT

nor is it for nothing that the chrysalids mate in the air
color di luce
green splendour and as the sun thru pale fingers.

An immediate consequence of the dichotomy between mud and light is the presence, throughout
the *Cantos*, of contrasted sets of imagery. To list
the themes and images by content is merely bewildering: a
narcotics charge, the drift of peach-blossoms, the visit to
Tiresias, the memoirs of Lincoln Steffens, the history of
China, a chronicle of transatlantic flights. If instead attention
be paid, along the lines just indicated, to *function*, much, if
not yet all, becomes luminous. In Canto XXIX, for instance,
we have several juxtapositions of this kind:

(1)   Past the house of the three retired clergymen
      Who were too cultured to keep their jobs.
      Languor has cried unto languor
              about the marshmallow-roast
      (Let us speak of the osmosis of persons)
      The wail of the phonograph has penetrated their marrow
      (Let us . . .
      The wail of the pornograph . . .)
              The cicadas continue uninterrupted.

(2)   The tower, ivory, the clear sky
      Ivory rigid in sunlight
      And the pale clear of the heaven
      Phoibos of narrow thighs,

The cut cool of the air,
Blossom cut on the wind, by Helios
Lord of the light's edge, and April
Blown round the feet of the God....

Languor, marshmallows, osmosis, culture Bostonian and gliding towards impotence. Against it rigid ivory, the 'cut cool', cut blossom, the light's edge, an April so embodied as to be blowable. In particular, the cut or cuttable or as-if-cut controls a whole sequence of sculpturesque imagery:

Rustle of airy sheaths,
      dry forms in the *aether*.   (Canto II).

And she went towards the window,
      the slim white stone bar
Making a double arch;
Firm even fingers held to the firm pale stone;   (Canto IV).

[the rain] Yet drinks the thirst from our lips,
      solid as echo,
Passion to breed a form in shimmer of rain-blur;   (Canto VII).

The grey stone posts
      and the stair of grey stone,
the passage clean-squared in granite: (Canto XVI).

There, in the forest of marble,
The stone trees—out of water—
The arbours of stone—
marble leaf, over leaf,
silver, steel over steel,
silver beaks rising and crossing,
prow set against prow,
stone, ply over ply,
the gilt beams flare of an evening   (Canto XVII).

Shelf of the lotophagoi,
Aerial, cut in the aether.   (Canto XX).

     ...and a milestone
an altar to Terminus, with arms crossed
back of the stone

Where sun cuts light against evening;
where light shaves grass into emerald   (Canto XLVIII).

These have been collected by the most rapid skimming. Their family includes definition of every kind (Imagism: Ching Ming), translucence, stone, clear water, many things—stone, water, air, light—laid 'ply over ply', shining metals, type-founders, artists and warriors aware of their work, writers of vivid and circumstantial accounts, in the later cantos the authors of exact and aphoristic observations:

Italy ever doomed with abstractions, 1850, wrote Zobi,
By following brilliant abstractions.   (Canto L).

> so that you cd/ crack a flea on eider wan
> ov her breasts
sd/ the old Dublin pilot
> or the precise definition   (Canto LXXVII).

Gaudier's word not blacked out
              nor old Hulme's, nor Wyndham's . . .
'definition cannot be shut down under a box lid'
but if the gelatine be effaced whereon is the record?
'wherein is no responsible person
              having a front name, a hind name, and an address'
'not a right but a duty'
              these words still stand uncancelled.
                              (Canto LXXVIII).

The lyric passages in the first thirty cantos, with their quality of intoxicated vision, their sculptured scenery, their specified colours and defined edges, generally serve the same thematic function. The later lyrics pin down more diverse states.

Against this very large classification (to which should be added definition achieved by strong rhythmic means) is the huge category of ignobility, muddle, and drift. Against death-less forms, metamorphoses. In Cantos I and II the seaman who journeyed to hell undamaged faces the seamen of treason-ous wills who sought to betray the god and were metamor-phosed into fish. Cantos XXVII and XXVIII consist almost entirely of metamorphoses in this mode, corpses rotting, men descended from frogs. The variety within this general category is, again, very great; and sub-distinctions become, again, sharper in the later Cantos. Sometimes the mode is frankly caricature, after the techniques developed in *Lustra*:

And Mr Lourpee sat on the floor of the pension dining-room
Or perhaps it was in the alcove
And about him lay a great mass of pastells,
That is, stubbs and broken pencils of pastell,
In pale indeterminate colours.
And he admired the Sage of Concord
  'Too broad ever to make up his mind'.
And the mind of Lourpee at fifty
Directed him into a room with a certain vagueness
As if he wd.
neither come in nor stay out
As if he wd.
go neither to the left nor the right
And his painting reflected this habit.   (Canto **XXVIII**).

In other places the mood is darker:

And from the stone pits, the heavy voices,
Heavy sound:
    'Sero, sero ...
'Nothing we made, we set nothing in order,
'Neither house nor the carving,
'And what we thought had been thought for too long;
'Our opinion not opinion in evil
'But opinion borne for too long.
'We have gathered a sieve full of water.' (Canto **XXV**).

The endless incongruities of modern business are manipulated so as to display the salesman's or financier's low cunning against the Tuscan cult of the intelligence: salience is given in the following passage to the endless violences to language and learning involved in the activities and laudation of a Zaharoff:

And Metevsky, 'the well-known philanthropist,'
Or 'the well-known financier, better known,'
As the press said, 'as a philanthropist,'

Gave—as the Este to Louis Eleventh,—
A fine pair of giraffes to the nation,
And endowed a chair of ballistics,
And was consulted before the offensives. (Canto XVIII).

This muddle has public ambience:

'Qu'est-ce qu'on pense . . .?' I said: 'On don't pense.
'They're solid bone. You can amputate from just above
The medulla, and it won't alter the life in that island.'
But he continued, 'Mais, qu'EST-CE qu'ON pense,
'De la metallurgie, en Angleterre, qu'est-ce qu'on
'Pense de Metevsky?'
'And I said: 'They ain't heard his name yet.
'Go ask at MacGorvish's bank.' (Canto XVIII).

The French Enlightenment is juxtaposed with a rotted aristocracy:

'Buk!' said the Second Baronet, 'eh . . .
'Thass a funny lookin' buk' said the Baronet
Looking at Bayle, folio, 4 vols. in gilt leather, 'Ah . . .
'Wu . . . Wu . . . wot you goin' eh to do with ah . . .
'. . . ah read-it?'
                    Sic loquitur eques.   (Canto XXVIII).

We may take the Second Baronet for Comic Relief. The gist of the discourse can be better seen in this account of an American millionaire:

Thing is to find something simple
As for example Pa Stadtvolk:
Hooks to hang gutters on roofs,
A spike and half-circle, patented 'em and then made 'em;
Worth a good million, not a book in the place;
Got a horse about twenty years after, seen him
            Of a Saturday afternoon
When they'd taken down an old fence,
Ole Pa out there knockin the nails out
(To *save* 'em.) I hear he smoked good cigars.
                                (Canto XXVIII).

246

Pa Stadtvolk is not a villain of the piece, his place is not among the 'liars and loan lice'. His obsession with 'something simple', the fantastic reward for his 'hooks to hang gutters on roofs', his illiteracy, his parsimonious saving of old nails, reflect a maniacal whittling of human concerns down to some almost non-existent point, as the ease with which his nickel's worth of shrewdness produced the jackpot focuses a nightmare economy based on starvation, muddle, and caprice. But still more important is his faintness of *directio voluntatis*. With Pa's

Spike and half-circle, patented 'em and then made 'em

may be contrasted certain Confucian dicta:

'The ethic of the man of high breed has its origin in ordinary men and women, but is, in its entirety, a rite addressed to heaven and earth.

Unwobbling Pivot, XX, iv.

'One would say that having this capacity for seeing clearly into himself and thereby directing his acts, he perforce came to the throne, perforce had these high honours, perforce this enduring fame and longevity.'

Unwobbling Pivot, XVII, ii.

The rhythms of the Yankee jargon in which the modern 'successful' are generally discussed, lines jerking back constantly to the starting-point like a colt on a lariat, enact by another means this poverty of motivation:

Baldy Bacon
        bought all the little copper pennies in Cuba:
Un centavo, dos centavos,
        told his peons to 'bring 'em in.'
'Bring em to the main shack,' said Baldy,
And the peons brought 'em . . .
        Nicholas Castano in Habana,
He also had a few centavos, but the others
Had to pay a percentage.
        Percentage when they wanted centavos,
Public centavos.

Baldy's interest
Was in money business.
   'No interest in any other kind uv bisnis,'
Said Baldy.   (Canto XII).

With the rhythms of this primitive *coup*, compare the orderly
chant of the sage:

And Kung said, and wrote on the bo leaves:
  If a man have not order within him
He can not spread order about him;
And if a man have not order within him
His family will not act with due order;
  And if the prince have not order within him
He cannot put order in his dominions.   (Canto XIII).

Examples of further dissociation could be multiplied
without end, since the main matter of the *Cantos* is to establish a hierarchy of values by dissociating actions, motives,
periods, customs, sensibilities, in this way. Order and disorder
take, and have taken, innumerable forms whose quiddities
are to be savoured. If the poet's task were simply to register
a luminosity and a muddle, there would be no reason why his
task should have been protracted to even one-hundredth of
its present length (over 500 pages so far). The job could be
done in a twelve-line lyric. We should beware of stamping all
the items in the *Cantos* either 'O.K.' or 'N.G.' But the cut-
vs.-muddled remains one of the major skeletal lines to be
grasped, and it has done no harm to isolate it. It may be
worth while before dealing with other matters to indicate
along these lines the organization of a whole Canto (LI).
  The opening has already been quoted:

    Shines
    in the mind of heaven God
    who made it
    more than the sun
    in our eye

This brief double hierarchy of light is juxtaposed with

    Fifth element; mud; said Napoleon.

Mediaeval light-metaphysics (Grosseteste, Erigena), associated by implication with the physics of the four elements, are suddenly confronted with the mud that impeded the ordered strategies of the *Grande Armée*. But there is in fact no full stop after Napoleon: the passage flows on without a break in recognition of the Emperor's resurrection of the Roman and Canon Laws against usury:

> Fifth element; mud; said Napoleon
> With usury has no man a good house
> made of stone, no paradise on his church wall
> With usury the stone cutter is kept from his stone
> the weaver is kept from his loom by usura
> Wool does not come into market
> the peasant does not eat his own grain
> the girl's needle goes blunt in her hand
> The looms are hushed one after another
> ten thousand after ten thousand....

and so on for sixteen more lines of recapitulation of Canto XLV. These rhythms merit close study. They shape the archaisms of Canto XLV into sober speech. Their main counterpoint is furnished by the opening line of the Canto, which strikes like a chime the single word, 'Shines.' The major theme is a dactylic chant,

> WOOL does not COME in-to MAR ket,

in sharply separate, almost spondaic syllables. Against this is played a slurred and softened speech, roughly dactylic again but muted to impede the natural momentum of the dactyl:

> the *peas*ant does not *eat* his own *grain*
> the *girl's needle* goes *blunt* in her *hand*
> the *looms* are *hushed one af*ter ano*ther*

The total effect is of something throttled, blurred, stilled. The dactyl throbs beneath mutes. The air of Hebraic chant, systole and diastole, is a further component in the elegaic feeling.

This intense absence of vehemence, a weight of statement

too solemn for rhetoric, is suddenly intersected by garrulous but useful technical instructions on fly-fishing:

> Blue dun; number 2 in most rivers
> for dark days, when it is cold
> A starling's wing will give you the colour
> or duck widgeon, if you take feather from under the wing ...
> ... can be fished from seven a.m.
> till eleven; at which time the brown marsh fly comes on.
> As long as the brown continues, no fish will take Granham.

These instructions, a blend of exact information on the habits of wild life, detailed particularity about colours and feathers, and intricate activities knowingly carried on for a purpose, (and that purpose a fundamental human activity, the taking of fish, here elevated by knowledge and technique into an art in a way that prepares for the elaborate solar and agricultural rituals of the next Canto) combine the peasant's wisdom with the skill of the man of leisure. The comment follows:

> That hath the light of the doer, as it were
> a form cleaving to it.
> Deo similis quodam modo
> hic intellectus adeptus
> Grass; nowhere out of place.

'Deo similis quodam modo' reflects the opening paralleling of divine and human light. 'Grass; nowhere out of place' contains both a natural order (e.g. grass growing where light and moisture are provided) and a civilized order imposed on the materials of nature, but by means in harmony with natural processes: a lawn, a garden, is, like fly-fishing, co-operative with the heavenly disposition of things. The next lines:

> Thus speaking in Königsberg
> Zwischen die Volkern erzielt wird
> a modus vivendi

—employ the corporate lawgiver and three languages to peg formal philosophic thought to ordered activity.

Suddenly the scene changes to Dante's Maleboge, abode of

the circling dragon who bore the poets downward on his back
in spiralling circles into the hell of the usurers and the violent
against art:

> circling in eddying air; in a hurry
> the 12: close eyed in the oily wind

('oily wind': a Dantean epithet; cf. 'l'aura morta'.)

> these were the regents; and a sour song from the folds
> > of his belly
> sang Geryone; I am the help of the aged;
> I pay men to talk peace;
> Mistress of many tongues; merchant of chalcedony
> I am Geryon twin with usura,
> You who have lived in a stage set.

> A thousand were dead in his folds;
> in the eel-fishers basket
> Time was of the League of Cambrai:

The Canto ends with the 'Ching Ming' ideograph of clarification: calling things by their right names. The Chinese characters extend their benediction over the poet's activities, and
pass their silent judgment on Geryon and *usura*.

Chapter 27

PLOTLESS EPIC

Le vieux commode en acajou:
beer-bottles of various strata.

I f many of the points in the previous chapter seem too obvious to need making, a reading of extant commentaries on the *Cantos* may provide excuse. It is usual to search for a subject-matter, a plot, a line of philosophic development, such as it has been Pound's principal achievement to dispense with. This statement may perhaps best be approached through Flaubert, the affinities of whose *mot juste* with 'Ching Ming' and the ideogrammic method have already been noted.

The resemblance of Pound's poetic activity to Flaubert's agonizing search for the phrase, the cadence, that would define his matter exactly is obvious at the most superficial level. A dip anywhere in the poem turns up unforgettable lines, rhythms, phrases. Achievements like

In the gloom, the gold gathers the light against it

have affected the most hostile with an intoxication like that experienced by the young Ford Madox Ford turning the pages of *Trois Contes*. *Le mot juste* extends however to much more than darkly evocative resonance of this order. There is just as much of the anvil and file about

Baldy Bacon
    bought all the little copper pennies in Cuba

(the stroke of genius being the affectionate epithet 'little'); or

252

Lift up their spoons to mouths, put forks in cutlets,
And make sound like the sound of voices

(which is hobbled if 'steaks' be substituted for 'cutlets', or the
closing cadence tampered with);

A mount, a bank, a fund a bottom an
institution of credit
a place to send cheques in and out of

(precision, exuberance, exasperation; but try putting commas
after 'fund' and 'bottom')

Atrox MING, atrox finis
the nine gates were in flame.

(hubris, phanopoeia).

Such language doesn't constitute a 'style', at least according
to current connotations of the word ('Le style, c'est l'homme').
Style has undoubtedly personal timbres (one would not
mistake a phrase out of the *Cantos* for a phrase out of *The
Waste Land* or *Ulysses*); but since the career of the French
novel between Stendhal and Flaubert, the only useful meaning
of the phrase 'good style' is 'language which renders its object
accurately'. Its object may be a character, a theory, an intention, the lilt of a voice, the smell of a room. No more
perspicacious judgment has been passed on *Ulysses* than Mr.
Eliot's neglected remark that it was Joyce's triumph not to
have a style, in the sense of a matrix into which to crush his
materials.

'Ineluctable modality of the visible: at least that if no
more, thought through my eyes'

and

'And just now at Edy's word as a telltale flush, delicate as
the faintest rosebloom, crept into her cheeks she looked so
lovely in her sweet girlish shyness that of a surety God's fair
land of Ireland did not hold her equal.'

are passages out of different parts of the same book. Joyce, of
course, handled directly the classical doctrine of decorum,

never questioned until long after the Renaissance; it is in the
same way that

> You do it wrong, being so majestical,
> To offer it the show of violence

and

> Art thou there, Truepenny?

are passages out of the same early seventeenth-century play.
Different cadences, different vocabularies, perform different
functions, register the tensions between different persons and
different facts. The doctrine of decorum at its best afforded
the artist an infinitely subtle adjustment of relative weights
and tensions, of the thing made to the thing perceived: the
conferring on the artifact of a degree of being precisely
adequate to a given experience. By the early nineteenth
century, however, even the most rule-of thumb apprehension
of even the schoolmaster's formulation of the three levels of
style had been discarded; a Wordsworth poured his diversity
of experiences into a more or less monotonous 'medium',
every page of Tennyson's *Becket* read exactly like any other
page, and into such keeping had the canons of poetic usage
passed that there was no one to protest when Butcher and
Lang innocently took 'elevated prose' like a pot in one hand,
and 'Homer' like jam in the other, and bottled away.

It was the last generation to be born under that shadow that
found *Ulysses* as formless as a telephone directory. To such
eyes the results of Joyce's study of the Flaubertian novel and
the classical rhetoricians were still invisible. To such minds the
Cantos still seem a rag-bag. (The early French reviews of
Madame Bovary show that the English critics of this dispensation were living in a world that had fought its continental
rearguard action seventy years before). Joyce commands to-
day, thirty years later, for irrelevant reasons far more lip-
service than Pound; understanding of his handling of language
cannot, however, be said to have much advanced. It is still
usual to point to Stuart Gilbert's quasi-mathematical table of
themes and symbols in *Ulysses* as proof of its 'form', as it is

usual to refer to *Tom Jones* or any detective novel as 'brilliantly constructed'. To Industrial Man 'construction' or 'form'
means a blueprint. An examination question at a mid-western
American University in 1944 invited the student to check the
one best answer to the following:

Hamlet's first soliloquy suggests that his melancholy is the
direct result of:

A—his father's death.
B—his mother's remarriage.
C—the ghost's revelations.
D—his uncle's refusal to let him return to Wittenburg.
E—his natural temperament.

To the 'knowledge' of the play so tested, any involvement of
the reader's whole perceiving self is a supererogatory addition
for post-graduate leisure. It is at the same institution,
thoroughly representative of American higher learning in
everything but the degree of insane thoroughness with which
it follows the contours of industrial society, that *Tom Jones*
is the novel *par excellence* because a diagram of its events can
be drawn with unexampled intricacy, and because a conversation on page 12 may be depended on to have consequences on page 324. *Ulysses*, of course, which in one of its
dimensions exists as a parody on these concerns, has been for
some years the happy hunting ground of their be-filing-
carded devotees.

It is because no satisfying diagram of the *Cantos* can be (at
least, has been) drawn that so many critics of repute have
confessed themselves unable to discern 'what it's all about'.
It is by now usual to announce, in capitals or in parentheses
depending on the degree of hostility or good-will involved, that
the poem is 'about' nothing (a concatenation of technical
exercises) or 'about' something or other deplorable and un-
American or un-British. The charge of anti-Semitism is
familiar, and there were once Arab attacks on the *Divina
Commedia* and the *Poema del Cid* as anti-Mohammedan.
(More than one scholar, by the way, has carefully diagrammed
The Canterbury Tales and then, because the four tales per

teller in some obvious balance didn't actually get written, dismissed the work, with a few remarks about characterization, as a noble ruin). That is where Flaubert comes in.

L'Education Sentimentale in at least one English translation is as dull as ditchwater. A young man is on a boat, he comes home, he goes to Paris, he rubs shoulders with various dull people, falls in love with a woman he can't manage to see, etc. etc. Nothing seems to lead to anything else, there is no conceivable reason for getting or staying interested, the plot, if we persevere, proves a tritely melancholy affair. We turn to our handbook and discover that it all goes much better in French, where we have *le mot juste* to keep us amused. Flaubert, that is, got away with it by applying an incomparable veneer to a narrative whose intrinsic banality would shame the clumsiest scribbler of science fiction. (This is precisely what Bernard Shaw and the public school system tell us about Shakespeare.) Pound's veneer is in the same way incomparable (in places; if he would only stop shoving his muttering fanatic's face through those lyric pages!) but Pound hasn't even Flaubert's excuse for a narrative, and that trick of gilding a vacuum has, now that every reader of Ellery Queen can recognize a well-constructed piece of literature, been exploded long ago.

What Flaubert actually did was arrange not primarily words but things; or words as *mimesis* of things. Out of an odour, a waft of talk, a plume of smoke, the flare of gaslight, the disposition, relative to the carpet and windows, of certain furniture in a certain room, the world of Frederic Moreau emerges with palpable and autonomous immediacy. The significant action of the novel, in contradistinction to the diagrammable 'plot', obstructed by dull descriptions, that emerges from a poor translation, consists in the interactions of, the tensions set up between, these items. That is the meaning of *le mot juste*. Here are the contemptuous incongruities of the contemporary newsmagazine ideogrammed in a paragraph:

'Un jour, plusieurs numéros du *Flambard* lui tombèrent

sous la main. L'article de fond, invariablement, était consacré à démolir un homme illustre. Venaient ensuite les nouvelles du monde, les cancans. Puis, on blaguait l'Odéon, Carpentras, la pisciculture, et les condamnés à mort quand il y en avait. La disparition d'un paquebot fournit matière à plaisanteries pendant un an. Dans la troisième colonne, un courier des arts donnait, sous forme d'anecdote ou de conseil, des réclames de tailleurs, avec des comptes rendus de soirées, des annonces de ventes, des analyses d'ouvrages, traitant de la même encre un volume de vers et une paire de bottes. La seule partie sérieuse était la critique des petits théâtres, ou l'on s'acharnait sur deux ou trois directeurs; et les intérêts de l'Art étaient invoqués à propos des décors des Funambules ou d'une amoureuse de Délassements.'

(II-iv).

'Les nouvelles du monde, les cancans.' 'Les condamnés à mort, quand il y en avait.' 'Des annonces de ventes, des analyses d'ouvrages.' These juxtapositions are precisely calculated. Equally accurate is the balancing of parts: six short sentences of desultory sampling followed by two that engage the ironic sense on smaller nuances. The component phrases are so cut and weighted as to give rhythmic definition to successive items.

There is nothing new about these observations, but their implications for the judging of English verse do not seem to have been much weighed. It is scarcely too much to say that it was the discovery of these techniques by French prose writers that made possible *vers libre*. This control of tone, this maintenance of an exact ironic distance, this sense of the weighting of successive phrases of contrasting length, runs directly from Flaubert through Laforgue into *Prufrock*. The organization of the paragraph just quoted does not differ in principle from that of one of the *Cantos*.

A particular word, the placing of a particular word, is 'inevitable' because it *belongs* to what is being rendered. A hieratic cadence has one function, a staccato cadence another. It is because this notion, familiar to the old rhetoricians, of an intrinsic relation between palpable linguistic gestures and human tensions and actions, has become so unfamiliar (so that 'style' is thought of as convertible with 'personality'), that the wit of the 'Oxen of the Sun' section of *Ulysses*, a comprehensive ideogrammic commentary on these matters, has gone unnoticed.

Ford Madox Ford twenty years ago in a little handbook on *The English Novel* provided a tiny tot's guide to the principle of 'rendering':

'If I say, "The wicked Mr. Blank shot nice Blanche's dear cat!" that is telling. If I say: "Blank raised his rifle and aimed it at the quivering black-burdened topmost bough of the cherry-tree. After the report a spattered bunch of scarlet and black quiverings dropped from branch to branch to pancake itself on the orchard grass!" that is rather bad rendering, but still rendering. Or if I say Monsieur Chose was a vulgar, coarse, obese and presumptuous fellow—that is telling. But if I say, "He was a gentleman with red whiskers that always preceded him through a doorway," there you have him rendered—as Maupassant rendered him.'

The second, Maupassant, example may be compared, in principle, with any of the snapshots in the later Cantos, which deal in very compressed rendering indeed: 'And Gaudier's eye on the telluric mass of Miss Lowell;' 'Newbolt who looked twice bathed.' With Ford's shot cat, compare a bit of hugger-mugger from Canto V, the 'telling' of which would be, 'Some-one saw John Borgia brought dead, on horseback, to the Tiber, and pitched in.'

John Borgia is bathed at last. (Clock-tick pierces the vision)
Tiber, dark with the cloak, wet cat gleaming in patches.
Click of the hooves, through garbage,
Clutching the greasy stone. 'And the cloak floated.'
Slander is up betimes.

Here is a second rendering:

And the next comer says, 'Were nine wounds,
'Four men, white horse. Held on the saddle before him . . .'
Hooves clink and slick on the cobbles.

Schiavoni ... cloak ... 'Sink the damn thing!'
Splash wakes that chap on the wood-barge.
Tiber catching the nap, the moonlit velvet,
A wet cat gleaming in patches.

It should finally be noted that Ford's horrible example, 'The wicked Mr. Blank shot nice Blanche's dear cat', is perfectly good as rendering, not of the shooting of the cat, but of a sentimental old lady's version of the shooting. Hence the Gerty MacDowell episode in *Ulysses* ('of a surety God's fair land of Ireland did not hold her equal') and the studious vulgarity of such verse as,

> ... and the prince come aboard,
> An' we said wud yew like to run her?
> And he run damn slam on the breakwater,
> And bust off all her front end,
> And he was my gawd scared out of his panties.
>
> (Canto XVIII).

or, less obviously,

> Oh yes, there are nobles, still interested in polo
> said the whoring countess of course there were nobles,
> Mr. Axon the usually so intelligent was
> after two lunches with Dortmund unable, in fact he was
> quite unable to play respectable chess and the younger
> Alexi after living with Murphy
> was observed to be grey in the gills
> through a presumed loss of vitality. . . .
>
> (Canto XXXV).

These 'prosaic' passages should be related not to the journalist's but to Flaubert's prose; Flaubert's alternations in paragraph length, and his variations of sentence length within paragraphs, correspond to the strophic structure of verse. Here the phrasing is as carefully controlled, the line-endings as suavely played against the sprawl of the syntax, as anywhere in the poem. The verse has a degree of formal being exactly adequate to the world it mirrors. There is no reason

why a public that has gotten as far as *vers libre* should continue a last-ditch insistence that it be canorous.

The 'action' of a Flaubert novel, we were saying, consists
of the progression of tensions among its items: rooms, streets,
men, gestures, speeches, cigarettes. The 'plot' in the usual
sense, whose unit is not the phrase but the chapter, can as we
have indicated, by a bad translator's or reader's levelling of
component perceptions to the status of identical bricks, be
made to seem hopelessly bald. Its aesthetic importance is
simply that of a major rhythm, like the fast-slow-fast of a
sonata. There is no intrinsic reason why it should possess
paraphrasable status. Thackeray, as Ford notes, had discovered (though he did little with) the possibility of a novel
without a hero. It was Pound's discovery that the logical end
of conscientious rendering was an epic without (in the usual
sense) a plot. (The exiguous plot of *Ulysses* has often been
complained of.) In the *Cantos* the place of a plot is taken by
interlocking large-scale rhythms of recurrence, whose principles we shall investigate more closely in chapter 29.

Once more, a cinematic example may help us consolidate
these ideas. In a 1929 essay reprinted in *Film Form* (pp. 45–
63), Eisenstein observes that a literally rendered plot (in
Aristotelian terms, the equation of *praxis* and *mythos*) is
intrinsically barren:

'For instance, murder on the stage has a purely physio-
logical effect. Photographed in *one* montage-piece, it can
function simply as *information*, as a sub-title.

Hence the least imaginative director, like the lowliest hack
purveyor of Amazing Stories, finds himself toying with
ideogram:

'*Emotional* effect begins only with the reconstruction of the
event in montage fragments, each of which will summon a
certain association—the sum of which will be an all-embracing
complex of emotional feeling. Traditionally:

1. A hand lifts a knife.
2. The eyes of the victim open suddenly.
3. His hands clutch the table.

4. The knife is jerked up.

5. The eyes blink involuntarily.

6. Blood gushes.

7. A mouth shrieks.

8. Something drips onto a shoe . . .

and similar film clichés.'

Clichés, certainly. But nevertheless these juxtaposed close-ups are an adumbration of ideogrammic *rendering*. Eisenstein's next observation carries us from the analytic to the synthetic:

'Nevertheless, in regard to the *action as a whole, each fragment-piece* is almost *abstract*. The more differentiated they are, the more abstract they become, provoking no more than a certain association.

As so often in Eisenstein's theorizing, the writing (or perhaps the translation) is hardly adequate to the insight. The implications of 'abstract' and 'association' are unfortunate; they turn our attention from the quiddity of the image to its penumbra. The insight, however, retains its value. There is no reason why the successive images, as they confront us, should be dominated by the schema of a familiar abstract action. We needn't be numbingly aware of a plot, of whose details we are receiving successive veri-similar close-up views. As the cinematic treatment increases in imaginative power, the obsession of verisimilitude retreats; the images take on independent force, in a concatenation of perpetually inflected surprise. In *Potemkin*, Eisenstein cut close-ups of statuary into a cannonade:

'In the thunder of the *Potemkin's* guns, a marble lion leaps up, in protest against the bloodshed on the Odessa steps. Composed of three shots of three stationary marble lions at the Alupka Palace in the Crimea; a sleeping lion, an awakening lion, a rising lion.'

The logical independence and aesthetic interdependence of successive images leads in the next paragraph to Plotless Epic:

'Quite logically, the thought occurs: could not the same thing be accomplished more productively by not following the plot so slavishly, but by materializing the idea, the impression, of *Murder* through a free accumulation of associative material? For the most important task is still to establish the idea of murder—the feeling of murder, as such. The plot is no more than a device without which one isn't yet capable of telling something to the spectator!'

The fragmenting of the aesthetic idea into allotropic images, as first theorized by Mallarmé, was a discovery whose importance for the artist corresponds to that of nuclear fission for the physicist. Plot, in the Dickensian sense, is obsolete. It would have been easy, and quite redundant, to weave into the *Cantos* a story; in fact, glimmerings of an autobiographical thread may be discerned, though its importance is not immediate and its function *vis-à-vis* the other material largely contrapuntal. Brought more to the foreground, it would be merely an irrelevant scaffolding, of one possible kind. Similarly, a philosophical system, a chronological or geographical ordering of events, even *progression d'effet* turning round a psychological climax after the manner of *The Waste Land*, would be no more relevant to the *Cantos* than a chain of anagrams.

Chapter 28

DIGRESSION—
FRENCH PROSE

and for all that old Ford's conversation was better,
consisting in *res* non *verba*
despite William's anecdotes, in that Fordie
never dented an idea for a phrase's sake.

Before tackling the replacement of paraphrasable plot by rhythms of recurrence, it will be well to relate the *Cantos* still more closely to the discoveries made in the nineteenth century by the writers of French prose. Pound is as closely indebted to Stendhal and Flaubert as Eliot to the French symbolists (who were also indebted to Flaubert). The nineteenth-century discoveries about the art of charging words were made in France, and primarily in prose. It is impossible to make sense either of Pound or of the bearings of any contemporary English verse without appreciating this fact.

Pound began to make use of these discoveries some years before the *Cantos* got under way. The epigrams in *Lustra* for example—

EPITAPH
Leucis, who intended a Grand Passion
Ends with a willingness-to-oblige.

—have much in common with the two-line paragraphs that punctuate *Bouvard et Pécuchet*:

'—Nous ferons tout ce qui nous plaira! nous laisserons pousser notre barbe!'

263

The transplantation of the French novel to English was undertaken, early in the present century, by Ford Madox Ford and Joseph Conrad. Ford's part in this process is still grievously underrated. Conrad possessed certainly the higher creative voltage. He was, however, as Dr. Leavis has remarked, in many respects a simple soul; it was Ford who was able to disengage technique from intuition sufficiently to make useful statements about narrative procedures. Hence Pound has left it on record that critical light, in the years immediately pre-war in London, shone from Ford Madox Ford (Hueffer) in so far as it shone on writing at all.

'The revolution of the word began so far as it affected the men who were of my age in London in 1908, with the LONE whimper of Ford Madox Hueffer. His more pliant disciples were Flint, Goldring, and D. H. Lawrence. Hueffer (Ford) read Flaubert and Maupassant in a way that George Moore did not. Impressionism meant for him something it did not for Mr Symons. . . .

'Madox Ford's aim toward the just word was right in his personal circle of reference. He was dealing mainly with visual and oral perceptions, whereinto come only colours, concrete forms, tones of voice, modes of gesture.

'OUT of these you build sane ideogram. You build your congeries, in validity.'

Polite Essays, pp. 50, 53.

This is not simply the post facto wisdom of 1935. As long ago as 1914, Pound was writing:

'It is he [Ford] who has insisted, in the face of a still Victorian press, upon the importance of good writing as opposed to the opalescent word, the rhetorical tradition. Stendhal had said, and Flaubert, de Maupassant and Turgenev had proved, that "prose was the higher art"—at least their prose.'

Polite Essays, p. 57.

Fourteen years later he prescribed specifically:

'. . . no man can now write really good verse unless he knows

Stendhal and Flaubert. Or, let us say, *Le Rouge et le Noir*, the first half of *La Chartreuse*, *Madame Bovary*, *L'Education*, *Les Trois Contes*, *Bouvard et Pécuchet*. To put it perhaps more strongly, he will learn more about the art of charging words from Flaubert than he will from the floribund sixteenth-century dramatists.'

Polite Essays, p. 180.

Pound of course learned directly from Stendhal and Flaubert; the present discussion may however be short-circuited, as to essentials, via Conrad and Ford.

FIRST: 'good writing as opposed to the opalescent word, the rhetorical tradition.'

SECOND: the time-shift.

It is impossible to give a fool-proof definition of 'good writing' in the sense delimited above. Pound's exclusion of 'the rhetorical tradition' may be especially prone to misunderstanding. We are *not* left with 'simple' Hemingwayese—actually, like its parent Steinese, a very highly figured and conventional language indeed, though corresponding perfectly to certain emotional states. Any metaphoric or syntactic audacity is admissible if it reveals the subject. The 'purest' style is a massive opalescent cliché if it doesn't. When the doctrine of decorum was in everyone's bones, the ground-bass, so to speak, of the manners, speech, worship, and writing of a civilization, the rhetoricians' tables of figures were useful educators' tools and compilations of practical wisdom. When the sense of decorum thickened, the vernacular manual of rhetoric became the dictionary of a dead language. It is seldom remembered that ethics and psychology were among the subjects taught as branches of rhetoric, and that the rhetoricians' figures, asyndeton, apostrophe, and the like, were actually the compressed essences of social and psychological situations, as Freud rediscovered apropos of the techniques of wit. (All of Freud's witty devices are listed in Cicero's *De Oratore*.) Joyce is the first English writer since Pope who has known how to make use of classical rhetoric.

The more mature a tradition, the more a Shakespeare can

265

concentrate his studies and energies on the unexplored, the less he has to find out all over again for himself; the more, also, he can take for granted in his audience. (The contemporary poet is positively hindered by the notions his audience entertains of serious ideas.) On the other hand, a complicated technical tradition is a serious menace to navigation when it goes derelict owing to the death of the perception that steered it. Manipulating the machinery comes to be mistaken for writing. The most familiar English example is the eighteenth- and nineteenth-century Miltonic cult.

Stendhal discarded the French equivalent of English Miltonics: 'poetry with its fustian à la Louis XIV.' Flaubert followed him. Ford and Conrad (and Joyce independently), knowing their Flaubert virtually by heart, undertook to clean up English prose as it existed at the opening of the present century—the forms of language utterly out of touch with any conceivable perception. Their remedy depended on slow and tireless honesty. Verbal manifestations were scrutinized and revised, from a standpoint of multi-lingual erudition, to bring them into the closest possible contact with situations as really intuited, and with things as seen, heard, smelt, and touched. *Ulysses*, like *Madame Bovary*, was seven years in the writing. Ford and Conrad spent nearly as long, while Joyce was still writing *Dubliners*, collaborating on *Romance*. It is unlikely that without those years of collaboration on what proved a wonderfully diverting but 'unimportant' book, either *Nostromo* or *Heart of Darkness* or Ford's two volumes of memoirs and the Tietjens novels would have been possible. This is from the first page of *Romance*:

'The black cane that had made the tap, tap, tap dangled by a silken cord from the hand whose delicate blue-veined, wrinkled wrist ran back into a foam of lawn ruffles. The other hand paused in the act of conveying a pinch of snuff to the nostrils of the hooked nose that had, on the skin stretched tight over the bridge, the polish of old ivory; the elbow pressing the black cocked hat against the side; the legs, one bent, the other bowing a little back—this was the attitude of Seraphina's father.'

The labour that set those details in relation to one another was identical in kind with the labour that adjusted the rhythms and images of a twenty-line passage in the *Cantos*. The language exists to present the man seen. And it *is* the language and not a stock response of the reader's that does present the man. His age and sober splendour are given in one vivid closeup of 'the hand whose delicate blue-veined, wrinkled wrist ran back into a foam of lawn ruffles'. Pound's verse owes much to these researches. His Lotus-eaters are

Borne over the plain, recumbent,
The right arm cast back,
   the right wrist for a pillow,
The left hand like a calyx,
Thumb held against finger, the third,
The first fingers petal'd up, the hand as a lamp,
A calyx.   (Canto XX).

The interest of the Imagists in visual images has been over-emphasized, largely through the resistance engendered by the unfamiliarity, for most readers, of this sort of snapshot. The English reader has a long-standing habit, isolated at last in our time by the campaign against Miltonic surge and thunder, of apprehending all verse not visually but viscerally, reading 'for the sound', drowsing over

  The moan of doves in immemorial elms,
   And murmuring of innumerable bees,

or feeling his entrails shoved about by caesurae. He is conditioned to feeling the effect of lines like

   Night's candles are burnt out, and jocund day
   Stands tip-toe on the misty mountain-tops

through the interaction of 'jocund', 'tip-toe,' and 'misty', without his having to *see* anything, Shakespeare's kind of optical particularity being overlaid with other devices to which the receiving set is better attuned.

Of *phanopoeia*, 'the casting of images on the visual imagination', the known maximum, according to Pound, was attained by the Chinese:

By the gate now, the moss is grown, the different mosses,
Too deep to clear them away!
The leaves fall early this autumn, in wind.
The paired butterflies are already yellow with August
Over the grass in the West garden . . .

Cathay: The River-Merchant's Wife: A Letter.

The red and green kingfishers
    flash between the orchids and clover,
One bird casts its gleam on another . . .

Cathay: Sennin Poem by Kakuhaku.

Spenserian watercolour, the accretion of detail about a lay figure (the method of description notoriously employed by Scott) differs utterly from this realization of quiddities. So does the other main kind of English non-auditory imagery, the argumentative simile—Satan's spear bearing the same proportion to a ship's mast as the mast would to a wand. It was by way of the Impressionist novel in the French manner that phanopoeia finally got a toehold in the English tradition: notably at the hands of Conrad, whose aim was 'above all, to make you see'.

*   *   *

To no technical device does Ford recur more frequently in his notes on the novel than the time-shift. There was also no device that he employed more freely, or with more consummate skill. The function of the time-shift is to do away with the plot—plot in the sense of a linear sequence of events. The 'story' is broken up into a number of scenes, conversations, impressions, etc., which function as poetic images and are freely juxtaposed for maximum intensity. In *The Good Soldier* and in Ford's various volumes of memoirs this device reaches a very high level of development. Illustration is difficult at less than chapter length; but here is a paragraph from Ford's memoir of Conrad, exhibiting two characteristic sutures:

'The writer exclaimed: Look! *Look!* . . . His companion unfolded the paper. The announcement went across two columns in black, leaded caps . . . *SUDDEN DEATH OF JOSEPH CONRAD.* They were demolishing an antiquated waiting-room on the opposite platform, three white-dusty men with pick-axes: a wall was all in broken zigzags. The writer said to himself: "C'est le mur d'un silence eternel qui descend devant vous!" There descended across the dusty wall a curtain of moonlight, thrown across by the black shadows of oak-trees. We were on a verandah that had a glass roof. Under the glass roof climbèd passion-flowers, and vine tendrils strangled them. We were sitting in deck chairs. It was one o'clock in the morning. Conrad was standing in front of us, talking. Talking on and on in the patches of moonlight and patches of shadow from the passion flowers and vines! The little town in which we were dominated the English channel from a low hill-top. He was wearing a dark reefer coat and white trousers.'

The drama of these juxtapositions needs no comment. Neither does its similarity to the method of the *Cantos*. The interested reader should examine *The Good Soldier*, a revolutionary book when it appeared in 1913, the year before *Ulysses* was begun. (Joyce's dramatic juxtapositions of mood and style have of course been complained of from 1922 to the present.)

What deprived Ford of revolutionary impact on the *avant-garde* (his failure to connect with the world of trade reviewers was rather a matter of literary politics) was the pre-Raphaelite elegance that muffled his discoveries. The time-shift, a pregnant dramatic device at the hands of Joyce and Pound, he passed off lightly as verisimilitude: the mind remembering in various, unordered pictures. That is why the time-shift gives his volumes of memoirs, and novels like *The Good Soldier* where he employs the device of a protagonist dazedly remembering, not so much an intensely dramatic as a genial and whimsical air. But the psychological pretext had only to be chiselled away from these books to yield a sequence of intensely illuminated scenes and images after the manner of the *Cantos*. This step Ford never took. Probably it would have offended his notion of good manners.

So much for major form, in which Ford, and Conrad to a

lesser degree, reached the threshold of later developments. In considering the dramatic salience of lesser detail they were less inhibited. The long and highly important section on novelistic technique on pages 179–215 of *Joseph Conrad: A Personal Remembrance* contains many useful remarks like the following:

'The most that the normal person carries away of a conversation after even a couple of hours is just a salient or characteristic phrase or two, and a mannerism of the speaker. . . . By the use of indirect locutions, together with the rendering of the effects of other portions of speech, you can get a great deal more into a given space. There is a type of reader that likes what is called conversations—but that type is rather the reader in an undeveloped state than the reader who has read much.'

This searchlight should be turned on the much-criticized Jefferson-Adams Cantos (**XXXI–XXXIV, LXII–LXXI**), which are put together out of passages like this:

'No man in America then believed me'
    J. A. on his Davila, recollecting.
Be bubbled out of their liberties by a few large names,
    Hume, probably not having read them.
Whether the king of the Franks had a negative on that
        assembly
'forward young man' wrote the critic
    on an unsigned J. A. (J. A. being then 53 and vice
                      president)
Pharamond on the banks of the Sala
    here again the french jargon
    not one clear idea what they mean by 'all authority'
                (Canto **LXVIII**)

Characteristic turns of speech and the torsos of quoted sentences are here built into an image of the quality of Adams' perceptions and the nature of his concern for definition. The superior immediacy of this method over prose panegyric (an immediacy exemplified in the richly informative anecdote of the critic who wrote 'Forward young man' on an anonymous vice-presidential document) is its ample justification for the reader who is willing to go slowly and ponder. It is in any case only to the reader willing to take in concrete detail that poetry is addressed.

In another place, Ford remarks that, with obvious exceptions, 'no speech of one character should ever answer the speech that goes before it.' As usual he fishes for psychological justification: 'This is almost invariably the case in real life, where few people listen, because they are always preparing their own next speeches.' Here again Ford's instinct served him better than his concern for verisimilitude would admit. As he himself later remarks of an imaginary example,

'If you gave all these long speeches one after the other you might be aware of a certain dullness when you re-read that *compte-rendu.* . . . But if you carefully broke up petunias, statuary, and flower-show motifs and put them down in little shreds one contrasting with the other, you would arrive at something much more coloured, animated, life-like and interesting and you would convey a profoundly significant lesson as to the self-engrossment of humanity.'

(p. 190).

Actually, this technique puts into the poet's hands means of achieving virtually simultaneous insights into a theme from diverse points of view: an adumbration of the ideogrammic method itself. The *Pisan Cantos* are full on this principle of 'little shreds one contrasting with the other':

and in Mt Segur there is wind space and rain space
  no more an altar to Mithras
from il triedro to the Castellaro
  the olives grey over grey holding walls
and their leaves turn under Scirocco
  la scalza: Io son' la luna
  and they have broken my house
the huntress in broken plaster keeps watch no longer
tempora, tempora, and as to mores

(Canto LXXVI).

271

A final principle of poetic life is given by Ford eight pages later; illustrating his remark that 'a good—an interesting—style will be found to consist in a constant succession of tiny, unobservable surprises', he writes,

'The catalogue in an ironmonger's store is uninteresting as literature because things in it are all classified and thus obvious: the catalogue of a farm sale is more interesting because things in it are contrasted. No one would for long read: Nails, drawn wire, ½ inch, per lb. . . . ; nails do., ¾ inch, per lb. . . . ; nails, do., inch, per lb. . . . But it is often not disagreeable to read desultorily "*Lot* 267. Pair rabbit gins. *Lot* 268, Antique powder flask. *Lot* 269, Malay Kris. *Lot* 270, Set of six sporting prints by Herring. *Lot* 271, Silver caudle cup . . . , for that, as far as it goes, has the quality of surprise.'

It will be observed that a particular kind of house assembled to the whim of a particular kind of owner, the focus of a delimited way of life, emerges from the five items in Ford's imaginary auction catalogue. The items, in other words, are not wholly incongruous. This is, once more, ideogram. In drawing attention to their power to excite attention Ford is testifying again to Aristotle's account of the essential poetic activity as the swift perception of relations among apparently incongruous things. We mentioned some chapters ago the seeming disparity, within a powerful but invisible order, of Pound's materials, and suggested that only the cement of habit prevented an analogous dynamism being discerned in, say, Wordsworth, whom hostile critics, as Mr. Eliot observes, found difficult but called silly. Ford's paragraph illustrates strikingly the extraordinary evocativeness of a few juxtaposed nouns, and provides some insight into Mr. Eliot's celebrated dictum about poetry communicating before it is understood. Before we are equipped for specific recognition of a single allusion, we can sense the quality of the white and radiant world that emerges from such lines as the following:

Cloud over mountain, mountain over the cloud
I surrender neither the empire nor the temples
        plural

nor the constitution nor yet the city of Dioce

each one in his god's name

as by Terracina rose from the sea Zephyr behind her

      and from her manner of walking

                    as had Anchises

    till the shrine be again white with marble

    till the stone eyes look again seaward

                  The wind is part of the process

                  The rain is part of the process

and the Pleiades set in her mirror

Kuanon, this stone bringeth sleep;

     offered the wine bowl

            grass nowhere out of place

              (Canto LXXIV).[1]

If, to cite Mr. Eliot for the third time, it is the supreme difficulty of criticism to make the facts generalize themselves it is nevertheless very nearly the whole business of poetry. That done, all things else will be added.

---

[1] This is good a place as any to note the principle of Pound's ellipses. Each of the fragmentary gists and piths gives prepositional or participial leverage to an unspecified verb, so that the whole comes alive with an urgency of generalized making and doing. 'And from her manner of walking' implies the way Venus will be *known*; 'till the stone eyes look again seaward' something complexly creative must be *done*. Fenollosa's derivation of all parts of speech from the verb should be closely studied. Pound has taken this hint to create, by hanging ellipses on generally inactive parts of speech, a major technique of poetic tension.

Chapter 29

GREAT BASS

Sed et universus quoque ecclesie populus,
All rushed out and built the duomo,
Went as one man without leaders
And the perfect measure took form.

The ways in which the facts generalize themselves in the *Cantos*, especially the later ones, into steady patterns of athletic beauty deserve, it goes without saying, continuous particular study. The present writer has derived much enlightenment from his attempts to select illustrations from the Pisan sequences. The five lines one would like to quote prove to demand the preceding three, and so on backwards through half a Canto. Sheer architectonics, despite the superficial fragmentary look of the page, can scarcely have been carried much further in poetry. Exemplification is unwieldy; a few hints will have to serve. The Elpenor passage in Canto I—

But first Elpenor came, our friend Elpenor,
Unburied, cast on the wide earth,
Limbs that we left in the house of Circe,
Unwept, unwrapped in sepulchre, since toils urged other.

*   *   *

'But thou, O King, I bid remember me, unwept, unburied,
'Heap up mine arms, be tomb by sea-bord, and inscribed:
'*A man of no fortune, and with a name to come.*
'And set my oar up, that I swung mid fellows.'

—releases certain potentials that are only realized when,

nineteen cantos later, after the myths of passion, the Malatesta
episode, the merchants, Kung, inferno, war, muck-raking, and
the vision of the Lotus-eaters, we hear from the chorus of

> the clear bones, far down,
Thousand on thousand.
> 'What gain with Odysseus,
'They that died in the whirlpool
'And after many vain labours,
'Living by stolen meat, chained to the rowingbench,
'That he should have a great fame
> 'And lie by night with the goddess?
'Their names are not written in bronze
> 'Nor their rowing sticks set with Elpenor's;
'Nor have they mound by sea-bord.
> 'That saw never the olives under Spartha
'With the leaves green and then not green,
> 'The click of light in their branches;
'That saw not the bronze hall nor the ingle
'Nor lay there with the queen's waiting-maids,
'Nor had they Circe to couch-mate, Circe Titania,
'Nor had they meats of Kalüpso
'Or her silk skirts brushing their thighs.
'Give! What were they given?
> Ear-wax.
'Poison and ear-wax,
> and a salt grave by the bull-field,
'*neson amumona*, their heads like sea crows in the foam,
'Black splotches, sea-weed under lightning;
'Canned beef of Apollo, ten cans for a boat load.'
> (Canto **XX**).

One dimension of this passage may be established by contrasting its surging unanimity with the later muted lament
from the stone-pits:

> 'Sero, sero . . .
'Nothing we made, we set nothing in order,
'Neither house nor the carving,

'And what we thought had been thought for too long;
'Our opinion not opinion in evil
'But opinion borne for too long.
'We have gathered a sieve full of water.'

(Canto **XXV**).

These dragging reiterated negatives, the double 'nothing', the hopeless 'thought' that has already and for too long been thought, the threefold nullity of 'opinion', are immediately set off by

notes and the chorus
Moving, the young fauns: Pone metum,
Metum, nec deus laedit;

but the major contrast is with the chorus of the drowned mariners five cantos earlier: 'heavy voices, heavy sound' counterpointing the gathering energy of protest of the drowned mariners taking up their chant by thousands. Clearly, there are degrees of failure.

The precision of definition achieved for these and each of the hundreds of other modes of being defined in the *Cantos* should not blind us to their mutual irradiation. It is too easy to be aware only of a series of disjunct medallions hung on a wall. But in this timeless bas-relief a complex intellectual drama is enacted. Denial of Pound's dramatic sense proceeds from the unaccustomed absence of a kind of stimulus he is being careful not to give: the sort of *progression d'effet* that relegates the greater proportion of the words to supporting or ancillary status, preparations for climaxes, to be submerged by the ultimate epiphany. To keep the reader in breathless anticipation (the secret of professional narrative) is to keep him from paying comprehensive attention to what is going on *now*. We embark on a long poem expecting it to take us somewhere; much of the difficulty of reading *Hamlet* is due to the conflict between this expectation, the practised reader's assurance that the significance of this or that speech or scene will be cleared up later, and his underlying awareness, borne upon him by the steady local intensity of the writing, that he must pause *now* and reflect, that what is missed at the instant of encounter will not later be restored. For all the components to claim equivalent importance is probably fatal to a satisfactory dramatic experience, as the critiques of *Hamlet* illustrate. Mr. Eliot is probably right in ascribing this unsatisfactoriness to Shakespeare's imperfect grasp of the emotions from which he started, and a consequent derangement of his architectonic skill; every scene and speech seems striving to be the definitive formulation of the play.

In the *Cantos*, on the other hand, while everything may be said to be as important as everything else, no action, single or multiple, is being offered the reader for dramatic participation. This is not to say that the experience of reading the poem is not continuously exciting. But there is no sweep up to and away from a climactic moment or symbol. Preliminary motifs are not discarded. The reader must remember all things and contemplate all things in a simultaneous present. What would seem to be inhuman demands so made are largely abrogated by the internal reverberations of similar themes, cunningly disposed throughout the poem.

Lists of the materials employed, as made by several commentators, make notoriously little sense. It is in the particular articulation given them by the poet that the materials have life. We have pointed out three mutually reverberating passages; their interrelations are controlled by such devices as the slowly gathering rhythm of the sailor-chorus:

> And beneath: the clear bones, far down
> Thousand on thousand.
>> 'What gain with Odysseus,
> 'They that died in the whirlpool
> 'And after many vain labours,
> 'Living by stolen meat, chained to the rowingbench,
> 'That he should have a great fame
>> 'And lie by night with the goddess?

Out of the sea the chant gathers momentum; its rhythmic definition is only fully achieved in the last two lines just quoted. And it is against this gathering impetus of stamp and sway that the 'heavy voices' of the stone-pits and the hurried unorchestrated colloquy with the single shade of Elpenor are to be weighed: one lost man whose personal doom ('I fell against the buttress') admits particular personal contact and recompense ('Heap up mine arms'); thousands on thousands of nameless dead achieving, in counterpoint with the hero's delights, a community of impersonal lamenting emphasis; and the drone of blighted voices without being, betrayed not by personal accident or heroic necessity but by an inner sapless-ness of the will.

The ramifications of a given passage may be pursued in-definitely. The chorus of the drowned seamen protests, in its immediate context, against the passionate drift of the Loto-phagoi, and the Odysseus of whom they are jealous overlaps the world of receptive aesthetic passion ('Circe to couch-mate') and the factive vigours of the Malatesta; 'The poor devils dying of cold, outside Sorano' counterweight the Renaissance exploits as the mariners do the Homeric ones. The seamen's chorus, in fact, makes contact with everything in the preceding *Cantos*: with the shored fragments of antiquarian passion in the first seven cantos, which in turn have affinities with the life of the Lotophagoi; with the Malatesta; with latter-day warfare—

> That's the trick with a crowd,
> > Get 'em into the street and get 'em moving;
> > > (Canto XVI).

with, negatively, commercial and infernal squalor. The Confucian canto presents an intuition of order devoid of such unnecessary deaths, held in tension with an acknowledgment of the autonomy of personal volition and personal doom:

> And Kung said, 'They have all answered correctly,
> 'That is to say, each in his nature.'

The cross-purposes and contretemps that in the actual world attend the incredibly wasteful realization of thought in matter are transposed by this latter dictum into a world of intellection and volition that can usefully encompass every direction of energy.

This last paragraph could hardly be intrinsically lucid without being thirty pages long; the reader is encouraged to check it, phrase by phrase, against his experience of the poem. Whatever formulation he eventually comes to approve, he cannot but be made aware of the weighing of passage against passage as the poem's modus of structural unity.

We have employed the analogy of reverberations running through the text as a means of controlling the steady accretion of material. It is possible to make this analogy more exact. Pound's theory of Great Bass in music throws much light on his poetic practices, and especially on the kind of organization the *Cantos* exhibit. Its rudiments were propounded as early as the preface to the Cavalcanti translations of 1910, a full statement is given in the little *Antheil* volume of 1924 (some sixteen cantos being then written); *Culture* (1938) contains several more comprehensive restatements.

In the *Cavalcanti* preface, we read:

'When we know more of overtones we shall see that the tempo of every masterpiece is absolute, and is exactly set by some further law of rhythmic accord. Whence it should be possible to show that any given rhythm implies about it a complete musical form, fugue, sonata, I cannot say what form, but a form, perfect, complete. *Ergo*, the rhythm set in a line of poetry connotes its symphony, which, had we a little more skill, we could score for orchestra.'

(p. 12).

In the 'Treatise on Harmony' that prefaces the Antheil volume, an intervening investigation of overtones has led to this statement:

'A SOUND OF ANY PITCH, OR ANY COMBINATION OF SUCH SOUNDS, MAY BE FOLLOWED BY A SOUND OF ANY OTHER PITCH, OR ANY COMBINATION OF SUCH SOUNDS, providing the time interval between them is properly gauged; and this is true for ANY SERIES OF SOUNDS, CHORDS OR ARPEGGIOS.

'The limits for practical purposes of music depend solely on our capacity to produce a sound that will last long enough, i.e. remain audible long enough, for the succeeding sound or sounds to catch up, traverse, intersect it.'

(pp. 3–4).

For the performer of music, this means that there is a precise speed at which a given piece *must* be played:

'The wobbling about by deficient musicians, the attempt to give life to a piece by abundant rallentandos and speedings up, results in reduction of all music to one doughy mass and all compositions to the one statement of the performing executant, said wobbly time is due to their NOT divining the real pace of the segment.

The 60, 72, or 84, or 120 per minute is a BASS, or basis. It is the bottom note of the harmony.'

Culture, p. 233.

In a poem the images persist for traversal or intersection in the reader's apprehension, in modalities governed by adroit rhythmic recall or imagistic analogy. For the poet and/or the reader of poetry, it means that the secret of major form consists in the precise adjustment of the intervals between disparate or recurrent themes or items or rhythms. And anything at all may be put into a poem, provided its mode and degree of definition, and its relation with the other things in the poem, be suitably managed.

'. . . Bach, consciously or unconsciously, never thought of using two chords except as parts, integral parts, of a progression, a rhythmic progression.'

Antheil, p. 6.

Pound, quite consciously, never thinks of using two motifs, two blocks of rendering, except as parts, integral parts, of a larger rhythm of juxtaposition and recurrence. This balancing and recurrence of motifs is what holds together single cantos. It also holds together the entire work, the temporarily unfinished condition of which doesn't diminish the structural

280

solidity of the portion existing, any more than the absence of a roof diminishes the interrelation of proportions among cathedral arches. Metaphor, conceived in Aristotle's way as a proportion among proportions, becomes in the *Cantos* the principle of major form. There are final stones to be laid in place, but there is not, as in the de Maupassant short story, a key to be turned in the puzzle-lock on the last page.

'The early students of harmony were so accustomed to think of music as something with a strong lateral or horizontal motion that they never imagined any one, ANY ONE could be stupid enough to think of it as static; it never entered their heads that people would make music like steam ascending from a morass.

'They thought of music as travelling rhythm going through points or barriers of pitch and pitch-combinations.

'They had this concept in their blood, as the oriental has his raga and tala. It simply never occurred to them that people would start with static harmony and stick in that stationary position.

Antheil, p. 5.

Poetry is not to be thought of as a concatenation of thickly-orchestrated *emotions fortes*. Every chord is an integral part of a rhythmic progression—

'—Rhythm—said Stephen—is the first formal esthetic relation of any part to part in any esthetic whole or of an esthetic whole to its part or parts or of any part to the esthetic whole of which it is a part.—'

Portrait of the Artist as a Young Man, p. 241.

The 'scholastic stink' here is part of the comic effect of Joyce's novel: an ingredient in its rhythm. It conduces also to exact if unexciting definition whose implications connect with our present topic. 'Rhythm' in the sense in which Pound is using the term in the Great Bass treatises is not to be thought of merely in short units, in the stamping of feet accompanying a single line.

'Any given rhythm implies about it a complete musical form.' The apparition of Elpenor in Canto I implies certain concomitants, the time for which is not 'right away'. To generalize the case of Elpenor *immediately* in terms of the other lost seamen of that voyage, in terms of the human wreckage of all enterprises, would not only crowd the poem too much, it would suggest far too simple relationships, for example, an insoluble dilemma for the Odyssean figures of the world, a Hamlet's impasse bulking the cost too large to justify any action. For the proper tragic stasis and the inhibition of irrelevant responses, these implications must be postponed for a definite interval, other material must be interposed, we must contemplate other dimensions of the factive personality (Malatesta, the Cid) other sacrifices (Cabestan's heart and the lady's suicide), other debacles (World War), leaders who betray as distinguished from leaders who involve their train in necessary attrition (Cantos XIV–XV), other modalities of order (Zagreus, Nerea, Kung). It demands, precisely, the interposition of nineteen cantos containing just these and no other materials, just so disposed. We hear at last from the chorus of mariners in Canto XX. We wait till Canto XXV, through a descending rhythm of increasing resistance and dispersal of energies, for the second major echo, the chorus from the stone-pits.

This account of large-scale rhythm, a ground-bass not imposed upon but demanded by the particular disjunct materials into which the total aesthetic idea of the *Cantos* has been, so to speak, prismatically fractured for purposes of poetic presentation, has been illustrated from three recurrences of a single theme established in Canto I. A similar account would of course apply to any sequence of motifs one might select. It applies within single cantos, very obviously in the looping recurrences of the Pisan sequence. In Canto LXXVI the modes of consciousness of the opening lines,

And the sun high over horizon hidden in cloud bank
lit saffron the cloud ridge
>   dove sta memora

interrupted by,

'Will' said the Signora Agresti, 'break his political
but not economic system'

recur immediately, indomitable—

But on the high cliff Alcmene,

> Dryas, Hamadryas ac Heliades
> flowered branch and sleeve moving
> Dirce et Ixotta e che fu chiamata Primavera
> in the timeless air,

and persist through modulations, negations, witty juxtapositions—

in the timeless air over the sea-cliffs
'the pride of all our D.T.C. was pistol-packin' Burnes'

to occupy the centre of the Canto in a continuous minor key
of loss and sorrow:

is measured by the *to whom* it happens
    and to what, and if to a work of art
        then to all who have seen and who will not . . .

                    ★ ★ ★

no cloud, but the crystal body
            the tangent formed in the hand's cup
    as live wind in the beech grove
            as strong air amid cypress
                    ★ ★ ★

                    nothing matters but the quality
of the affection—
in the end—that has carved the trace in the mind
dove sta memoria
                    ★ ★ ★

Such excision indicates the continuity of feeling, though it
does violence to the cunning with which these recurrences are
spaced. The entire canto should be examined most carefully.
It will be noted, for example, that in the citations just given

the phrase 'dove sta memoria' occurs in two contexts.[1] The reader presumably knows its source in the Cavalcanti 'Donna mi pregha' canzone:

> In quella parte
> > dove sta memoria
> Prende suo stato
> > sí formato
> > > chome
> Diafan dal lume
> > d'una schuritade

translated by Pound in Canto XXXVI,

> Where memory liveth,
> > it [*love*] takes its state
> Formed like a diafan from light on shade.

'Dove sta memoria'—'where memory liveth'—connected by Cavalcanti, via neoplatonic psychology, with mediaeval light-metaphysics (the sun as source of physical light being analogous with the focus of intellectual *virtu*), is connected by Pound first with the suffusion of clouds by hidden light—

> And the sun high over horizon hidden in cloud bank
> lit saffron the cloud ridge
> > dove sta memora

(memory hypostasized as part of an extra-mental world of forms; memories illuminating present clouds and cankers); then six pages later with the quality of the possessed and personal mental world—

> > > nothing matters but the quality
> of the affection—
> in the end—that has carved the trace in the mind
> dove sta memoria

[1] The inconsistent spelling of 'memoria' in the Canto has troubled some readers; but see above, page 216, footnote. 'Memora' is given marginally as a variant in Pound's editing of the canzone, *Make It New*, p. 364.

(memories as ingredients of the mental make-up, lovely or otherwise, and determined according to the individual's bestowal of affection. Cavalcanti's canzone is of *Amor*, and the entire motif is caught up five cantos later: 'What thou lov'st well shall not be reft from thee.') Between these occurrences of the 'dove sta memoria' motif, and determining both the progression from the physical metaphor to the ethical statement and the weight of emotion carried ultimately by the latter, come literally dozens of other themes, all delimiting 'the quality of the affection'. These groupings are not fortuitous. They are the very texture of the *Cantos*. Everything is weighted by its context, and everything functions as part of the context of everything else. This order is not excogitated. It is the function of a tact, a scrupulous fidelity to the contours of his experience, which in turn registers the intensity wherewith— over how many years!—Pound has contemplated his world of forms:

> As the sculptor sees the form in the air
> before he sets hand to mallet
> and as he sees the in, and the through,
> the four sides.

Chapter 30

CONFUCIUS

The blossoms of the apricot
blow from the east to the west,
And I have tried to keep them from falling.

Pound's Confucian, as distinguished from his ideo-grammic, interests, are sometimes supposed to be a relatively late enthusiasm. The abruptness of the incursion of Chinese history into the *Cantos*, in a section written toward the end of the 1930's, is perhaps responsible for this view. Canto XIII, however, was written in the early '20's, and a letter quoted in Margaret Anderson's autobiography (*My Thirty Years' War*) displays Pound, about the time of the first drafts of the early *Cantos*, offering *The Little Review* an essay on Confucius.

These chance data are put before the reader to offset the frequent assertion that the author of *A Draft of XXX Cantos* had nothing but a rigorous aestheticism to sustain his long poem. There would be no difficulty in showing that the ethos of the *Cantos* is Confucian from the very first, or that, as our juxtaposition of Confucius and the Imagist Manifesto has implied, Pound's conception of aesthetic honesty showed from the first an intrinsic alignment with concepts of personal and governmental honesty, and with inspection of the moral and emotional quality of cultures and civilizations.

Those who demand most loudly some paraphrasable principle of order in the early Cantos are the same who complain of the didacticism of the later ones. These matters may be set in a less confusing relation by considering some paragraphs from an important essay of 1935:

'No man who is building anything more than a suburban villa can be expected to have his construction always on the market, always finished, with all the scaffoldings taken down. . . .

'At 50 one cannot make any complete statement without reference to details already set in order. "Ut doceat, ut moveat, ut delectet." This classification I got from a certain Agricola, who presumably had it of antiquity. Without this "in partes tres" I see no very sane criticism.

' "Doceat, moveat" should be fused in the delectet in any great work of art. Separate, they belong to action and as action they pass in time, with the day or the hour contingent. The need of teaching goes when the scholar has learned, the need of moving, with the mass action intended. But begun at the wrong end or hind end, the delectet is prone to mean mere literature of escape.'

Polite Essays, pp. 49–50.

On an earlier page (33) we find this cross-light:

'Dante wrote his poem to MAKE PEOPLE THINK, just as definitely as Swinburne wrote a good deal of his poetry to tear the pants off the Victorian era and to replace the Albert Memorial by Lampascus.'

These statements do not contradict Pound's earlier remark that

'In writing poems, the author must use his *image* because he sees it or feels it, *not* because he thinks he can use it to back up some creed or some system of economics.'

Gaudier-Brzeska, p. 99.

There is nothing to prevent the human dynamics of the creed or the system of economics being seen and felt. The Bank of Siena (Cantos XLII–XLIV) captured Pound's imagination. So did the correspondence of Jefferson and Adams, and the philosophy of Confucius. What is fatal to poetry is the intrusion (as in *The Princess* or *The Dynasts*) of uncorrelated formulae, apprehended only at the level of formula, clung to by a portion only of the author's mind in satisfaction of some unexplored emotional need.

The emotional exploration that underlay *Personae* corresponds to a Confucian injunction. So does the concern for precise observation and verbal exactness that becomes strikingly manifest with the *Lustra* volume.

'Intelligence that comes from sincerity is called nature or inborn talent; sincerity produced by reason is called education, but sincerity [this activity which defines words with precision] will create intelligence as if carved with a knife-blade, and the light of reason will produce sincerity as if cut clean with a scalpel.'

Unwobbling Pivot, III-xxi.

We have spoken of Pound's conviction of the intrinsic importance of the poet, as custodian of the word, to society, and of his conviction of the automatic leavening function of any honestly directed activity. In the *Unwobbling Pivot* we read,

'[The sincere man] concentrates in a pervading study, searches benevolently as if he were watching over a rice field, he looks straight into his own thoughts, he clarifies the just distinctions (between one thing or category and another), and continues thus with vigour.'

(II-xx-19).

There can be no doubt of Pound's passionate conviction of the utility of Confucian doctrine. 'Confucius is more concerned with the necessities of government, and of governmental administration than any other philosopher.' On the other hand, 'Greek philosophic thought is utterly irresponsible. It is at no point impregnated with a feeling for the whole people.' Having characterized the latter as 'mainly highbrow discussion of ideas among small groups of consciously superior persons', he quotes from the preface to Rackham's edition of Aristotle's *Politics*:

'Hence the tendency to think of the End not as the sum of the Goods, but as one Good which is the Best. Man's welfare is thus ultimately found to consist not in the employment of all his faculties in due proportion, but only in the activity of the highest faculty, the "theoretic" intellect.'

Culture, pp. 29, 30, 342.

It is here that Pound detects the seed of the 'schismatic tendency' symbolized by Blake's Urizen and by the 'Split Man' in Wyndham Lewis' *Apes of God*. Confucius on the other hand, 'and his interlocutors live in a responsible world, they think for the whole social order.'[1] Hence—

> better gift can no man make to a nation
>   than the sense of Kung fu Tseu
>   who was called Chung Ni
> nor in historiography nor in making anthologies
>
> (Canto LXXVI).

These are the components 'doceat, moveat,' without which 'the delectet is prone to mean mere literature of escape', For the filling out of the allusions in the *Cantos* the reader is referred to Pound's translations of the Confucian texts. All that is proposed in the rest of this chapter is illustration of a few of the points of contact between the Chinese doctrines and Pound's undertaking in his long poem.

From the point of view of poetic practice, perhaps the most important hookup can be sensed in the following group of citations:

(1) 'What heaven has disposed and sealed is called the inborn nature. The realization of this nature is called the process. The clarification of this process (the understanding or making intelligible this process) is called education.

'You do not depart from the process even for an instant. What you depart from is not the process. Hence the man

[1] Contrast the Greek epic of venturesome individuality (Canto I) with the Chinese intuition of total, solar, religious, communal, and personal harmony (Canto LII). These are two of the main axes of reference in the poem.

who keeps rein on himself looks straight into his own heart at the things wherewith there is no trifling: he attends seriously to things unheard.'

Unwobbling Pivot, I-i-1, 2.

(2) 'No man who is building anything more than a suburban villa can be expected to have his construction always on the market, always finished, with all the scaffoldings taken down. . . . At 50, one cannot make any complete statement without reference to details already set in order.'

Polite Essays, p. 49.

(3) 'All poetic language is the language of exploration. Since the beginning of bad writing, writers have used images as ornaments. The point of Imagism is that it does not use images as *ornaments*. The image is itself the speech. The image is the word beyond formulated language.

'I once saw a small child go to an electric light switch and say "Mamma, can I *open* the light?" She was using the age-old language of exploration. The language of art. It was a sort of metaphor, but she was not using it as ornamentation.

'One is tired of ornamentations, they are all a trick, and any sharp person can learn them.'

Gaudier-Brzeska, p. 102.

(4) 'Great works of art . . . cause form to come into being. By "the image" I mean such an equation; not an equation of mathematics, not something about *a*, *b*, and *c* having something to do with form, but about *sea*, *cliffs*, *night*, having something to do with mood.

'The image is not an idea. It is a radiant node or cluster; it is what I can, and must perforce, call a VORTEX, from which, and through which, and into which, ideas are constantly rushing.'

Gaudier-Brzeska, p. 106.

(5) 'When you don't understand it, let it alone. This is the copy-book maxim whereagainst sin prose philosophers, though it is explicit in Kung on spirits.

'The mythological expression permits this. It permits an

expression of intuition without denting the edges or shaving off the nose and ears of a verity.'

Culture, p. 127.

The general provenance of some of these we have met before. No. 3, metaphor as exploration, we have discussed apropos of ideogram. No. 4 is the 'objective correlative'. The reader should have no difficulty in seeing how these two principles, exploration of experience and consolidation of imagery, point forward to the claim made for poetry, myth, or image, as an organic statement capable of yielding moral and emotional nourishment, rather than a propositional cross-section of reality (No. 5). He should also notice how statements (1) and (2) are connected with the problems of artistic sincerity.

What is common to all five of these observations is the notion of organic unfolding, personal in (1), ideological in (2), linguistic in (3), and aesthetic in (4). No. 5 does not label so readily; 'mythological expression' may be understood at the level of philosophy, religion, psychology, group culture, or major poetry.

'Organic unfolding' may be defined at various levels. Most obviously, a historical process is postulated. A process unfolding in time enters the poem with Canto 53, and Cantos 53–71 comprise the most important part of the work.

'What heaven has disposed and sealed is called the inborn nature. The realization of this nature is called the process.'

In the life of a civilization heaven disposes and seals in co-operation with the sage, the city-founder, the framers of the constitution. A nation, like a poem or a child, has literally a time of conception; its history consists of the realization of an initial vision from which it will depart at its peril. 'Kung is to China as is water to fishes;' Cantos 53–61 trace the dynastic lessons elsewhere summed up by Pound as follows:

'The dynasties Han, Tung, Sung, Ming rose on the Confucian idea; it is inscribed in the lives of the great emperors, Tai Tsong, Kao Tseu, Hong Vou, another Tai Tsong, and

Kang Hi. When the idea was not held to, decadence super-
vened.'

Cantos 62–71 exhibit John Adams as the Great Emperor of
America, registering in a hundred writings and actions a
detailed concept of national probity which unfolds in time
(Cantos 31–4, 37) until the Civil War blots it from men's minds
(see Appendix 3 below). The Confucian vision, the American
constitution, an aesthetic concept ('as the sculptor sees the
form in the air'), a volitional manifestation, are all *trouvailles*,
innovations not to be violated ('And Kung said "Respect a
child's faculties from the moment it inhales the clear air" ');
the poet who compromises with the right word, the man who
does not 'abandon every clandestine egoism and letch toward
things extraneous to the real man in order to realize to the
full the true root', the Emperor who allows himself to be 'had
by the eunuchs', the President who puts the Constitution in
jeopardy, perform parallel acts of treason.

It will be seen from this how Pound's view of history is
continuous with his view of poetry, how both find confirmation in his study of Confucius and how the presence of history
in his major poem is the reverse of accidental. Noting once
more the stress, private and public, on the quality of implicit
wholeness at whatever point a cross-section is taken, combined with the quality of growth, of exploration, of there
being always something still to come, we may develop further
these themes as they touch the poet *qua* poet. At the level of
aesthetic perception it is now becoming commonly recognized
that integrity and development are not antithetical notions.
We are accustomed to line after line being resonant, cadenced,
in a sense complete in itself, without being equatable with the
whole poem. We are accustomed to the notion that a scene
out of *Hamlet* makes good reading in isolation, and to the
contrasting notion that no scene or passage is really intelligible without reference to the whole play; nor the play excerpted from the entire output of Shakespeare, or from the
morphologies of 'the mind of Europe . . . which abandons
nothing en route'. It is possible, that is, to intuit the principles

of *Tradition and the Individual Talent* as much with respect to the word in the line as to the poet in the tradition.

It may now be suggested that these principles, far from being of aesthetic validity merely, are analogical and applicable at personal, political, and spiritual levels of experience. The author of *Tradition and the Individual Talent* has in fact so applied them; *Four Quartets* is Mr. Eliot's most profound application of his early vision of history:

Every phrase and every sentence is an end and a beginning ...

         ... the pattern is new in every moment,
And every moment is a new and shocking
Valuation of all we have been.

In *Four Quartets* Mr. Eliot has realized a wisdom that engages with, without violating, the drives and preoccupations of a creative lifetime.

To say that in the *Ta Hio* Pound found a comparable wisdom ready-made would imply a clumsy antithesis. His labours over the ideograms have made their nutriment his own, as the successive translations[1] show. Pound's translation of *The Unwobbling Pivot*, *The Great Digest* and *The Analects*, his discovery of vivid imagistic and syntactic equivalents for intellectual forms embodied in the utterly alien modality of Chinese characters, the whole articulated by a tone at once tough, sensitive, resilient, and utterly new in English prose, is as much a creative achievement as Mr. Eliot's metamorphic processing of St. John of the Cross, the Ferrar community, his childhood memories, Dante, and a rose-garden.

On reflection this claim may become less absurd than it perhaps at first sounds. The gap between any Chinese and any English is in a way as absolute as that between an experience of dawn desolation and the words arranged on the page in the second part of *Little Gidding*:

In the uncertain hour before the morning
    Near the ending of interminable night
    At the recurrent end of the unending

[1] See Appendix 2.

After the dark dove with the flickering tongue
Had passed below the horizon of his homing . . .

It is silly to talk as though the poet 'simply went home and wrote it down'; equally silly to suppose that the translator of Confucius simply thumbed his dictionary and scribbled out the results. It was necessary for Mr. Eliot to fix that tone, to feel out a metrical pattern (a rhythmic correspondence with *terza rima*), to invent the local rhythms line by line (no two of the above five are alike), to hit upon the portentous syntactic paralleling of expressions of time with which the section opens, to fuse the departing bomber with the Pentecostal visitant, and invent the astonishing image of the *dark* dove. Similarly, Pound in his cell in Pisa bringing for hours to the pages of Confucius the weight of a lifetime's experience saw visions, evidently, burning in every ideogram. Certain characters in the *Chung yung* which prompted a 'traditional' translator to write nothing more exciting than:

'Confucius remarked: "The power of spiritual forces in the Universe—how active it is everywhere! Invisible to the eyes, and impalpable to the senses, it is inherent in all things, and nothing can escape its operation." '

emerge in *The Unwobbling Pivot* startlingly transfigured:

'1. Kung said: The spirits of the energies and of the rays have their operative *virtu*.

'The spirits of the energies and of the rays are efficient in their *virtu*, expert, perfect as the grain of the sacrifice.

'2. We try to see them, and do not see them; we listen, and nothing comes in at the ear, but they are in the bones of all things and we can not expel them, they are inseparable, we can not die and leave them behind us.'   (II-xvi).

Whether or not 'the grain of the sacrifice' and 'the bones of all things' are in the ideograms, it was poetic genius that saw them there.

If the reader will now turn back to the five paragraphs quoted earlier in this chapter he will have no difficulty discerning their applicability to this translation, considered both as a linguistic tour de force achieved in the month of October 1945, and as the realized and articulated flowering of the drives and interests of a lifetime.

The Confucian ethos as understood by Pound connotes the opposite of the passivity with which China is usually associated. There is an initial distinction between probity and mere busy-ness:

'Chung-Ni (Confucius) said: The master man finds the centre and does not waver; the mean man runs counter to the circulation about the invariable.' (I-ii-1).

But what is distinguished from unfocussed extroverted energy is not inanition:

'Kung said: Hui's mode of action was to seize the unwavering axis, coming to an exact equity; he gripped it in his fist and at once started using it . . . .' (I-viii).

The arena of use is inner as well as outer:

'He concentrates in a pervading study, searches benevolently as if he were watching over a rice field, he looks straight into his own thoughts, he clarifies the just distinctions [between one thing or category and another], and continues thus with vigor.' (I-xx-19).

The unwavering axis is a centre about which something turns; a permanent modality comprehending countless particular deeds. In the language of poetic organization,

'The image is not an idea. It is a radiant node or cluster; it is what I can, and must perforce, call a VORTEX, from which, and through which, and into which, ideas are constantly rushing.'

Gaudier-Brzeska, p. 106.

This concordance between an early poetic and a recent ethical formulation gives us the clue to the function of Confucian congeries in the *Cantos*. The sincerity proper to the poet as poet consists in perseverance at the task of rendering, in 'images' (=poems), concepts ('Vortices') which are perfectly real and definite but which language cannot handle as directly as it handles chairs and cows. These concepts are not static diagrams:

'An *idée fixe* is a dead, set, stiff, varnished "idea" existing in a vacuum.

'The ideas of genius, or of "men of intelligence" are organic and germinal, the "seed" of the scriptures ...[1]

'The academic ass exists in a vacuum with a congeries of dead fixed ideas which may be "good" and not quite dead, or rather which MIGHT be useful were they brought to focus on something....

'Let us deny that *real* intelligence exists until it comes into action.'

Jefferson and/or Mussolini, pp. 21, 18.

This intelligible vortex, which is the end for which the poem exists, 'from which, and through which, and into which, ideas are constantly rushing,' is defined through a careful selection of these in-rushers, the tangible things and actions on which language takes direct hold. Thus the words that can be looked up in a dictionary and the fields of reference that can be checked in the encyclopaedia are not the content of the poem. Verse that mentions cows, sheep, and grass need not be 'about' cows, sheep, and grass, but may exist to render with intellectual intensity—an intellectual intensity making use of the senses—a certain mode and degree of spiritual tranquillity. And intense concentration on that mood or mode is the necessary condition of the poet's being able to render it: 'Not the idea but the degree of its definition determines its aptitude for reaching to music.' In Confucian language,

'Finding the precise word for the inarticulate heart's tone means not lying to oneself, as in the case of hating a bad smell or loving a beautiful person, also called respecting one's own nose.'

Great Digest, VI, 1.

[1] Cf.   Canto LXXXIII: 'That he eat of the barley corn / and move with the seed's breath.'

And the carrying into action of this knowledge, for the poet the making of the poem, for the reader the co-operative discovery of its meaning, 'also serves to clarify the self-knowledge.' It is in this way that poetry ameliorates the body politic; hence Flaubert's statement that if people had *read* his *L'Education Sentimentale* the war of 1870 wouldn't have happened.

'He who possesses this sincerity does not lull himself to somnolence perfecting himself with egocentric aim, but he has a further efficiency in perfecting something outside himself.

'Fulfilling himself he attains full manhood, perfecting things outside himself he attains knowledge.

'The inborn nature begets this knowledge naturally, this looking straight into oneself and thence acting. These two activities constitute the process which unites outer and inner, object and subject, and thence constitutes a harmony with the seasons of earth and heaven.'

Unwobbling Pivot, III-xxv-3.

This sense of the public function of the poet is as old as the Greek reverence for Homer and lasted in Europe until the time of Dr. Johnson. It took the anarchic cult of poetry as self-expression, reflex of a philosophy that divided the mind from things and knowledge from the will, to make unintelligible the words of Sir Philip Sidney:

'For suppose it be granted, (that which I suppose with great reason may be denied,) that the Philosopher in respect of his methodical proceeding, doth teach more perfectly than the Poet: yet do I thinke, that no man is so much *Philophilosophos*, as to compare the Philosopher in mooving, with the Poet.

'And that mooving is of a higher degree then teaching, it may by this appeare: that it is wel nigh the cause and the effect of teaching. For who will be taught, if hee bee not moved with desire to be taught? and what so much good doth that teaching bring forth, (I speak still of morrall doctrine) as that it mooveth one to doe that which it dooth teach? for as *Aristotle* sayth, it is not *Gnosis*, but *Praxis* must be the fruit.

297

And howe *Praxis* cannot be, without being mooved to practise, it is no hard matter to consider.'

Pound tells us that 'the whole of the *Divina Commedia* is a study of the "directio voluntatis" (direction of the will).'

This account of the poet's characteristic activity parallels exactly the generalized Confucian account of the realization of 'the process' by 'the man of breed'. He seeks to lay hold on 'the unwavering axis' by a process of self-scrutiny, 'finding the precise words for the inarticulate heart's tone.' His grasp of this centre is manifested in intellectual, domestic, or public actions, as the poet's grasp of his concepts is manifested in the making of poems. The action clarifies the self-knowledge as the poem clarifies its meaning; and leavens the condition of public affairs as poetic achievement leavens that of language and so of life:

'One humane family can humanize a whole state; one courteous family can lift a whole state into courtesy; one grasping and perverse man can drive a nation into chaos. Such are the seeds of movement [*semina motuum*, the inner impulses of the tree].'

Great Digest, IX-3.

Interest in a philosophy which makes possible this parallel is not simply a poet's way of flattering poetry. The point is not that the poet is the prototype of the man of breed, but that the complete natural man is the paradigm of the poet. This was indeed, with somewhat different connotations, another Renaissance commonplace which the collapse of a hylomorphic philosophy (*'Descartes a coupé la gorge de la poésie'*) rendered meaningless. Only in our own generation has it once more become possible to see aesthetic activities as normal and as parallel (not identical) with the cardinal processes of rectificative volition. (The subject of such a poem as *Ash Wednesday* is at one level the purification of the will, at another level the aesthetic act itself.) Kung's

'Without character you will
be unable to play on that instrument
Or to execute the music fit for the Odes.'

(Canto XIII).

delimits this disciplined post-Romantic awareness; and Pound's final Confucian translations may if assimilated prove a decisive event in current intellectual history, a completion of the movement toward clarifying art's status inaugurated by Pater, and a rediscovery of how *recta ratio factibilium* and *id quod visum placet* geared with all making and all knowing in such wise as to make separate treatises on the purpose of art superfluous for the philosophers of antiquity and the high middle ages.

The Odysseus-persona of the opening Canto presents the poet as explorer, as presider at rites, as indefatigable quester after chthonic wisdom. In Canto XXIII the Odyssean persistence, discernible still in fragments through textual and editorial opacities—

> ('Derivation uncertain.' The idiot
> Odysseus furrowed the sand.)
> alixantos, aliotrephès, eiskatebaine, down into,
> descended, to the end that, beyond ocean,
> pass through, traverse . . .

—appears in allotropic forms of patent civic efficacy; Gemisto the Neoplatonist thinks for the commonweal:

> 'Never with this religion
> 'Will you make men of the Greeks.
> 'But build wall across Peloponesus
> 'And organize, and . . .

and the tenacity of the fabulous voyager animates the physicist:

> 'J'ai
> Obtenu une brûlure' M. Curie, or some other scientist
> 'Qui m'a coûté six mois de guérison.'
> and continued his experiments.

The *dramatis personae* of the *Cantos*, artists, warriors, statesmen, sages, are engaged in parallel activities, faring forward, making successive statements with reference to details set in order. The undertaking of the poem, the discovery of verbal equivalents for the 'inarticulate heart's tone' of successive phases of civilization, points toward the definition of just such a congeries of intelligible concepts containing the multiform flux of particular ideas, persons, and actions, as we have previously described: the proper end of poetry, and analogous with the grasp upon the unwavering moral axis of the Confucian 'man of true breed'.

'Happiness, rage, grief, delight. To be unmoved by these emotions is to stand in the axis, in the centre; being moved by these passions each in due degree constitutes being in harmony. That axis in the centre is the great root of the universe; that harmony is the universe's outspread process [of existence].

'From this root and in this harmony, heaven and earth are established in their precise modalities, and the multitudes of all creatures persist, nourished on their meridians.'

Unwobbling Pivot, I-i-4.

Almost in the dead centre of the scheme of one hundred Cantos we find impersonality passing into the dispassionate anonymous ('by no man these verses'), fused with the immemorial rhythms of 'Sun up; work: sundown; to rest:'

> Autumn moon; hills rise above lakes
> against sunset
> Evening is like a curtain of cloud,
> a blurr above ripples; and through it
> sharp long spikes of the cinnamon,
> a cold tune amid reeds.
> Behind hill the monk's bell
> borne on the wind.
> Sail passed here in April; may return in October
> Boat fades in silver; slowly;
> Sun blaze alone on the river. . . .

(Canto **XLIX**).

Around this axis, the emotional tonality of which is unique in the poem, are grouped the men who are 'moved by these passions each in due degree': the great Emperors, the brothers Adams, Jefferson, Odysseus, Sigismundo Malatesta, Cosimo, first Duke of Tuscany. The 'outspread process of existence' is rendered in image after image, rhythm after rhythm, field after field of interest, of reference, or of action, filling in grade after grade the modes of positive and negative action and passion on an immense simultaneous scale.

In absence of air-pockets, in sharpness of definition on detail after detail, in the kind of continual relevance to contemporary problems that alone can guarantee, through its engagement of the poet's whole personality, the permanent interest of the work for future generations, the *Cantos* invites application of the highest criteria. It is safe at least to say that there has been no effort at moral definition of comparable scope since the *Commedia*; though a contemporary has no means of estimating relative success.[1] Any intuition of the undeviating sincerity that went into the realization of such a scheme should render Pound's local imprudences not only comprehensible but nugatory. If Mussolini was not altogether the seamless factive intelligence Pound imagined him to be, it was necessary, we may say, for Pound to invent him.

The power of Pound's invention, a corollary of his lifelong tenacious devotion to the arts, permitted him to hold mode after mode of feeling steadily in focus while his firm lines were chiselled to its image. The inferior poet does not discover what his feelings were even when he has finished writing them, and consequently never writes anything accurately. He never 'sees the form in the air'. His verse, in its rudderless inability to realize a foreseen and complexly discriminated project, is, like the Confucian mean man's life, not a 'circulation about the invariable', but merely 'a set of obsolete responses'. Impossible, to such a mindless executant as Pound has more than once been accused of being, the suppression of heckling contingencies that brought the eighty-third Canto out of the death-cells in Pisa:

> First came the seen, then thus the palpable
> Elysium, though it were in the halls of hell.

[1] ' ... But there is no competition—
There is only the fight to recover what has been lost
And found and lost again and again: and now, under conditions
That seem unpropitious. But perhaps neither gain nor loss.
For us, there is only the trying. The rest is not our business.'
—*East Coker*, V.

No rage or fear disturbs his focussing of 'the moon nymph immacolata'; the control of tone and feeling is more remarkable in the *Pisan Cantos* than ever before, than even in *Mauberley* and *Propertius*. Line after line carves its mutation of the inarticulate heart's tone:

<pre>
        Death's seeds move in the year
                            semina motuum
            falling back into the trough of the sea
            the moon's arse been chewed off by this time
    semina motuum
            'With us there is no deceit'
                said the moon nymph   immacolata
                Give back my cloak, *hagoromo*.
                had I the clouds of heaven
                    as the nautile borne ashore
                in their holocaust
                    as wistaria floating seaward
        with the sea gone the colour of copper
            and emerald dark in the offing . . .
                                    (Canto LXXX).
</pre>

It is indeed in these last sequences, a *Paradiso* in counterpoint, that the definition of unwavering modalities at length commences; in the preceding Cantos rather they inhered by implication in actions in turn implicated in bewildering tangles of circumstantiality, or else were visible only in silhouette against a background of ignorance, vulgarity, and crassness. (It should be particularly emphasized that the idyllic passages in the first thirty Cantos are, in keeping with Greek palpitation and Renaissance grandiloquence, generally speaking less sculpturesque than hypnotic, clean-limbed but sensuous, and in any great quantity a drug; the lady who emerges most clearly from the first half of the poem is Circe). With the Cantos now midway through their final third, we can see the constellation of positives emerging unequivocally at last: Hellenic and Tuscan and eighteenth-century acquacities held in durable tension by the unwavering vision of Kung fu tse.

These positives are not afterthoughts, or recent discoveries brought to the top at long last by the impact of *la tristesse*. They are, in ways the reader can learn to see, implied in the poem from the very first, from the first descent of the swift ship to the tenebrous home of undying intelligence. They are implicit, furthermore, in every interest and activity of Pound's from his earliest researches into 'what had been written, and how', and his first Imagistic campaign, now nearly forty years back, for the rectification of language and the excision of unnecessary words. Every sentence in the one-page digest of Confucius he composed in 1933 invites analogical application to the poetic themes we have discussed in this book; I give the passage that the reader may make the connections for himself:

'The doctrine of Confucius is:

'That you bring order into your surroundings by bringing it first into yourself; by knowing the motives of your acts.

'That you can bring about better world government by amelioration of the *internal* government of your nation.

'That private gain is not prosperity, but that the treasure of a nation is its equity.

'That hoarding is not prosperity and that people should employ their resources.

'One should respect intelligence, "the luminous principle of reason," the faculties of others, one should look to a constant renovation.

' "Make it new, make it new as the young grass shoot."

'One should not be content with the second-rate, applying in all these the first principle, namely the beginning with what is nearest to hand, that is, one's own motives and intelligence. You could further assert that Kung taught that organization is not forced on to things or on to a nation from the outside inward, but that the centre holds by attraction.

' "The humane ruler acquires respect by his spending, the inhumane, disrespect, by his taking."

'Shallow critics fail to understand ideas because they look on ideas as a stasis, a statement in a given position, and fail to look where it leads. The people who fail to take an interest in Kung fail, I think, because they never observe WHAT Confucian thinking leads to.

For 2,500 years, whenever there has been order in China or in any part of China, you can look for a Confucian at the root of it.'

Jefferson and/or Mussolini, pp. 112–13.

'You bring order into your surroundings by bringing it first into yourself; by knowing the motives of your acts.' This recall of post-Nietzschean man from voluntarist juggernauting to volitionist sincerity that does not exclude contemplation renders the poet's 'sense of graduations' no longer

> Quite out of place amid
> Resistance to current exacerbations,

and makes it possible once more to find meaningful contemporary parallels to the similes of Sidney:

'So as Amphion was sayde to move stones with his Poetrie, to build Thebes. And Orpheus to be listened to by beastes, indeed, stony and beastly people....

'. . . it is not riming and versing that maketh a Poet, no more than a long gown maketh an Advocate. . . . But it is that fayning notable images of vertues, vices, or what els, with that delightfull teaching which must be the right describing note to know a Poet by.'

We have been trying to adequate our understanding to poetry that needs no Apologie.

> But to have done instead of not doing
> > this is not vanity
> To have, with decency, knocked
> That a Blunt should open
> > To have gathered from the air a live tradition
> or from a fine old eye the unconquered flame
> This is not vanity.
> > Here error is all in the not done,
> > all in the diffidence that faltered, . . .

APPENDIXES

THIS HULME BUSINESS

before the world was given over to wars
Quand vous serez bien vieille
remember that I have remembered.

(Too many cards are still being held too close to too many chests for a history of events in London 1900–1920 to be written. The necessary research doesn't in any case come within the scope of the present volume. The following pages, however, contributed by Pound to *The Townsman* of January 1938, are reprinted here partly as an indication of the unreliability of extant formulations, partly for the light they throw on the attention given in the *Pisan Cantos* to men whom literary historians would lead one to believe negligible. Ford's *Return to Yesterday* furnishes invaluable light for the same period.)

Among the infinite stinks of a foetid era is that arising from the difficulty of not being able to do a man justice without committing some sort of inflation. I attempted to do Hulme justice in the last pages of Ripostes (A.D. 1910).

Without malice toward T. E. H. it now seems advisable to correct a distortion which can be found even in portly works of reference. The critical LIGHT during the years immediately pre-war in London shone not from Hulme but from Ford (Madox etc.) in so far as it fell on writing at all.

To avoid mere argument or expression of opinion, let me put it as datum *pour servir*. I used to see Ford in the afternoons and Yeats at his Monday evening, Yeats being what Ford called a 'gargoyle, a great poet but a gargoyle', meaning by gargoyle a man with peculiar or gothic opinions about writing.

The 'image' does exist in the early Yeats, syntactical simplicity is in the pages of 'The Wind Among the Reeds'. Ford knew about WRITING. The general tendency of British criticism at the time was toward utter petrifaction or vitrifaction, and Henry Newbolt was as good an example of the best ACCEPTED criteria as can be unearthed.

It detracts no jot from the honour due Hulme that he had no monopoly of London literary life and did not crowd out other interests. A proper map of that London for the Lustrum 1909 to '14 should include:

1. The great men: Henry James, W. H. Hudson (visible to the eye of the present recorded at Miss Hunt's parties).

2. Swinburne and Meredith, not personally inspected by me, Three hundred or more novelists, some of 'em meritorious and few wanting to write durable books.

3. Mr. Yeats' friends, Sturge Moore included.

4. Of the Rhymer's club there remained, apart from Yeats, Rhys, Plarr, Selwyn Image, Edgar Jepson, and Radcliffe. Maurice Hewlett, Fred Manning, Bridges, Newbolt (above mentioned) were interested in criteria.

The EVENT of 1909–10 was Ford Madox (Heuffer) Ford's 'English Review', and no greater condemnation of the utter filth of the whole social system of that time can be dug up than the fact of that review's passing out of his hands. Its list of contributors should prevent critical exaggeration of our Frith Street cenacle without in the least damaging Hulme's record. This is in no way an attempt to inflate the reputations of D. H. Lawrence (born in the English Review) or of any of the minor writers who being minor were not less than some of the Frith Street group.

Hulme stopped writing poetry. He had read Upward. His evenings were diluted with crap like Bergson and it became necessary to use another evening a week if one wanted to discuss our own experiments or other current minor events in verse writing, Tagore, Frost, Selver's struggles with the Slovak and Czech poets, etc., or to receive Monsieur Barzun's philippics and news from Paris. J. B. Fletcher's library of French poets was useful.

Hulme was the largest object in his dining club, his satellites in 1909 being Storer, Flint, Tancred, with the occasional appearance of Colum and the 'darrk man frum th' narth who wrote the "gilly of Christ" ' and later took to printing his name in Gaelic orthography. Desmond Fitzgerald was in fairly regular attendance but not to be classed as a satellite.

Hulme's broadside may have come later as a godsend when published. I have no doubt that the bleak and smeary 'Twenties' wretchedly needed his guidance, and the pity is that he wasn't there in person to keep down vermin. God knows Messrs. Lewis and Eliot must have had a lonely time in your city during that fifteen years' interval.

E. P.

Appendix 2

SECOND THOUGHTS

'Renovate, dod gast you, renovate'

A curriculum in poetics could be extracted from Pound's two versions of the *Ta Hio*, the earlier first published in 1928 and the later (entitled *The Great Digest*) dated 'D. T. C., Pisa; 5 October—5 November, 1945'. The final version, along with *The Unwobbling Pivot*, has gone strangely unnoticed. It brings something totally new into English prose.

'Things have roots and branches; affairs have scopes and beginnings. To know what precedes and what follows, is nearly as good as having a head and feet.'

In the earlier version, this admirable gnomic verse read:

'The creatures of nature have a cause and effects; human actions have a principle and consequences: to know the causes and the effects, the principles and the consequences, is to approach very near to the rational method whereby one attains perfection;'

—well enough, but leery of defining its terms. The unembarrassed reliance of the later version on images is more philosophic at the same time as it is more poetic. 'The rational method whereby one attains perfection' is not merely circumlocutory, it has an unwanted air of extraneous discipline, of Sandow-exercising the soul. 'Having a head and feet' unites by a

310

homely image moral perfection with the most obvious physical marks of human integrity.

The more parallel verses one inspects, the more apparent is the virtue of trusting to unglossed images. 'Mythological expression . . . permits the expression of intuition without denting the edges or shaving off the nose and ears of a verity.' Compare—

'This proves that there is nothing which the sage does not push to the last degree of perfection' (1928).

'Hence the man in whom speaks the voice of his forebears cuts no log that he does not make fit to be roof-tree.' (1945).

*   *   *

'A prince who cherishes those who have incurred general and merited hatred, and who hates those who hold the general affection, outrages men's natural feelings. Disasters will come upon him.' (1928).

'To love what the people hate, to hate what they love is called doing violence to man's inborn nature. Calamities will come to him who does this, the wild grass will grow over his dead body.' (1945).

*   *   *

'One should first know the target toward which to aim, that is, one's ultimate destination; and then make up one's mind; when one's mind is made up, one can then have the spirit calm and tranquil; and with the spirit calm and tranquil one can then enjoy that unalterable repose which nothing can trouble; and having succeeded in enjoying that unalterable repose which nothing can trouble, one may then meditate and form a judgment upon the essence of things; and having meditated and formed a judgment upon the essence of things one may then attain that desired state of perfection.' (1928).

'Know the point of rest and then have an orderly mode of procedure; having this orderly procedure one can "grasp the azure", that is, take hold of a clear concept; holding a clear concept one can be at peace (internally), being thus calm one can keep one's head in moments of danger; he who can keep his head in the presence of a tiger is qualified to come to his deed in due hour.'(1945).

311

As this last example indicates, Pound's expanding technical resource has accompanied a steadily more complex intuition of his matter. French or Italian can be translated in some measure mechanically. We can read 'la plume de ma tante' and put down 'the pen of my aunt' without bothering to notice the dynamics of sentence and paragraph. (It is because most translation *is* done in this way that the capital importance of Flaubert, for example, remains a blank in the mental decorations of so many well-read Anglo-Saxons). The most elementary acquaintance with Chinese ideograms, even the two pages of 'terminology' prefixed to Pound's 1945 *Great Digest*, makes it plain that the translator of Confucius cannot even begin without possessing, rethinking, and recreating his matter. Of one ideogram, Pound comments:

'The action resultant from this straight gaze into the heart. The "know thyself" carried into action. Said action also serving to clarify the self-knowledge. To translate this simply as "virtue" is on a par with translating rhinoceros, fox, and giraffe indifferently by "quadruped" or "animal".'

It follows that the Confucius translation of 1945 is creative work of a high order: comparison with the earlier draft gives warrant for calling it one of Pound's most important poems. The two halves of poetic process, perception and realization, 'the capacity to see ten things where the ordinary man sees one, and where the man of talent sees two or three, PLUS the ability to register that multiple perception in the material of his art', are engaged to the full in this series of complex meditations on the black-letter ideograms. Though the disparity is not always so striking, the verse of the *Pisan Cantos* (composed in the same months) registers a gain in technical and emotional maturity over that of the earlier sequences in exactly the same way. The quality of mind of a major poet comes out in any chance phrase:

'Kung said: Hui's mode of action was to seize the unwavering axis, coming to an exact equity; he gripped it in his fist, and at once started using it, careful as if he was watching his chicken-coop, and he never let go or lost sight of it.'

A parallel sample from anything that has previously been offered as Confucius in English gives us all the cross-light we need:

'Confucius remarked of his favorite disciple, Yen Huei: "Huei was a man who all his life sought the central clue in his moral being, and when he got hold of one thing that was good, he embraced it with all his might and never lost it again." '

(Ku Hungming's version, ed. Lin Yutang.)

The difference is radical, not superficial. Pound's version is not merely to be described as the more picturesque. His intention is to 'make it new', according to the ideogram he has so often cited, of axe, tree, and wood-pile. Something new goes into the reader's mind. The tangled concepts, not so much of Confucius as of moral being, that he brings to the text are forcibly trimmed, cleared, and ordered; 'He gripped it in his fist, and at once *started using it*' briskly deranges a quietist conception of 'virtue'. The function of the traditional translation is, on the other hand, to disturb nothing. The loosest and commonest ethical terminology is employed precisely because it *is* loose and common. As the familiar counters are shuffled, 'the moral sense,' 'the moral law,' 'the sense of justice,' 'the mean,' we are reassured to find that we need derange no furniture, that we knew it all before, that all wisdoms are after all one, the wisdom of Confucius and that of the old lady down the street who remarked only yesterday that the main thing in life was to be moderate. We are allowed, that is, to hear as much of the orchestral score as can be played on a badly-tuned flute.

THE CANTOS—
FURTHER NOTES

... and for ending
Is smothered beneath a mule,
a poet's ending,
Down a stale well-hole, oh a poet's ending.

(This material has been shoved into the last appendix in hopes that the reader will not discover it until it is unlikely to harm him. There has been no attempt whatever at completeness; allusions have in general gone unidentified, whole blocks of verse have been lumped under captions. The intention has been to set up a few practical finger-posts to save the reader's time in getting the hang of a difficult poem.

If anyone supposes that the diagrammatic cross-sections here provided are the meat of this book or its perhaps triumphant result, the preceding three hundred pages have been wasted. The diagrams are not meant to simplify the poem, but only to simplify the information here offered. In addition, the writer has tried to scatter as many suggestions as possible without making statements that can be argued about in isolation from Pound's text.)

MAJOR FORM

Yeats has reported one plan of organization in *A Packet for Ezra Pound*; Pound's own remark about permanent, recurrent, and casual themes implies another; inklings of an Inferno-Purgatorio-Paradiso analogue have in recent years reached recipients of Pound's letters. It is futile to argue about the 'right' plan, or to imply that Pound doesn't know his own mind because all three suggestions are traceable to him. Ten thousand different-looking cross-sections, all equally 'correct', can be taken of any complex organism. A slight change in the angle of cut will reveal a wholly new surface. One may suggest dozens of classifications depending on what one wants to emphasize. To reinforce our technical account in chapters 25 and 26 we emphasized the interplay of two contrasting streams of imagery:

Cut	Lumpy
Clear	Opaque
Defined	Soggy
Sculptured	Confused
Stone	Mud
Water	Murk
Volition	Drift
Light	Gloom

These might be parcelled out among various Cantos to yield a convincing structural prospectus. A different level of organization would be revealed by dissociating:

1–51   Timeless frieze.
52–71   Action unfolding in time.
74–84   Remembered co-presence.

Again, taking as a key Pound's dictum that the history of culture is the history of ideas going into action, one would get:

1   Overture: poetic action.
2–16   Supply of ideas.
17–30   Greek ideas in action: Renaissance and Contemporary.
31–41   Jeffersonian ideas in action: America and Italy.
42–51   Stasis: Folk-wisdom and summary.
52   Cosmic Order.
53–61   Ideas in action: China.
62–71   Ideas in action: Adams.
74–84   Stasis: Contemporary crisis in guise of personal lyric.

Again, one might, on a hint in Canto 52, trace Kung and Eleusis as interwoven threads.

Kung	Eleusis
Ruler	People

Volitional	Traditional
Directed will	Choric ritual
Politics	Religion
Human works	Natural fertility
Action	Passion

etc.

The reader familiar with the poem will have no difficulty thinking of other schemae, all revealing some dimension of its life.

The plan adopted below is intended to highlight as many internal relations as possible at a single view. It omits a great deal but at least indicates one way in which the poem hangs together, a way which our previous concentration on technical organization has compelled us to scamp. The reader need not be told that he is at liberty to quarrel with the details of the following analysis, because there is strictly speaking nothing to quarrel about. What follows is not a set of answers to a puzzle, but an exegetical tool whose usefulness, like that of any other tool, will depend on the hands into which it falls.

CANTO I

This is an overture on several levels. We may distinguish:

(1) Cultural overlayering. 'In any case the classic culture of the Renaissance was grafted onto mediaeval culture, a process which is excellently illustrated by Andreas Divus Justinopolitanus' translation of the *Odyssey* into Latin.' (*Make It New*, p. 33). The relevant portion of Divus' text may be examined in *Make It New*, pp. 138–41. In the Canto, the mediaeval is represented by Anglo-Saxon (*Seafarer*) rhythms. The fusion points forward to the classical/renaissance counterpoints in cantos 17–30.

(2) Persona. The poet as Odysseus. 'He saw the cities of many peoples and he learnt their ways. He suffered many hardships on the high seas in his struggles to preserve his life and bring his comrades home. But he failed to save those comrades, in spite of all his efforts. It was their own sin that

brought them to their doom, for in their folly they devoured the oxen of Hyperion the Sun, and the god saw to it that they should never return.' In one sense, the substance of the *Cantos* is what Odysseus sees, as that of *The Waste Land* is what Tiresias sees. The distinction between these two personae gives us one measure of Pound's poem. Tiresias the shade, fore-suffering all, is capable only of psychic action, motions of fascination, revulsion, purgation. Odysseus, *polumetis*, many-minded, fertile in stratagems, is engaged in active ameliora-tion of conditions for himself and his men, involved as factive protagonist in what he sees. Eliot and Pound are conducting their analyses at different levels which do not contradict one another.

(3) Descent to Tiresias. Visit with the dead as indispensable prologue to homecoming. Invocation of chthonic wisdom, encyclopaedic intelligence. Rhythms, rituals, to coerce in-telligibility out of events. Elpenor episode: piety to fore-runners and gone companions.

With Elpenor's death compare that of Lionel Johnson in *Mauberley*: 'by falling from a high stool in a pub.' Odysseus. Pound's memorial to Johnson ('pile high mine arms') was a collected edition of the latter's works ; the inscription ('a man of no fortune and with a name to come') has its counterpart in Pound's preface thereto.

CANTOS II–XVI

These cantos may be compared to the pages of 'terminology' prefixed to the translation of *The Great Digest*. A thematic concordance of modes of moral being later to be inspected in action in a wide variety of contexts. More specifically:

2–7 PASSION. Myths, metamorphoses, modes of love and violence.

Helen theme: Danae, Troy in Auvergnat, Eleanor of Acquitaine, 'Doom goes with her in walking;' summation in XLVI: 'Aurum est commune sepulchrum . . . helandros kai heleptolis kai helarxe.' (breaker of men, of cities, of order.)

Cunizza theme: fidelity, Procne, Cabestan's lady, fructive passion: 'Winter and summer I sing of her grace.'

The theme of Canto 2 is the artist's struggle to bring form (Browning's *Sordello*, Pound's *Cantos*) out of flux (the Sordello documents, the sea). So-shu, who also churned in the sea, was an Emperor who built roads (form out of flux again, at the political level; you churn the fluid to get a solid). The metamorphosed impious seamen were solidified in punishment by Bacchus, and in epiphanization by Ovid.

3: Glory and decay. 4: Fatal passion. 5: Declines and murders. 6: Legalisms vs. troubadour passions. 7: James and Flaubert in XIX century hell.

One key to these cantos is at the opening of VIII: 'These fragments you have shelved (shored).' Another in VII: 'And the passion endures. Against their action, aromas. Rooms, against chronicles.'

8–11 ACTION. Sigismundo Malatesta. The factive personality imprinting itself on its time, its mark surviving all expropriation. 'A codex once of the Lords Malatesta' furnishes the text for civilized activity at the end of XXX. Innumerable relics 'Olim de Malatestis' haunt the later cantos.

'And they want to know what we talked about?
　　"de litteris et de armis, praestantibusque ingeniis,

Both of ancient times and our own; books, arms,
And of men of unusual genius,
Both of ancient times and our own, in short the usual
　　　　　　　　　　　　　　　　　subjects
Of conversation between intelligent men." ' 　(XI).

12 CUNNING: placed as incestuous and abortive.

13 KUNG: each aphorism gears with other motifs in the poem.

14–15 INFERNO: 'The place lacking in interest, / last squalor, utter decrepitude.'

16 PURGATORS: Blake, Dante, Augustine, 'burglar alarms.'
　　ELYSIAN FIELDS: *earned* paradise (distinct from the passionate drift of the lotus-eaters in XX). 'and by their

fountains, the heroes, / Sigismundo, and Malatesta Novello, / and founders, gazing at the mounts of their cities.'

WORLD WAR: a litmus paper distinguishing modes of moral being.

CANTOS XVII–XXX

Much of the modern world may be seen as the ossified heritage of the Renaissance; the Renaissance being the period when Greek ideas, apprehended with various degrees of clearness, suddenly went into action. These Cantos weave their lock-stitch through renaissance Venice and the nineteen-twenties.

17: SECOND OVERTURE. Cultural overlayering. Elements of dawn and magnificence in Greece and renaissance Italy.

18–19: COMMERCE & WAR. Munitions trade, revolutionaries, traders in far countries.

20: LOTUS-EATERS. Contrast second part of XVI, and see ch. 29 above.

21–23: TRIPTYCH: (1) Confusion, source of renewals.
(2) Confusion, dissipation, muddle.
(3) Bringers of order, conquerors, artists in living. Hymn to Aphrodite the ground bass to a panorama of scientists,[1] platonists, poets, voyagers, troubadours. (See end of ch. 12 above: periploi).

24–26: TRIPTYCH: (1) Venice: maturity.
(2) Venice: inner death—'dead words keeping form.'
(3) Venice: decline. Luxuria. Decline of will into wrangle.

[1] 'We have ceased to believe that we conquer anything by having Alexander the Great make a gigantic "joy-ride" through India. We know that conquests are made in the laboratory, that Curie with his minute fragments of things seen clearly in test-tubes . . . makes conquests.'
Make It New. p. 255

Not successive stages but simultaneous strands, as the frequent dates remind us. [1]

27–28: METAMORPHOSES. (slither, not persistence of vital form)

29:   REPRISE.   Helen theme (Pernella) ⎫   ⎧Cunizza.
              Muddle.   ⎭   ⎩Clear-cut.

30:   'Nothing is now clean slayne ⎫   ⎧Final tableau: AF-
      But rotteth away.'   ⎪   ⎪FIRMATION of a high
                                   ⎬   ⎨and busy civiliza-
      'Balls for yr. honour!'   ⎪   ⎩tion.
                                   ⎭
                    Il Papa mori.

CANTOS XXXI–XLI

This is where the reader must go carefully. We move in for a close-up on matter developed in Cantos 8–11, 13, 23, and elsewhere: the statesman as artist. Politics, like writing poetry, is a practical art, using what materials are available, with an eye to the best work feasible, mobilizing a plenum of practical knowledge to cope with circumstances continually new.

Simultaneously, we inspect a *new* set of concepts going into action. The complete change in the tone of the verse marks the supersession of dark lordly magnificence rooted in Greek irresponsibility by the brisk shrewd rationality of the Enlightenment.

The American constitution was an innovation. The new sequence begins with Jefferson. With the first lines of Canto XXXI we are plunged into an utterly changed mental climate, which has shaken off the incubus of tradition constantly enacted in the heavy sway and chant of the Renaissance cantos. The opening panorama of Jefferson's encyclopaedic interests displays him detached from the past, selecting and conserving, building his new nation amid a new mental

[1] Cf.: 'You can't know an era merely by knowing its best. Gourmont and James weren't the whole of the latter half of a century. There are all strata down to the bottom, the very. You get the Middle Ages from Mussato, in a way you do not, I think, get them from Dante without Mussato; and Mussato is again a summit.'

Make It New. p. 16.

freedom. A passage from the Pisan sequence (LXXIV) enforces the Confucian axis of this alert detachment:

> Yaou chose Shun to longevity
> who seized the extremes and the opposites
> holding true course between them
> shielding men from their errors
> cleaving to the good they had found
> holding empire as if not in a mortar with it
> > nor dazzled thereby

'As if not in a mortar with it.'

External clues to the organization of these eleven cantos will be found in *Jefferson and/or Mussolini* (1935; written 1933). Definition of the exact claims there made is more important than wrangle about the justice of their application to Mussolini. A few paragraphs relevant to the *Cantos* follow:

'(1) In one sense American history or the history of American development runs from Jefferson through Van Buren and then takes a holiday; or is broken by a vast parenthesis, getting rid of the black chattel slavery, and then plunging fairly into unconsciousness.

'We were diddled out of the heritage Jackson and Van Buren left us. The real power just oozed away from the electorate. The *de facto* government became secret, nobody cared a damn about the *de jure* ...

(page 97).

Hence the constructive period in America runs from the Revolution to the Bank War (Cantos 31–4, 37). 38 and the latter half of 41 are the ensuing 'unconscious'. And after 1840 the continuation of the Jefferson current must be looked for elsewhere. Pound found it in the awakening Italy of 1922–1933.

'(2) The challenge of Mussolini to America is simply:
'*Do the driving ideas of Jefferson, Quincy Adams, Van Buren, or whoever else there is in the creditable pages of our history, FUNCTION actually in the America of this decade to the extent that they function in Italy under the DUCE?*

x   321   K.E.P.

'The writer's opinion is that they DON'T, and that nothing but vigorous realignment will make them, and that if, or when, they are made so to function, Mussolini will have acted as stimulus, will have entered into American history, as Lenin has entered into world history.

'That don't, or don't necessarily, mean an importation of the details of mechanisms and forms more adapted to Italy or Russia than to the desert of Arizona or to the temperament of farms back of Baaaston. But it does definitely mean an orientation of will.'

(page 104).

(PARENTHESIS: The reader's blood-pressure may be saved by Pound's explicit disavowal of 'advocating fascism in and for America'. 'I think the American system *de jure* is probably quite good enough, if there were only 500 men with guts and the sense to *use* it, or even with the capacity for answering letters, or printing a paper.'—page 98.)

It is important to grasp, amid the shifting details of these eleven cantos, Pound's intuition of a clear forward current running from Jefferson through Adams, Jackson, Van Buren, to the distributionist economists (Canto XXXVIII states the gist of Douglas' monetary analysis) to the regeneration of Italy:

(3) 'After [the revolution] Jefferson governed our forefathers for twenty-four years, and you might almost say he governed for forty-eight. There was the slight cross-current of Quincy Adams, but there was the intensively Jeffersonian drive of Van Buren.

'When I say twenty-four years I count Jefferson's eight years as President and the sixteen wherein he governed more or less through deputies, Madison and Monroe. (page 14).

As further light, there may also be cited:

(4) The reduction of Jefferson's thought to sixteen permanent principles (pp. 114–19).

(5) The Bank War (pp. 120–4, 95–6). This, the gist of the Van Buren canto (XXXVII), has become less esoteric since

the impact of Schlesinger's *Age of Jackson* (1945). In 1935 Pound was compelled to write, 'The war of the 1830's is not to be found in the school-books. Jackson is regarded as a tobacco-chewing half-wit, or tuppenny militarist, the murderer of a few Indians, and the victor of New Orleans; Van Buren either vilified or forgotten.'

The sequence may be graphed as follows:

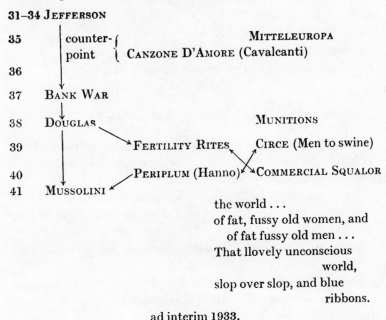

31–34 JEFFERSON

35   counter- {   MITTELEUROPA
        point { CANZONE D'AMORE (Cavalcanti)

36

37   BANK WAR

38   DOUGLAS   MUNITIONS

39   FERTILITY RITES   CIRCE (Men to swine)

40   PERIPLUM (Hanno)   COMMERCIAL SQUALOR

41   MUSSOLINI

> the world ...
> of fat, fussy old women, and
>   of fat fussy old men ...
> That llovely unconscious
>   world,
> slop over slop, and blue
>   ribbons.

ad interim 1933.

CANTOS XLII–LI

This section is a gathering of energies, a consolidation of motifs, marked by a steady ground-bass of folk-wisdom: the bank of Siena founded on 'the abundance of nature with the whole folk behind it,' the catalogue of communal wrongs wrought by usury in 45, the appeal to the public jury in 46, the resurgence of fertility in 47, the balancing of popular wisdom (Hawaiian navigators, fly-fishermen) against financial trickery in 48 and 51, the tranquil lyric of 49 passing into communal chant.

The foundation and career of the Monte dei Paschi in Cantos XLII–XLIV is the second *episode* in the poem (the first is the Malatesta sequence, VIII–XI). At the beginning of Canto LII Pound glosses its significance:

And I have told you of how things were under Duke
                                          Leopold in Siena
And of the true base of credit, that is
                                          the abundance of nature
with the whole folk behind it.
'Goods that are needed' said Schacht (anno seidici)
commerciabili beni, deliverable things that are wanted.
                              neschek is against this, the serpent.

Social Credit, an Impact (1935) gives further details:

'Banks differ in their INTENTION. Two kinds of bank stand in history: Banks built for beneficence, for reconstruction; and banks created to prey on the people.

Three centuries of Medici wisdom went into the Monte dei Paschi, the *only* bank that has stood from 1600 to our time.

'Siena was flat on her back, without money after the Florentine conquest.

'Cosimo, first Duke of Tuscany, had all the Medici banking experience behind him. He guaranteed the capital of the Monte, taking as security the one living property of Siena, and a certain amount of somewhat unhandy collateral.

'That is to say, Siena had grazing lands down toward Grosseto, and the grazing rights worth 10,000 ducats a year. On this basis, taking this for his main security, Cosimo underwrote a capital of 200,000 ducats, to pay 5 per cent. to the shareholders, and to be lent at $5\frac{1}{2}$ per cent; overhead kept down to a minimum; salaries at a minimum and all excess of profit over that to go to hospitals and works for the benefit of the people of Siena. That was in the first years of the 17th. century, and that bank is open to-day. It outlasted Napoleon. You can open an account there tomorrow.

'And the lesson is the very basis of solid banking. The

CREDIT rests *in ultimate* on the ABUNDANCE OF NATURE, on the growing grass that can nourish the living sheep.

'And the moral is in the INTENTION. It was not for the conqueror's immediate short-sighted profit, but to re-start life and productivity in Siena, that this bank was contrived.

(pages 10–11).

Schema:

42–44 MONTE DEI PASCHI

45   The indictment against USURA.

46   Indictment in another mode. Explicit clearing of air:

'Nineteen years on this case.'
        This case, and with it
the first part, draws to a conclusion,
of the first phase of this opus, Mr. Marx, Karl, did not
foresee this conclusion, you have seen a good deal of
the evidence, not knowing it evidence, is monumentum
look about you, look, if you can, at St. Peter's
Look at the Manchester slums, look at Brazilian coffee,
or Chilean nitrates. This case is the first case
Si requieres monumentum? . . .

19 years on this case / first case. I have set down part of
The Evidence. Part / commune sepulchrum
Aurum est commune sepulchrum. Usura, commune
    sepulchrum.
helandros   kai heleptolis   kai helarxe.
Hic Geryon est. Hic hyperusura.

47   Tiresias: fertility: power over wild beasts. Reprise of Canto I, with new inflections.

48   New images for a reprise of moral motifs. *Grasp on reality* (Browning, the puppy's pedigree, divers voyagers); *continuity* (the pedigree, seafaring traditions, peasant festivals unthwarted by Christianity or Fascism); *slither & illusion* (bond sales, loud speakers, election of Mr. Rhumby); *lithe energy* (falling Mars); *senescence* (the vanished houses and pavements; the old man with a basket of stones).

49 Chinese lyric pastiche: impersonal twilit peace. The senescent emotion of the old man with the basket of stones subtly transformed into the equable sustaining rhythm of immemorial civilization. This is one of the pivots of the poem: the emotional still point of the *Cantos*.

50 Italy: 1750 through Napoleon ('Mars meaning, in that case, order') to the post-Waterloo slump. Advent and withdrawal of factive personality.

51 FINALE of first half:

CANTOS LII–LXXI

At this point a continuous action in time suddenly intersects the poem. LII is a major pivot: the Li Ki's (*Book of Rites*) prehistoric affirmation of total order, celestial, ritualistic, agricultural, aesthetic.[1] This wisdom goes into action in China, is consolidated by Confucius, and its career is traced to the emperor who ascended the throne in the year of John Adams' birth. At LXII the scene is switched to America; the process continues to unroll in Adams' actions.

This connection is not gratuitous. The European discovery of China is recorded in LX; Confucian ideas helped feed the Enlightenment, which in turn nourished the Revolution of Jefferson and Adams.

52 — COSMIC ORDER
53 GREAT EMPERORS; KUNG
54–61 KUNG in ACTION.
62–71 → ADAMS IN ACTION.

[1] Cf. communal component of Greek wisdom in XLVII: 'Begin thy plowing/when the Pleiades go down to their rest.' XLVII + XLIX→LII.

CANTOS LXXIV–LXXXIV[1]

At XXXI and at LXXIV marked technical innovations initiate a new phase in the poem. The first of these is the shift from predominantly emphatic to predominantly denotative rhythms, and the introduction, apropos of Jefferson, of tessellated quotations marking the statesman's registration of fact, a technique that comes to flower in the Adams sequence. The second, which initiates the Pisan sequence, depends on extremely rapid shifts of tone, shorthand juxtaposition of masses of material, a continual graceful irony of parable, and single cantos as complexly organized as former entire sequences. Confronted with this, our skeletal graphings, which now show tendencies to expand into pages, must be abandoned for still more cursory thematic indications.

What is going on in the *Pisan Cantos* is no longer survey (Inferno-Purgatorio) but affirmation (Paradiso). Unpromising opportunities are cunningly seized. The internment camp becomes the modern world. Thematic vocabulary (I–XL), narrative and documentation (XLI–LXXI), are followed by meditation and digestion, a personal synthesis, the going of a lifetime of ideas into *inner* action (sustainment, nutriment, passage of knowledge into wisdom) amid catastrophes hacking cruelly at the will. A few of the most prominent motifs:

(1) Merciles Beauté (Chaucer). A new inflection of the Helen theme. 'Your eyen two wol sleye me sodenly.' 'Beauty is difficult.' 'Cythera egoista.' The intransigent forms, the implacable métier. Beauty 'a brief gasp between clichés,' its manifestations in these times unspeakably precious.

(2) Treasured memories continually sorted and ordered, their nutritive irreplaceability continually affirmed:

> and that certain images be formed in the mind
> to remain there
> *formato locho.*

Bringing these images into order is the achievement of wis-

---

[1] According to Pound, Cantos 72 and 73 loop forward to the unwritten 85–100, and have been held in reserve at this time to obviate confusion.

dom; the order into which they are brought is the mirror of wisdom.

(3) *Periplum*. (See LIX: 'periplum, not as land looks on a map/but as sea bord seen by men sailing.') 'The great periplum brings in the stars to our shore,' we are told on the first page of the sequence. Things disparate in space and time are united by the experiencing mind. The poet-as-Odysseus *persona* strong once more, specifically Odysseus on his raft, after shipwreck, driven 'as the winds veer'.

(4) 'Each in the name of his god.' (Micah IV, 5). Pound's sense of the autonomy and particularity of varying modes of order receives constant expression. Echoes from Confucius (especially the *Analects*), Scotus Erigena, the Old Testament, Homer, Cavalcanti, go into one ideal order while retaining their more localized contexts and validities. (This is the exact opposite of the eclectic shopping for phrases of which Pound has been accused. Such allusions are not 'phrases', but insights into compatible modes of life.) In a group of Old Testament motifs (Leviticus XIX, Micah IV) the Jewish law receives the Poundian compliment of Confucian analogy; it itself condemns the usurer and the counterfeiter.

(5) Epiphanies of concentration camp banalities, with emphasis on the quality of affection possible even in that context: 'Doan you tell no one I made you that table.' The aesthetic 'distance' of witty analogies is not hardness; it is convertible with affective comprehension: this is itself one of the motifs of the poem.

(6) The spectator's detachment, contemplating an ideal order which he does not enter except in his mind, is conveyed by a whole series of insect and beetle analogies; ants, lizards, green midges, butterflies, wasps, beautifully fulfil without fumble or hiatus their proper modes of being. Analogies are present on the one hand with the autonomy of innumerable modes of intelligible order (the ant makes no apologies to the butterfly), on the other hand with the unfaltering certainty of action of the ideal poet or statesman (the ant knows no gap between theory and practice).

Such tabulation could go on at great length; enough has

been done to show that the range of reference is not haphazard. The total action of the sequence may be very sketchily indicated as follows:

I: SYNTHESIS OF FEELING AND FACT

74. (25 pages) Recapitulation and memories. Public and personal experience gradually achieve stereoscopic focus.

75. Indestructible affirmation: Janequin's music. Metamorphoses in a mode that does not (as in XXVII–XXVIII) sap the integrity of the concept.

76.   *Lyric fact*   *Physical fact*

Desolation of spirit underlying rapid alternation of opposites.

77. Kindly memories   78.   Unrighteous war
Counterpoint, issuing in lynx-chorus
Perennial form, in touch with folk-rhythms, affirmed against welter.

II: SYNTHESIS OF KNOWLEDGE AND DESIRE

80. (23 pages) The struggle with recalcitrant beauty as focus of personal history (Cf. *Mauberley*). Artist as Odysseus. Closing ideogram of England as it was when Pound left it about 1920.

81. Artist-explorers. 'Pull down thy vanity' and affirmation of accomplishment.

82. Back-swing of emotional pendulum: Regrets and consciousness of death as death.

83. Descent of rain and peace from heaven (Hudor et Pax) as outer and inner worlds achieve fusion. Elegiac treatment of factive elements and persons.

84. Toughening: troubles chalked up to experience. 'Out of all this beauty something must come.'

*   *   *

It is repeated that there can be no finality about such out-
lines, however elaborately done. The one above has been
scamped even in its own area of reference. Nothing has been
said about the subtle and elaborate variations of verse texture,
or the scale of emotional intensity, surprisingly varied even in
the most superficially unpromising sections. Mr. Eliot's
remark about the superficies of Jonson reflecting only the lazy
reader's fatuity should be consulted again. The Chinese
chronicle is as brilliant as anything in the poem: obviously so
at, for example, the end of Canto LVIII:

> Atrox MING, atrox finis
> > the nine gates were in flame.
> Manchu with Ousan put down many rebels
> Ousan offered to pay off these Manchu
> who replied then with courtesy:
> we came for peace not for payment.
> > came to bring peace to the Empire
> in Pekin they cried OUAN SOUI
> > a thousand, ten thousand years, A NOI
> eijen, ouan soui; Ousan, Ousan
> > peace maker Ousan, in the river, reeds,
> > flutes murmured Ousan
> Brought peace into China; brought in the Manchu
> Litse thought to gain Ousan,
> > roused Ousan and Ousan
> remembered his father
> > dead by the hand of Litse.
> > > $\tau\acute{a}\delta'$ $\mathring{\omega}\delta'$ $\check{\epsilon}\chi\epsilon\iota$[1]

At the other end of the scale is this bare document:

> 4 to 5 million balance in the national treasury
> Receipts 31 to 32 million
> Revenue 32 to 33 million
> The Bank 341 million, and in deposits
> 6 millions of government money
> (and a majority in the Senate)

[1] *Agamemnon*, line 1415; = 'Haec ita se habent.' Clytemnestra's
brag of murder. See *Make It New*, p. 150.

Public Money in control of the President
from 15 to 20 thousand (id est a fund for the secret service)
(Canto XXXVII).

These facts are set down in a cool rage that implies the superfluity of comment: the puny '15 to 20 thousand' in the final line drives home its own story. This balance sheet is as eloquent as the whirling excitement of the Ousan finale. There is no reason to suppose that a line drawing need carry less charge than a Wagnerian tableau.

We have made a sketch-map of the surface presented by one cross-section of the poem. We may close with two more sectionings:

HISTORY

1. Homeric clarity
(adventuring individualism)

2–30. The West till the Renaissance. 'In the gloom, the gold/Gathers the light against it.' Clear Greek speculative stream running into marshes. Homeric clarity turning into a nightmare incubus. Civilization staggering into rot. Beauty in shelved fragments.

52. Li Ki's universal order
(feeling for whole people)

53–71. Continual self-renewal of a concept of communal order. 'History is a school book for princes.' 'Kung is to China as is water to fishes./War, letters, to each a time.' China—France—America. 'Foundation of every government in some principle/or passion of the people.' 'Few of the human race have had opportunity like this/to make election of government, more than of air, soil, or climate.'

31–51. Responsible rule in America, Italy. Abundance of nature entering lives of the people. 'Having drained off the muck by Vada/From the marshes, by Circeo, where no one else wd. have drained it.' 'The light has entered the cave. Io! Io!/ The light has gone down into the cave.'

74–84. Universal shipwreck. Order which has collapsed at public level subsumed into and conserved by poet's mind, which becomes depository of an ideal order capable of going once more into action. Personal meditation and regeneration. 'Out of all this beauty something must come.'

VOLITION

Inferno (see above, p. 41, footnote).
Voyage of Odysseus to Tiresias,
'Who even dead has yet his mind
entire.'

Dante the live man among the dead.

Purgatorio

'And we sit here . . .
    there in the arena . . .' ⟵⟶ Directio Voluntatis.

'So this is, we may take it, ⟵⟶ ' "this was the state of things
    Mitteleuropa.'   in 1785 . . ." (Mr. Jefferson.)'
                ' "The revolution," said Mr.
                    Adams,
                "Took place in the minds of the
                    people." '

'Sun up; work
sundown; to rest
dig well and drink of the water
dig field; eat of the grain
Imperial power is? and to us what is it?'

'How drawn, O GEA TERRA,
    what draws as thou drawest
        till one sink into thee by an arm's width
embracing thee. Drawest,
    truly thou drawest.
Wisdom lies next thee,
    simply, past metaphor.'

Paradiso

'quand vos venetz al som de l'escalina

$\eta\theta os$ gradations

These are distinctions in clarity

ming 明[1] these are distinctions.'

The ideogram of 'the total light process'—Sun and moon together.

BIBLIOGRAPHY

In this book I have tried to anthologize Pound's prose, insofar as it bears on the procedures of the *Cantos*. One could make a separate anthology of passages throwing light on the *contents* of the epic, a third of his judgments on and propaganda for particular men and works of art.

The following list of his publications in book form is arranged and annotated for the reader's convenience. In the present state of the publishing trade it is impossible to guess what will or will not be in print when this book appears.

1. BASIC WRITINGS

The Cantos of Ezra Pound, New York, New Directions, 1949. There is no British counterpart to this omnibus volume of Cantos I through LXXXIV. The separate parts were published in London by Faber and Faber as follows: *A Draft of XXX Cantos* (1933); *Eleven New Cantos* (1934); *The Fifth Decad of Cantos* (1937); *Cantos LII–LXXI* (1940); *The Pisan Cantos* (1949). The first four of these volumes are now published by Faber and Faber in one volume as *Seventy Cantos* (1950).

Personae, New York, Liveright, 1926; reissued with additional poems, New York, New Directions, 1949. All the verse up to the *Cantos* that Pound wishes to preserve. Again, no British counterpart; the *Selected Poems* edited by T. S. Eliot (Faber and Faber, 1928; new edition, 1949) would be satisfactory but for the omission of the *Propertius*.

Make It New, New Haven, Yale University Press, 1935; London, Faber and Faber, 1934. Pound's solidest volume of literary scholarship: Troubadours, Arnaut Daniel, Elizabethan Classicists, Translators of Greek, French Poets, Henry James and Remy de Gourmont, the Imagist platform and list of

'Don'ts', Cavalcanti (including the crucial 'Mediaevalism' essay, the 'Donna mi priegha' text, translation, and notes). The text of Divus' Latin from which Canto I is paraphrased appears on pages 138–141. The introductory 'Date Line' demands careful digestion.

Polite Essays, London, Faber and Faber, 1937; New York, New Directions, 1940. Contains the long 'How to Read', decidedly one of the pieces the beginning Poundling should read first. The critics of *Ulysses* haven't begun to follow up 'James Joyce et Pécuchet'.

Culture, New York, New Directions, 1938. *Guide to Kulchur*, London, Faber and Faber, 1938, is the same book, printed from the same type; but in the opinion of the American publisher American readers want polite titles on their tables; cf. cult of Grandma Moses. An attempt to perform for our time the functions of the French *Encyclopaedia* and Landor's *Conversations*; unbelievably witty, varied, and compressed. The apparent scrappiness is cunningly calculated to bring a dozen bodies of knowledge into relation. Not for a quick reading.

The Unwobbling Pivot and the Great Digest, New York, New Directions, 1947. Dated 'D.T.C., Pisa; 5 October–5 November, 1945', these are Pound's basic Confucian studies. An earlier version of the *Great Digest*, first published in 1928, is available from New Directions as *The Ta Hio of Confucius* (see appendix II). Pound's new version of the *Analects* has appeared in the New York *Hudson Review* (Spring and Summer, 1950). The *Analects* are among the most important 'sources' for the *Pisan Cantos*.

The Letters of Ezra Pound, 1907–1941, ed. D. D. Paige, New York, Harcourt Brace, 1950; London, Faber and Faber, 1951. An autobiography, backstage history of contemporary literature, and quarry of exegetical aids. This volume appeared when the present book was in proof; it changes nothing, but would have enabled me to condense somewhat.

2. OTHER PROSE

The Spirit of Romance: an attempt to define somewhat the

charm of the pre-renaissance literature of Latin Europe. London, Dent, 1910; New York, Dutton, 1910. The quality may be gauged from an excerpt on Dante in *Polite Essays*.

Gaudier-Brzeska, a memoir, London and New York, John Lane, 1916. (reissued with 30 instead of 38 illustrations, London, Laidlaw and Laidlaw, 1939). Contains a valuable exposition of Vorticist aesthetics, largely represented in Part I of the present work.

Pavannes and Divisions, New York, Knopf, 1918. Contains the translated *Dialogues of Fontenelle* separately published in London in the previous year, the essays on Troubadours and Elizabethan Classicists reprinted in *Make It New*, and *inter alia* valuable notes on Arnold Dolmetsch and the light thrown on *vers libre* by his musicological discoveries. 'The Serious Artist', though largely superseded by later essays, still deserves reading.

Instigations, New York, Boni and Liveright, 1920. About half of *Make It New* reprinted from this important collection. Contains Fenollosa's *Chinese Written Character*.

Indiscretions, or Une revue de deux mondes, Paris, Three Mountains Press, 1923. Memories of Idaho and New York. An experiment in autobiography, reprinted in the *Quarterly Review of Literature*, (U.S.A.), Winter, 1950.

Antheil and the Treatise on Harmony, Paris, Three Mountains Press, 1924. 'Ching Ming' in yet another dimension. Valuable for the light it throws on the musical structure of the *Cantos*.

ABC of Economics, London, Faber and Faber, 1933. Less valuable than it should have been. The best of Pound's work on economics belongs to subsequent years; a reprint of the relevant Italian pamphlets in translation is promised by Mr. Peter Russell as this is written.

ABC of Reading, London, Routledge, 1934; reissued by Faber and Faber 1951; New Haven, Yale University Press, 1934; reissued by New Directions 1951. An invaluable extension of the principles of 'How to Read' for the use of students of the English component alone.

Social Credit: an impact, London, S. Nott, 1935 (Pamphlets on the New Economics, No. 8). Of great assistance for the middle Cantos.

Jefferson and/or Mussolini, London, S. Nott, 1935; New York, Liveright, 1935. Invaluable for the middle Cantos.

If this be treason . . . , Siena, 1948. Five radio addresses, including a Joyce obituary and examination of Cummings' *Eimi*.

An Introduction to the Economic Nature of the United States. Translated from the original Italian by Carmine Amore. London, Peter Russell, 1950. This is the first of a series of 'Money Pamphlets' from the same publisher, and obtainable from him at 114 Queens Gate, London S.W. 7.

3. EARLY COLLECTIONS OF VERSE (superseded by the 1926 *Personae*).

A Lume Spento, Venice, 1908. Pound's first published work, and one of the scarcest of modern first editions.

Personae of Ezra Pound, London, Elkin Mathews, 1909.

Exultations of Ezra Pound, London, Elkin Mathews, 1909.

Provenca: Poems selected from *Personae, Exultations*, and Canzoniere of Ezra Pound, Boston, Small, Maynard & Co., *circa* 1910.

Canzoni of Ezra Pound, London, Elkin Mathews, 1911. Contains many false starts never reprinted.

Ripostes of Ezra Pound, whereto are appended the complete poetical works of T. E. Hulme, with prefatory note. London, S. Swift and Company, 1912; Boston, Small, Maynard & Co., 1913.

Personae and Exultations of Ezra Pound, London, E. Mathews, 1913.

Canzoni and Ripostes of Ezra Pound, whereto are appended the complete poetical works of T. E. Hulme, London, E. Mathews, 1913.

Cathay, London, Elkin Mathews, 1915.

Lustra of Ezra Pound, London, E. Mathews, 1916. (*Cathay* included).

Quia Pauper Amavi, London, The Egoist Ltd., 1919. (Contains 'Langue d'Oc', 'Mœurs Contemporaines', three Cantos in a very early draft later cancelled and the best parts salvaged, and the *Propertius*.

Umbra: the early poems of Ezra Pound, all that he now wishes to keep in circulation from 'Personae', 'Exultations', 'Ripostes', etc. With translations from Guido Cavalcanti and Arnaut Daniel and poems by the late T. E. Hulme. London, E. Mathews, 1920.

Hugh Selwyn Mauberley, London, The Ovid Press, 1920.

Poems, 1918–1921, including three portraits and four cantos, by Ezra Pound. New York, Boni and Liveright, circa 1921.

Alfred Venison's Poems: Social Credit themes by the Poet of Titchfield Street, London, S. Nott, 1935 (Pamphlets on the New Economics, No. 9). These poems are among those added to the 1949 reissue of *Personae.*

4. MISCELLANEOUS.

The Sonnets and Ballate of Guido Cavalcanti; with translation and introduction by Ezra Pound. Boston, Small, Maynard & Company, *circa* 1912.

Certain Noble Plays of Japan: from the manuscripts of Ernest Fenollosa, chosen and finished by Ezra Pound, with an introduction by William Butler Yeats. Churchtown, Dundrum, The Cuala Press, 1916. (Contains Nishikigi, Hagoromo, Kumasaka, Kagekiyo).

Noh, or Accomplishment, a study of the classical stage of Japan, by Ernest Fenollosa and Ezra Pound, London, Macmillan, 1916. Contains the above four plays and others, with essays and explications, chiefly arranged by Pound from Fenollosa's papers.

Catholic Anthology, 1914–1915, edited by Ezra Pound, London, Elkin Mathews, 1915.

Passages from the letters of John Butler Yeats, selected by Ezra Pound. Churchtown, Dundrum, The Cuala Press, 1917.

The Natural Philosophy of Love, by Remy de Gourmont, translated with a postscript by Ezra Pound. London, the Casanova Society, 1926. The claim of this on Pound's attention was vindicated nearly 20 years later in the insect motifs of the *Pisan Cantos.*

Imaginary Letters, Paris, 1930. Reprinted from the wartime *Little Review.* Tryout of an urbane expository persona, patient educator of society ladies. By implication, Pound's designation of the most receptive available English stratum.

Guido Cavalcanti: Rime. Edizione rappezzata fra le rovine. Genova, Marsano S. A., Anno IX (1931). The heart of this sumptuous and all but inaccessible edition is reprinted in *Make It New.*

Profile, an anthology collected in MCMXXXI, Milan, 1932. 'Merely the poems that I happen to remember': an ideogrammic history of contemporary verse, invaluable as illumination of the *Pisan Cantos.*

Active Anthology, London, Faber and Faber, 1933. The best part remains the preface, reprinted in *Polite Essays.*

The Chinese Written Character as a Medium for Poetry: an Ars Poetica, by Ernest Fenollosa, with foreword and notes by Ezra Pound. London, S. Nott, 1936; New York, Arrow Editions, 1936. Probably less accessible than the reprint of Fenollosa's essay in *Instigations,* but the preface (an interesting tie-up with Mr. Ogden's 'Basic') and the notes (comments on many particular ideograms, with specimen analysis and translation of a whole poem) make this particular edition worth looking up.

INDEX

341